ROCK
CHRONICLE

ROCK
CHRONICLE

A 365 day-by-day journal
of significant events
in Rock history.

by DAN FORMENTO

ROCK CHRONICLE

Delilah

DISTRIBUTED BY

THE PUTNAM PUBLISHING GROUP

N E W   Y O R K

BOOK DESIGN: ED CARAEFF
COVER DESIGN: VIRGINIA RUBEL

DEDICATION

To my sister Darlene, my biggest fan.

ACKNOWLEDGMENTS

I would like to give special thanks to
Ellyn Ambrose, Stephanie Bennett,
Stan Kaufman, Darlene Kwiatkowski,
Joyce Knapp, Michelle Maglionico,
Jeannie Sakol, and Jack Uram.

Additional writing and research
by Alan Tullio and Tim Brown.
Edited by George Taylor Morris.

Thanks to Una Fahy, Virginia Rubel,
Richard Schatzberg, Catherine Greene
and Melissa Smith.

Special thanks to Alan Betrock
for selected photos from
the Alan Betrock collection.

BEATLES FLUNK THE AUDITION! Decca Records A&R man Dick Rowe isn't impressed with the Fab Four's version of "Please Mr. Postman" and several other songs during an audition set up by Beatles manager, Brian Epstein. Rowe tells Epstein "guitar groups are on their way out!" (1962)

1966   Simon and Garfunkel's "The Sounds of Silence" tops American singles charts.

1972   Edgar Winter and White Trash disband. Winter then forms **The Edgar Winter Group,** which later hits with the single, "Frankenstein."

1974   Polydor Records is the first to jump album prices a dollar, to $6.98. Other labels soon follow.

**1974   ** A notable West Coast doctor reports that loud rock music can reduce sex drive and may cause brain damage.

1975   Yoko Ono joins **Patti Smith** and 60 others for original readings at the New York Poetry Project's Annual New Year's Day Extravaganza.

1976   Robert Plant takes his first step from the wheelchair confinement that followed a crippling auto accident in Greece a year earlier.

🎵 **RECORD RELEASES** include the **Beach Boys** "Barbara Ann" (1966) . . . **T. Rex** "Bang A Gong" (1970) . . . and **Fleetwood Mac** "Go Your Own Way" (1977).

Birthdays:
COUNTRY JOE McDONALD, El Monte, California, 1942. Mid sixties · anti-war singer-crusader with Country Joe and the Fish. Best known for "I feel Like I'm Fixin' To Die Rag."

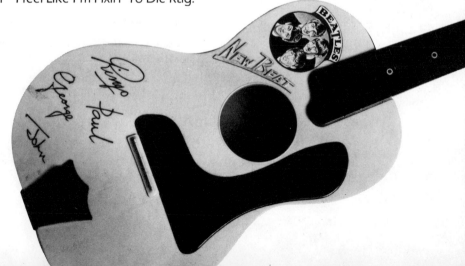

TWO VIRGINS LOCKED UP! Authorities at Newark Airport in New Jersey confiscate the entire shipment of album sleeves from the first John Lennon-Yoko Ono LP *Two Virgins* because the cover shows the couple in a frontal nude pose. Tetragammaton Records agrees to repackage the album in a plain brown wrapper. (1968)

1974   **Tex Ritter,** the singing cowboy star of movies and records, dies of a heart attack at age 67. Ritter is survived by son, John, now the star of TV's *Three's Company.*

1974   Gold Record awarded to **Chicago** for sales of a half-million copies of "Just You and Me."

1975   **The Allman Brothers Band** is honored by the Georgia State Department of Corrections as "The Outstanding Community Organization Of The Year."

1975   **John Lennon** awarded a favorable ruling from U.S. District Court Judge Richard Owen that allows the former Beatle to gain access to U.S. immigration files to aid in his fight to become an American citizen.

1979   The murder trial of **Sid Vicious** begins in New York City. **The Sex Pistols** singer is accused of murdering girlfriend, **Nancy Spungen,** in her Greenwich Village apartment three months earlier.

1981   **David Bowie** single "Scary Monsters" is released.

Birthdays:
ROGER MILLER, Fort Worth, Texas, 1936. A successful country and pop singer, Miller is best known for his hit single "King Of The Road."

Notes:

A BEACH BOY GETS HIS! But Carl Wilson says "no" to the invitation in the mail from Uncle Sam that tells him he's been drafted. The Beach Boys singer is later indicted by a Federal Grand Jury for draft evasion, but wins his case after an exhausting five-year court battle. (1967)

1974   After an eight-year seclusion, **Bob Dylan** hits the road with a concert in Chicago, the first of a 39-date tour in 25 cities. Much of the tour is recorded and later issued as the double-live LP *"Before the Flood,"* starring Dylan and the Band.

1976   Record releases this day include **Gary Wright** "Dream Weaver" . . . **Dr. Hook and the Medicine Show** "Only Sixteen" . . . and **Queen** "Bohemian Rhapsody."

1982   *Double Fantasy* and *"Starting Over"* both top American record charts. The LP and single will stay at #1 for seven weeks, as fans continue to mourn the death of John Lennon.

🎵 **GOLD RECORDS** awarded to **Don McLean** for "American Pie" (1972) . . . and to **Jim Croce** for "Time In A Bottle" (1974).

Birthdays:

GEORGE MARTIN, London, England, 1926. Best known as record producer for the Beatles. Also noted for successful productions for Jeff Beck, America, and the Little River Band.

STEVE STILLS, Dallas, Texas, 1945. Founder of Buffalo Springfield, then partner in supergroup Crosby, Stills, Nash & Young before engaging in various solo projects.

JOHN PAUL JONES, born John Baldwin, Kent, England, 1946. Producer/Arranger/bassist/keyboardist for Led Zeppelin. Recording session credits include work with the Rolling Stones, Donovan, Dusty Springfield and Herman's Hermits.

Notes:

THE TOP TEN IS BORN! *Billboard* magazine introduces the first pop music chart that ranks records based on national sales. Joe Venuti, a Big Band violinist, grabs the first #1 chart position. The race for the Top Ten begins. (1936)

1965   **Fender,** the premiere manufacturer of fine electric guitars, is sold to CBS for $13 million.

1968   A drunken **Jimi Hendrix** is arrested in Gothenburg, Germany, after trashing his room at the Opelan Hotel.

1978   **Fleetwood Mac's** original leader and founder **Peter Green** marries **Jane Samuel** in Los Angeles.

1978   **Ozzy Osbourne** rejoins Black Sabbath, replacing his own replacement **Dave Walker.** The bizzare singer would soon quit again.

1979   **The Star Club** in Hamburg, Germany, reopens amid a resurgence of interest in the Beatles' early history. None of the Fab Four attends the gala opening.

1979   Jazz great **Charles Mingus,** bassist and composer, dies of a heart attack at age 57 in Cuernavaca, Mexico.

🎵 **GOLD RECORDS** awarded to **George Harrison** for his triple album set *The Concert For Bangla Desh* (1972) . . . and to **Elton John** for his double LP *Goodbye Yellow Brick Road* (1974).

🎵 **RECORD RELEASES** include the **Foundations** "Build Me Up Buttercup" (1969) . . . and **Phoebe Snow** "Poetry Man" (1975).

Notes:

_____

_____

_____

_____

_____

_____

_____

_____

THE INTRODUCTION TO FM RADIO! The Federal Communications Commission hears the first demonstration of FM radio as a service which would give an improved signai, freer from interference than AM. A year later the first FM transmitter is "On the air." (1940)

1967 Folk singer **Jesse Winchester** decides Canada is a better place to be than the U.S. Army, after receiving the news he's been drafted. Winchester later opts for permanent Canadian citizenship, even though he's allowed to return to the U.S. under President Carter's blanket amnesty for draft evaders.

1976 Former **Beatles** bodyguard and road manager **Mal Evans** is shot to death by Los Angeles police after threatening his live-in companion with a rifle during an argument. The police say Evans turned the rifle on them when asked to surrender.

1978 **The Sex Pistols,** the pioneers of Punk Rock, make their American concert debut in Atlanta, Georgia.

1979 *Saturday Night Fever,* the movie soundtrack album that launched the **Bee Gees** and others to new career heights, marks its 25-millionth sale.

1979 **Southside Johnny** is hospitalized with cuts from a broken cocktail glass after stumbling over a stage monitor during a concert encore in Sacramento, California.

Birthdays:

SAM PHILLIPS, founder of Phillips Records, 1923. It was on his Sun label that Elvis Presley, Jerry Lee Lewis, Johnny Cash and others made their first recordings.

DOC NEESON, Belfast, Ireland. Founder of the Keystone Angels, later called the Angels, and now Angel City. Neeson takes his name from an early fascination with famed gunslinger Doc Holliday.

Notes:

THE KING TAKES A FINAL BOW! After several appearances before screaming TV studio audiences, Elvis Presley makes a final appearance on *The Ed Sullivan Show.* (1957)

1964   **The Rolling Stones** begin their first headline tour of Great Britain. The **Ronettes** open the show at the Harrow Granada. The following June, The Stones will tour as the headline band for the first time in the U.S.

1968   Two popular singles are released on the same day. **Paul Mauriat's** "Love Is Blue" and the theme to *Mission: Impossible* by **Lalo Schifrin.**

1975   *The Wiz* opens on Broadway to enthusiastic reviews. The black version of *The Wizard of Oz* later becomes a movie starring **Diana Ross** as Dorothy and **Michael Jackson** as the scarecrow.

1977   **The Sex Pistols'** outrageous behavior leads the British record label EMI to drop the group from their roster of artists. Not least among the embarrassing string of incidents attributed to the punk band's loss of a label was their use of profanity on a live British TV show.

1977   **Kiss** is awarded a Platinum Record for sales of a million copies of the LP *Rock and Roll Over.*

Birthdays:
SYD BARRETT, Cambridge, England, 1946. The original guitarist and founder of Pink Floyd, Barrett was responsible for the band's early direction. He left Pink Floyd in 1968.

Notes:

_____

_____

_____

_____

_____

_____

Elvis Presley

COME FLY WITH "V" Long an innovator of fine guitar design, Gibson patents the "Flying V" guitar and looks forward to its future as a favorite among many rock guitarists. (1958)

1964 **Cyril Davies** dies of leukemia. Davies was a founding member of the band **Blues Incorporated,** featuring **Mick Jagger** and **Keith Richards,** later of the **Rolling Stones.**

1972 **Bread** is awarded a Gold Record for the single "Baby I'm A Want You."

1975 **Led Zeppelin** fans wreak havoc at Boston Garden while waiting in line all night for ticket windows to open. By morning, concession stands are looted, doors unhinged and seats smashed, firehoses ripped and left running. Boston mayor, Kevin White, cancels the concert after surveying the damage, estimated at $30,000.

1976 Record industry executive, **Kenneth Moss,** is sentenced to 120 days in jail after he pleads guilty to involuntary manslaughter in the death of **Average White Band** drummer **Robbie McIntosh.** McIntosh OD'd on heroin at a party given by Moss in Los Angeles the previous September.

1980 **Hugh Cornwell** of **The Stranglers** draws eight weeks in prison on a pot possession conviction.

Birthdays:

MIKE McCARTNEY, Liverpool, England, 1944. The brother of Beatle Paul formed a satirical group, Scaffold, using the name Mike McGear and had a #1 hit in England in 1968, "Lily The Pink."

PAUL REVERE, Harvard, Nebraska, 1946. The founder of the popular sixties dance-pop band, Paul Revere and The Raiders, stars on the Dick Clark project *Where The Action Is.*

KENNY LOGGINS, Everett, Washington, 1948. Moderately successful as a songwriter for The Nitty Gritty Dirt Band and in 1970, half of Loggins & Messina. After the breakup with Jim Messina in 1976, even more successful as a solo artist.

Notes:

JANUARY 8

WHAT'S GOING ON UP THERE! A far cry from the folksy *Hootenanny* or pop *Hit Parade* TV shows that preceded it, the TV premiere of the weekly dance show "Hullabaloo" causes some raised eyebrows, mostly because of the mini-skirted go-go girls. (1965)

1966   The **Beatles**' *Rubber Soul* tops the American LP charts.

1973   **Carly Simon** is awarded a Gold Record for the single "You're So Vain."

1973   **Yoko Ono's** first album *Approximately Infinite Universe* is released on Apple Records, featuring **John Lennon** and the Plastic Ono Band.

1979   **Rush** is named "The Canadian Ambassadors of Music" by the Canadian government.

Birthdays:

ELVIS ARON PRESLEY, Tupelo, Mississippi, 1935. Singer, guitarist, songwriter and film star. From his "Heartbreak Hotel" in 1955 to more record sales than any other recording artist (over 500 million) and more than 30 film appearances. Credited as "The King" of Rock 'n' Roll.

DAVID BOWIE, born David Robert Jones, London, England, 1947. To avoid confusion with Davy Jones of the Monkees, he changed his name to Bowie in 1968 and has since recorded several successful LPs including *Ziggy Stardust, Young Americans* and *Scary Monsters.* His stage credits include *The Elephant Man* on Broadway and in film, *The Man Who Fell To Earth.*

TERRY SYLVESTER, Liverpool, England, 1947. Replaced Graham Nash as rhythm guitarist in The Hollies.

ANTHONY GOURDINE, Brooklyn, New York. Major pop influence in fifties and sixties as Little Anthony & The Imperials.

ROBBY KRIEGER, Los Angeles, California, 1941. Originally with the Psychedelic Rangers, Krieger joins The Doors in 1965 while a physics and psychology major at UCLA. Vocalist for The Doors after the death of Jim Morrison.

Notes:

JANUARY 9

THE BRITISH INVASION MOVES AHEAD! Two major releases from English bands that will later top the charts. The Zombies "Tell her No" and "Heart of Stone" from The Rolling Stones. (1965)

1973   Lou Reed marries a New York City cocktail waitress named Betty.

1976   Graham Parker and **The Rumour** sign their first record deal with Phonogram Records in England.

1977   Peter Frampton follows up his multi-million selling *Frampton Comes Alive* with the release of the *I'm In You* LP, a somewhat disappointing comeback for A&M Records.

1977   Emmylou Harris marries **Brian Ahern,** her producer, in Halifax, Novia Scotia.

1979   The Bee Gees, Rod Stewart, Donna Summer, Earth, Wind & Fire, John Denver, Olivia Newton-John and other performers play a benefit concert for UNICEF, the United Nations International Childrens' Emergency Fund. Each artist performs one song and donates all future rights and royalties of the song to UNICEF. The gala event raises more than $50 million.

1979   The K-Mart Department stores pull **Steve Martin's** comedy LP *Let's Get Small* off the record shelves for being in "very bad taste."

Birthdays:

JOAN BAEZ, Staten Island, New York, 1941. Singer-guitarist known as "Queen of Protest" for her anti-war and civil rights work in the sixties and early seventies.

JAMES PATRICK PAGE, Middlesex, England, 1945. Originally a London session player, Page joined the Yardbirds as a replacement for Jeff Beck and in 1968 formed Led Zeppelin. His independent recording projects include the movie soundtrack for *Death Wish II*

DAVID JOHANSEN Born 1950. Former guitarist-vocalist with New York Dolls, later embarking on a successful solo career.

Notes:

JUST A BOY AND HIS GUITAR! The RCA Victor studios have never been the same since this day when Elvis Presley came by for his first recording session for the label playing "I Got A Woman" followed by "Heartbreak Hotel." (1956)

1976 Blues great **Howlin' Wolf** dies in Chicago. He was a major influence on the styles of **Eric Clapton, Jeff Beck** and many other blues-oriented rock guitarists.

Birthdays:

JIM CROCE, Philadelphia, Pennsylvania, 1943. Singer and songwriter who grabbed national attention in 1972 with "Don't Mess Around With Jim" and "Bad Bad Leroy Brown" after nearly a decade of musical obscurity. Croce died in a plane crash in Louisiana in 1973.

ROD STEWART, Glasgow, Scotland, 1945. Discovered while playing harmonica on a train platform by legendary bluesman Long John Baldry. Began singing career with Hoochie Coochie Men before joining Jeff Beck Group, then Small Faces. His solo career started in 1969 and has moved through a string of Gold and Platinum albums.

PAT BENATAR, Long Island, New York, 1952. Operatic student turned rock singer, discovered while waitressing at the New York comedy club Catch A Rising Star, where she auditioned on amateur nights. Her debut LP bore the hit single "Heartbreaker" and she's been awarded two consecutive Grammys.

DONALD FAGEN, Founding member of **Steely Dan,** a studio oriented rock-jazz influenced group with Platinum credentials.

Notes:

DISCO-A-GO-GO NUMBER ONE! Multi-colored neon lights and mini-skirted dancers in cages highlighted the opening of America's first discoteque on Sunset Boulevard in Los Angeles. The Whiskey-A-Go-Go was modeled after similar clubs in Europe and was an instant success. (1963)

1969 **JETHRO TULL'S** debut LP *This Was* and the single from **Joe South**, *Games People Play*, both released on the same day.

1977 Rolling Stone, **Keith Richards,** is convicted of cocaine possession by a London court and fined $1300. The charges stem from an auto accident involving the guitarist after which the police found 130 grams of coke in his car.

1980 **The Pretenders** debut LP is released, featuring the songs "Brass in Pocket" and "Mystery Achievement."

Birthdays:

DENNIS GREENE, born Frederick Greene, New York City, 1949. He formed **Sha Na Na** with a number of friends in 1969 for a performance at a fifties nostalgia dance at Columbia University. The initial acceptance of their routine led to a recording contract and weekly TV show.

CLARENCE CLEMMONS, Noted saxaphone player for the E Street Band, most often the backing band for Bruce Springsteen.

Keith Richards

A HIT TO PLEASE EVERYONE! Just a year after they flunked their first audition, the Beatles released "Please Please Me," which was to become their first hit single. (1963)

1963 **Bob Dylan** takes part in a BBC Radio play in London titled "The Madhouse on Castle Street" during which he sings "Blowin' In The Wind" and "Swan On The River". The latter song is never recorded by Dylan.

1974 **Redbone's** "Come and Get Your Love" is released as a single.

1979 **Aynsley Dunbar** joins **Jefferson Starship** as the drummer, replacing John Barbata, injured months earlier in a car crash.

1981 The White House record library expands to include albums from **Bob Dylan, Kiss** and **The Sex Pistols** from a donation of 800 albums by The Recording Industry Association of America.

Birthdays:

"LONG" JOHN BALDRY, London, England, 1941. Singer, songwriter and guitarist, Baldry got his start with folk-bluesman, Jack Elliot, in the mid-fifties. Baldry later formed the Hoochie Coochie Men, Steampacket and Bluesology and weaned future stars Rod Stewart, Elton John and Brian Auger, among others.

MAGGIE BELL, Glasgow, Scotland, 1945. An original member of Stone The Crows, the gravel-voiced rocker tried for a solo career in 1973. Bell eventually became a founding member of Midnight Flyer in 1979.

Notes:

_____

_____

_____

_____

_____

_____

_____

_____

WHO'S HIS BEST FRIEND! Fans at the Rainbow Theater in London are thrilled by comeback performance of Eric Clapton after two years away from the music scene suffering from depression and heroin addiction. The Who guitarist Pete Townshend helps Clapton beat addiction and organizes the Rainbow Concert to celebrate. (1973)

1974   A small riot by fans breaks out when **Steve Miller** is inadvertently not invited to his own "after-concert" party at Tower Records in Los Angeles. The overflow crowd fights in the street and police close down the store. Thirty-seven injuries, including 17 cops, and 8 arrests.

1976   **Greg Allman** is subpoenaed by a grand jury investigating a drug ring.

1979   **Donny Hathaway** dies in a fall from a fifteenth-floor room at New York's Essex House Hotel. The 33-year-old singer, composer and arranger was recording a second album with **Roberta Flack** earlier in the day. Police couldn't say whether Hathaway jumped or fell accidentally.

🎵 **RECORD RELEASES** include **Little Richard** "Good Golly Miss Molly" (1958) . . . the **Beatles** "I Wanna Hold Your Hand" and **Bob Dylan** "The Times They Are A Changin' " (1964) . . . and **Cream** "Sunshine Of Your Love" (1968).

Notes:

_____

_____

_____

_____

_____

_____

_____

JANUARY 14

SUCCESS IN THE CHANGE OF A NAME! The time has come for Davie Jones to become David Bowie and avoid confusion with the very popular Davy Jones of the Monkees. First use of the new name appears on his fourth single, "I Can't Help Thinking About Me" by David Bowie and the Lower Third. (1966)

1967   Golden Gate Park in San Francisco is the site of the first "Be-In," with thousands of "flower children" getting off to the music of the **Jefferson Airplane,** the **Grateful Dead, Quicksilver Messenger Service, Big Brother and the Holding Company** and others.

1969   "Monterey Pop" opens in Los Angeles. The eighty-minute film documents the legendary 1967 Monterey Pop Festival, which starred **Janis Joplin, Jimi Hendrix, The Who,** and the **Jefferson Airplane.**

1970   An exhibition of **John Lennon's** erotic lithographs opens in London. The art gallery is closed by police two days later and eight of the prints are removed to be used as evidence for possible prosecution under the Obscene Publications Act.

1973   **Phil Lesh** of the **Grateful Dead** is busted on drug charges at his home in Fairfax, California.

1978   **The Sex Pistols** call it quits with a farewell concert at the Winterland in San Francisco.

🎵**RECORD RELEASES** include **Little Richard** "Tutti Frutti" (1956) . . . and **Sonny and Cher** "The Beat Goes On" (1967).

Birthdays:

ALLEN TOUSSAINT, New Orleans, Louisiana, 1938. Singer, keyboardist, producer and arranger, his first LP is recorded in 1958, *Wild Sounds of New Orleans.* He later provides material for Wings, The Band, Little Feat, and others.

Notes:

WHO'S FIRST! Only a thousand copies are pressed by Brunswick Records to test the first Who single "I Can't Explain," but 100,000 more are immediately put into circulation when the single hits #8 on the charts. (1965)

1966   **The Supreme's** "My World Is Empty Without You" is released.

1966   **The Rolling Stones** awarded a Gold Record for the *December's Children* LP.

1967   **The Rolling Stones** sing a censored version of "Let's Spend The Night Together" in an appearance on *The Ed Sullivan Show,* changing the lyrics to "let's spend some 'time' together."

1968   **John Fred** and his **Playboy Band** awarded a Gold Record for the single "Judy In Disguise."

1970   **Diana Ross** quits **The Supremes** and goes solo.

1972   "American Pie" tops the American singles charts, but singer-composer **Don McLean** refuses to discuss what the lyrics to the hit actually mean.

1972   **Elvis Presley** draws the largest single TV audience ever with a live, worldwide concert telecast from the Honolulu International Center.

1977   **David Bowie's** *Low* LP is released.

1979   **Linda McCartney** is voted one of the top ten "most watchable women" by The International Bachelors' Club.

Birthdays:

CAPTAIN BEEFHEART, born Don Van Vliet, Glendale, California, 1941. Began with Frank Zappa before forming the Magic Band.

RONNIE VAN ZANDT, Jacksonville, Florida, 1949. Founding member of Lynyrd Skynyrd. Singer-songwriter on such hits as "Sweet Home Alabama" and "Free Bird" before his death in a plane crash in 1977.

MELVYN GALE, 1952. Bassist for Electric Light Orchestra, Gale joined ELO as replacement for Michael Albuquerque.

Notes:

THE CAVERN CLUB OPENS! This early Liverpool, England, rock club was much like any other until the Beatles took up residency there. This is the place where Brian Epstein would first set eyes on his future fortune. (1957)

1965 **The Temptations'** "My Girl" is released.

1972 **David Seville** dies in Beverly Hills, California, after many successes with the **Alvin and The Chipmunks** novelty records of the early sixties.

1975 **Paul Beaver** dies of a stroke in Los Angeles. The electronic synthesizer wizard has brought the Moog to popularity with Beaver and Krause, and used it effectively on film soundtracks for *The Graduate, Catch 22, Performance,* and *Rosemary's Baby.*

1976 *Frampton Comes Alive* is released by A&M Records. The carefully produced double-live LP tops the charts for 17 weeks and sells ten million copies in its first year.

1979 The divorce is finalized for **Cher** and **Greg Allman,** four years after papers were filed. Cher filed them nine days after the wedding.

1980 **Paul McCartney** is busted by customs officials at Tokyo International Airport when nearly a half-pound of pot is discovered in his suitcase. The former Beatle is detained for nine days before being kicked out of Japan.

Birthdays:

WILLIAM FRANCIS, Los Angeles, California, 1942. Keyboardist for Dr. Hook and the Medicine Show, a band formed from studio musicians who worked together on the film soundtrack of *Who Is Harry Kellerman?*

SANDY DENNY, England, 1947. After one album with the Strawbs, she joined Fairport Convention in 1968, then quit a year later to pursue a solo career. Sandy, considered one of the best British female vocalists in rock, died in '78.

Notes:

A MIGHTY BIG START! The #1 song in Great Britain is Manfred Mann's "The Mighty Quinn," a Bob Dylan composition. Dylan's version of the song will not be heard by fans until the release of *The Basement Tapes*. (1968)

1969 **Led Zeppelin's** first album project is released. Simply titled *Led Zeppelin*, the LP will appear on the record charts for 73 weeks, but never reach #1.

1977 **The Marshall Tucker Band** and **Charlie Daniels** headline the first in a series of benefit concerts for ex-Allman Brothers Band roadie, **Scooter Herring.** Herring faced 75 years in prison and $300,000 in legal fees for cocaine trafficking, a conviction that comes, in part, from damaging testimony given in court by Greg Allman. The benefit brings him about $5,000.

Birthdays:

MICK TAYLOR, Hertfordshire, England, 1948. Originally a member of John Mayall's Bluesbreakers, Taylor replaced Brian Jones as guitarist for The Rolling Stones in 1969. Known as the only member of The Stones "to leave the band alive," Taylor joined the Jack Bruce Band in 1974 for a short-lived stint and now records solo and makes occasional guest appearances on LPs by other artists.

The Pretenders

THE BEST IS NOT ENOUGH! Pete Best, the original drummer for the Beatles, is awarded a settlement in his suit against the Liverpool group, thought to be considerably less than the $8 million he claims he's due. Best sues after Ringo tells a *Playboy magazine* interviewer that Best "used to take little pills to make him ill." (1969)

1973 **The Rolling Stones** benefit concert at the Los Angeles Forum raises $200,000 for the Pan American Development Fund to aid victims of a devastating earthquake in Nicaragua. **Mick Jagger** kicks in another $150,000 of his own money, knowing his mother-in-law had to literally crawl from the ruins to survive.

1973 **Pink Floyd** begins the first recording sessions for their classic *Dark Side of the Moon* LP at EMI Studios in London.

1974 **Bad Company** is formed by singer **Paul Rodgers** and drummer **Simon Kirke** of **Free,** guitarist **Mick Ralphs** of **Mott The Hoople,** and **King Crimson** bassist **Boz Burrell**.

1975 **Minnie Ripperton** releases "Lovin' You."

1978 Platinum Record is awarded to **Billy Joel** for his *The Stranger* LP.

1980 Plasmatics lead singer **Wendy O. Williams** is allegedly fondled and beaten by Milwaukee police as they arrest her after a **Plasmatics** concert. Williams is charged with "simulating masturbation on stage."

1980 The **Pretenders** debut LP enters British charts, while **Pink Floyd** dominates American charts with *The Wall,* in its third month at #1.

Birthdays:

ELMORE JAMES Durant, Mississippi, 1918. Legendary bluesman cited as major influence to the styles of Eric Clapton, George Harrison and others.

BOBBY GOLDSBORO, Florida, 1941. Sixties pop singer best known for #1 single "Honey" in '68.

Notes:

RECYCLING THE HITS! The first serious pop culture film of the late sixties is recognized with a Gold Record for its soundtrack based on various rock hits. *Easy Rider* makes a brash statement of the times and the use of cocaine and LSD, backed with the music of Steppenwolf and many others. (1970)

1974 **Bob Dylan's** concert in Miami causes a traffic jam unequaled since Woodstock. Many fans leave cars unattended and walk the entire nine miles to the event.

1976 **John Lennon, Paul McCartney, George Harrison** and **Ringo Starr** are offered $30 million by rock promoter Bill Sargent if the four musicians agree to play together, on the same stage, under the name "The Beatles." The answers are no, no, no and no!

Birthdays:

PHIL EVERLY, Brownie, Kentucky, 1939. With brother Don, The Everly Brothers are formed in 1957. The first hit single, "Bye Bye Love," sparks a career which lasts on and off until 1973.

JANIS JOPLIN, Port Arthur, Texas, 1943. Began singing on the local bar circuit at 17 before joining Big Brother and the Holding Company in 1966. Attracted worldwide attention with an appearance at the Monterey Pop Festival, followed by a solo career in 1968 and death in 1970.

ROD EVANS, Edinburgh, Scotland, 1945. Original member and lead singer for Deep Purple, later replaced by Ian Gillan in 1969.

ROBERT PALMER, Yorkshire, England, 1949. Singer and guitarist first with Vinegar Joe, then as solo artist in 1973 leaning heavily on R&B flavored rock.

DEWEY BUNNELL, Yorkshire, England, 1951. Guitarist and singer for America, the band he formed in 1970 on a U.S. Air Force base in England. First American hit in 1972, "Horse With No Name," followed by "Ventura Highway," "Tin Man," and others.

Notes:

Bob Dylan

ROCK OF AGES ROLLS TO REST! Alan Freed, the father of rock radio DJs, dies in a Palm Springs hospital of uremia. He was one of the first to program black music for a white audience and even gave it a name, "Rock 'n' Roll," coined from the lyrics of a Bill Haley tune. After tremendous popularity in the fifties, Freed was indicted for payola in 1960 and died before he could answer charges of income tax evasion involving income from "commercial bribery." (1965)

1968   **Bob Dylan's** Woody Guthrie Memorial Concert is held at Carnegie Hall in New York City, featuring Guthrie folk songs sung by **Dylan, Judy Collins, Richie Havens** and **Pete Seeger.**

1972   A Gold Record is awarded to the **Rolling Stones** for their Greatest Hits LP *Hot Rocks*

1974   **Stevie Wonder** makes a successful comeback in concert at the Rainbow Theater in London, five months after a near fatal auto accident.

1982   **Ozzy Osbourne** hospitalized with rabies after he bites the head of a dead bat thrown on stage by a fan in Des Moines. The incident forces cancellation of all Ozzy concerts, including the scheduled live nationwide broadcast by The Source Network.

1982   **Charlie Daniels, Rick Derringer, Phil Lynott** and **Carmine Appice** headline a UNICEF benefit concert at The Savoy in New York City.

🎵 **RECORD RELEASES** include the **Silhouettes** "Get a Job" (1958) . . . the **Beatles** album debut *Meet The Beatles* (1964) . . . the **Bee Gees** "Words" (1968) . . . and the **Doobie Brothers** "What A Fool Believes" (1979).

Birthdays:

ERIC STEWART, Manchester, England, 1945. Lead guitarist with 10cc, a band which emerged from the group Hotlegs.

GEORGE GRANTHAM, Cordell, Oklahoma, 1947. Original drummer for Poco, formed with Buffalo Springfield members Richie Furay and Jim Messina.

PAUL STANLEY, New York City, 1952. Cofounder of theatrical rock group Kiss. Like other Kiss members, guitarist Stanley is never seen out of make-up.

Notes:

GEORGE AND PATTI TIE THE KNOT! Tears everywhere as Beatle George Harrison weds actress Patricia Boyd after a brief courtship. Patti played one of the schoolgirls in the train scene near the start of the film *A Hard Days Night,* the production which brought the two together. (1966)

1967   The Rolling Stones' "Ruby Tuesday" is released. **Cream's** first hit single, "I Feel Free," enters the British charts.

1974   Bob Dylan is invited to the Georgia Governor's mansion by **Jimmy Carter** following Dylan's Rolling Thunder Revue concert date in Atlanta. Chip Carter is the one to suggest the get-together so Dylan can try some real Southern cooking.

1977   Al Stewart is threatened on stage during a concert in Bellingham, Washington, by a lunatic fan who claims to be a character in one of Stewart's songs.

1978   The *Saturday Night Fever* soundtrack LP is #1 on the *Billboard* magazine album chart, a position it will hold for 24 weeks.

Birthdays:

RICHIE HAVENS, New York City, 1941. Faststrumming folk singer who made his mark in the late sixties with anti-war songs and particularly with his appearance at Woodstock.

JIM IBBOTSON, Philadelphia, 1947. Bassist with the Nitty Gritty Dirt Band, he joined in 1970 to replace original bassist Ralph Taylor Barr.

Notes:

THERE'S MUSIC IN THOSE GROOVES! Amidst the flurry of inventions in the late 19th century, the announcement of The Columbia Phonograph Company being formed in Washington, D.C., is one that would change musical habits considerably. The offshoot of the original company is today's Columbia Records. (1889)

1959   Buddy Holly makes his last recordings in his New York City apartment.

1967   The Spencer Davis Group, featuring Steve Winwood's vocals, hits #1 on British singles charts with "Keep On Runnin'."

1971   The Jimi Hendrix Memorial Foundation is established by his father, designed to award five music scholarships each year to talented young people in Washington State.

♪ RECORD RELEASES Include **Nancy Sinatra** "These Boots Are Made For Walking" (1966) . . . and **Hall & Oates** "Rich Girl" (1977).

Birthdays:

SAM COOKE, Chicago, Illinois, 1935. One of the most popular R&B pop singers of the fifties and sixties, Cooke started singing gospel, and later recorded his own songs, including "Shake" and "You Send Me." He died of gunshot wounds in Los Angeles in 1964.

STEVE PERRY of Journey born in 1953.

Sam Cooke

HELLO! GOODBYE! Another short-lived supergroup that helped shape the sound of the sixties releases a farewell album, *Goodbye Cream.* The Cream legacy is carried on in tunes like "Badge," composed by Eric Clapton and George Harrison. (1969)

1972 Blues singer **Big Maybelle** dies in Cleveland, Ohio.

1974 *The Exorcist* premieres and introduces America to the music of **Mike Oldfield.** The opening theme to his million-selling "Tubular Bells" is the score for the film's title sequence.

1977 **Carole King's** *Tapestry* LP becomes the longest running pop album to date on *Billboard's* Hot 100 chart, marking its 302nd week. **Pink Floyd's** *Dark Side of the Moon* will surpass it in 1980.

1978 **Terry Kath,** guitarist with **Chicago,** accidentally kills himself with his own 9mm pistol during a party in Los Angeles. Kath tells witnesses the gun is empty as he puts it to his head and pulls the trigger.

1979 **Toto** is awarded a Platinum Record for their debut LP *Toto.* A million-seller first time out.

1979 **Brian Wilson** of the Beach Boys is divorced from his wife of fifteen years, Marilyn Rovell. She was just sixteen years old when they wed.

Birthdays:

ROBIN ZANDER, born 1953. Vocalist with Cheap Trick.

Beach Boy Brian Wilson

JANUARY 24

TO BEATLE OR NOT! Brian Epstein came, saw and heard the Beatles and then was signed to be their manager. Interestingly, Epstein never countersigned the contract because he had given his word about what he intended to do and "that was enough." (1962)

1970 **Santana's** "Evil Ways" is released.

1976 A rock concert in Las Vegas is now described as "a public rendition of music in a permanent institution, consisting of several individual compositions performed by a musician or group of musicians utilizing electronically amplified instruments, which music is characterized by a persistent, heavily accented beat and a great degree of repetition of simple musical phrases." The vivid dissection by the Las Vegas County Commissioners.

1981 **Blondie's** "The Tide Is High" from the *Auto-American* LP is #1 on the singles chart.

1981 **Adam & The Ants** debut, *Kings of The Wild Frontier,* is biggest selling LP in England.

Birthdays:

DOUG KERSHAW, Tiel Ridge, Louisiana, 1936. Fiddler best known for his work with Bob Dylan and for the song "Louisiana Man."

NEIL DIAMOND, Brooklyn, New York, 1941. Singer, composer and guitarist with sixties pop roots and an eighties adult image, Diamond penned songs for Elvis Presley, Ray Charles, and the Monkees among others. His long string of hits include "Solitary Man," "Kentucky Woman" and "Cracklin' Rosie."

WARREN ZEVON, 1947. Satircal rock singer, songwriter and keyboard player. Late seventies FM hits include "Werewolves Of London" and "Excitable Boy."

JOHN BELUSHI, Chicago, 1949. A comic actor made famous from *Saturday Night Live,* he and Dan Aykroyd formed the Blues Brothers in the late seventies, and scored a hit with "Soul Man." Belushi died in 1982.

Notes:

BALDING BEATLEMANIA! John and Yoko completely shave their heads and declare 1970 is "Year One." The hair is then donated to Black House, an interracial community center in North London and is auctioned off to raise funds. (1970)

1978 **Bob Dylan's** second benefit concert for boxer, Rubin "Hurricane" Carter, lasts seven hours at the Houston Astrodome, and stars Stevie Wonder, Steve Stills and Ringo Starr. Dylan immortalized the boxer in the song "Hurricane."

1980 **Paul McCartney** wins freedom from a Tokyo jail nine nights after being busted for possession of a half-pound of pot.

♪ **RECORD RELEASES** include the **Beatles** "She Loves You" (1964) . . . and **Creedence Clearwater Revival** "Proud Mary" (1969).

Birthdays:

ANITA PALLENBERG, girlfriend of Rolling Stone Brian Jones, then Keith Richards, with whom she bore son Marlon. Co-starred with Mick Jagger in the film *Performance.*

CHINA, daughter of Grace Slick and Paul Kantner of the Jefferson Airplane/Starship. Was to be named God but parents opted for China, a name that could be changed again "to something more normal as she gets older, if she wants to"—Paul.

Notes:

Paul McCartney

THAT'LL BE THE DAY! Buddy Holly has his first recording session for Decca Records, a label that drops him later that year, and the same label that passes on the Beatles in 1962. (1956)

1956 **Buddy Holly** and the **Crickets** first appear on *The Ed Sullivan Show*.

1963 **The Four Seasons** release "Walk Like A Man."

1970 "Instant Karma" becomes **John Lennon's** first solo project of the seventies. He writes, records and mixes the song with producer Phil Spector all in the same day.

1970 Jefferson Airplane drummer **Spencer Dryden** marries **Sally Mann.**

1973 A Gold Record is awarded to **Creedence Clearwater Revival** for their Greatest Hits LP *Creedence Gold*.

1977 **Kiss** wins a Peoples' Choice Award for the ballad "Beth," an uncharacteristic song for the hard rock band.

1977 **Fleetwood Mac** founder **Peter Green** is committed to a mental institution after threatening his accountant with a rifle.

1978 *Billboard* magazine reports tie between **Kiss** and **Elvis Presley** for earning the most Platinum Albums in a single year, three each in 1977.

1979 **Bob Dylan** forms his own record company, Accomplice Records.

1979 **Jackson Browne** and **Graham Nash** play the first of three benefit concerts to help the Pacific Alliance fight nuclear power plant construction.

1979 The "**Gizmo**" guitar synthesizer is first demonstrated.

Notes:

BEE GEES U.S. DEBUT! The young Brothers Gibb are paid the astronomical sum of $50,000 for their American opener at the Anaheim Convention Center in California, the same sum the Beatles got for their first Hollywood Bowl concert. (1968)

1968 **Otis Redding's** biggest hit record, "Sittin' On The Dock Of The Bay" is released after his death.

1969 **Peter, Paul and Mary** awarded a Gold Record for *Album 1700.*

1980 Capricorn Records files bankruptcy in Macon, Georgia, leaving the **Allman Brothers Band, Marshall Tucker Band,** and other southern rock groups without a record label.

Birthdays:

NICK MASON, Birmingham, England, 1945. Drummer for Pink Floyd since the day it was formed. Originally played with Sigma 6 with Roger Waters and Rick Wright.

BOBBY "BLUE" BLAND, born Robert Calvin Bland in Rosemark, Tennessee, 1930. One of the leading vocalists of the mid fifties with tunes like "Farther Up The Road" and "Stormy Monday."

JANUARY 28

THE ODD COUPLE! The Dorsey Brothers' band swings in a different direction with the introduction of Elvis Presley to national TV on CBS's *Stage Show,* the first of six Elvis appearances. (1956)

1967 **The Rascals** "I've Been Lonely Too Long" is released. Also "Love Is Here And Now You're Gone" by **The Supremes** and the **Buffalo Springfield**'s "For What It's Worth."

1968 **Roger Daltry** is sued for divorce by his wife of four years, Jacqueline.

1970 **Jimi Hendrix** headlines Madison Square Garden at the Vietnam Moratorium Committee's Winter Festival for Peace.

1978 **Ted Nugent** carves an unusual autograph at a fan's request, with a Bowie knife on the man's arm.

1982 **Jackson Browne** and wife, **Lynne Sweeney,** become parents to their first child together, **Ryan Daniel Browne.**

BATTLE OF THE BANDS! The Marquee Club in London is packed for the great guitar face-off between Jimi Hendrix and The Who, staging a dual concert as part of a tribute to the late Beatles manager, Brian Epstein. (1967)

1978   Rare original versions of "Somebody To Love" and "White Rabbit" are released for the first time by Columbia Records on the LP *The Great Society* with **Grace Slick.**

1974   **Bob Dylan** brings wife, **Sara,** on stage as a spectator during a concert at Nassau Coliseum in New York. She sits quietly on a sofa.

1975   **Elton John** is awarded a Gold Record for "Lucy In The Sky With Diamonds."

1979   **Emerson, Lake and Palmer** disband after ten years following a financially disasterous concert tour and poor reviews of their final LP *Love Beach.*

1981   *Creem* magazine publisher, **Barry Kramer,** is found dead in his Birmingham, Michigan, apartment at age 37.

🎵 **RECORD RELEASES** Include the **Four Seasons** "Working My Way Back To You" and **Bobby Fuller Four** "I Fought The Law" (1966) . . . **Bread** "Everything I Own" (1972) . . . and the **Atlanta Rhythm Section** "So Into You" (1977).

Birthdays:

DAVID BYRON, London, 1947. Vocalist for Uriah Heep, a band that evolved from a number of groups Byron and Mick Box played in together. He exits the group in the mid seventies.

TOMMY RAMONE, New York City, 1952. Drummer for the Ramones, formed in 1974, the band got its start playing the same New York club circuit from which emerged Patti Smith and Talking Heads.

Notes:

JANUARY 30

GET BACK THE FINAL TIME! The Beatles make their final public appearance, a free lunchtime concert on the roof of Apple Headquarters in London, where they record "Get Back." The session is also filmed for the movie *Let It Be.* (1969)

1973 **Kiss** play their first gig at the Coventry Club in Queens, New York.

1974 **Greg Lake** is arrested for skinny-dipping in a Salt Lake City hotel pool, clearly visible from the street.

1974 **Bob Dylan** plays Madison Square Garden in NYC and records "Knockin' On Heaven's Door" for the *Before The Flood* LP.

1976 Platinum Record is awarded to **Kiss** for their million-seller "Kiss Alive."

1982 **"Lightnin' " Hopkins** dies of cancer in Houston, Texas. The most recorded blues artist in history.

1982 CBS announces Ambient Sound Records, a new label for old Doo Wop Artists.

🎵 **RECORD RELEASES** include **Herman's Hermits** "Can't You Hear My Heartbeat" (1965) . . . **Janis Joplin** "Me And Bobby McGee" and **Ike and Tina Turner** "Proud Mary" (1971).

Birthdays:

MARTY BALIN, Cincinnati, Ohio, 1943. Singer for the Jefferson Airplane, a group he launched from his Matrix Club in San Franciso, 1965. He later dropped out, then rejoined the group as Jefferson Starship. His first solo LP is released in early 1980's.

STEVE MARRIOT, London, England, 1947. Guitarist and singer with Humble Pie following disbanding of Small Faces, which he organized in 1965.

Notes:

JANUARY 31

CASH IN THEIR CHIPS! Bob Weir and Phil Lesh of The Grateful Dead are busted along with 17 others after a Dead concert in New Orleans. Group members claim it was all a set-up. (1970)

1970   **Creedence Clearwater Revival** film their first TV special.

1976   **Hall & Oates'** "Sara Smile" and **David Bowie's** LP *Station To Station* released.

1978   **Blood, Sweat and Tears** sax man **Greg Herbert** dies of accidental drug overdose in an Amsterdam hotel room during BS&T's European tour.

1979   **The Clash** begins first U.S. tour with **Bo Diddley** as the opener.

Birthdays:

PHIL COLLINS, London, England, 1951. Drummer and vocalist for Genesis as a replacement for John Mayhew in 1970. Moved to lead vocals with the departure of Peter Gabriel and has since developed successful solo LPs and brought Genesis to the top of the charts.

JOHNNY "ROTTEN" LYDON, London, England, 1956. Notorious leader of The Sex Pistols and then Public Image Limited.

TERRY KATH, Chicago, Illinois, 1946. Founding member of Chicago Transit Authority as guitarist and singer, then with Chicago until his death in 1978.

PHIL MANZANERA, 1951. Guitarist for Roxy Music since 1971, after early work with Quiet Sun.

The Grateful Dead

LET'S GET SMALL! RCA Victor unveils the first 45 RPM record playing system. It's the first time a record and a record changer are specifically made for each other. (1949)

1964   The **Beatles** "I Wanna Hold Your Hand" hits #1 on American singles charts and stays there for seven weeks.

1968   **Lisa Marie Presley** is born to Elvis and Priscilla at Baptist Memorial Hospital in Memphis. As heir to her father's estate, Lisa can collect on her 24th birthday, 1992.

1969   **Fleetwood Mac's** "Albatross" leads British singles charts to become the group's first #1 hit record. When it's re-released in 1973, it again makes it into the Top Five.

1971   **Neil Young** is recorded live in Los Angeles. The tapes are issued as *Young Man's Fancy,* a popular bootleg.

1974   Health problems force founder and guitarist, **Eric Bell,** to quit **Thin Lizzy.**

♪ **RECORD RELEASES** include the **Four Seasons** "Dawn (Go Away)" . . . and **Tommy Roe** "Dizzy" (1969).

Birthdays:

DON EVERLY, Brownie, Kentucky, 1937. He and brother Phil formed the Everly Brothers.

RAY SAWYER, Alabama, 1937. Singer with Dr. Hook and the Medicine Show. He himself is group symbol and namesake because of his eyepatch.

Notes:

_____

_____

_____

_____

_____

_____

_____

EVERYDAY ENDS TONITE! Buddy Holly performs for the last time at the Surf Ballroom in Clear Lake, Iowa. Tomorrow, Holly, Richie Valens and J.P. Richardson are to travel by plane to Fargo, North Dakota. (1959)

1974 **Keith Emerson** suffers slight injuries to his hands when his ''rigged'' piano explodes prematurely during a San Francisco date with **Emerson, Lake and Palmer.**

1978 **Van Halen** signs with Warner Brothers Records, remembered by drummer **Alex Van Halen** as ''the day I signed my life away.''

1979 **Sid Vicious** of the **Sex Pistols** dies of a heroin overdose in Greenwich Village, not far from the apartment where he allegedly murdered his girlfriend. The end for the 21-year-old punk star comes only a day after he's bailed out of Rikers Island Prison.

🎵 **RECORD RELEASES** include the **Coasters** ''Charlie Brown'' (1959) . . . and **Carly Simon-James Taylor** ''Mockingbird'' (1974).

Birthdays:

GRAHAM NASH, Lancashire, England, 1942. Singer and guitarist with the Hollies, before becoming part of Crosby, Stills and Nash in '69. Various solo albums.

SKIP BATTIN Bassist replacement for John York of the Byrds in '69, followed by a career with the New Riders of the Purple Sage and the Flying Burrito Brothers.

DEREK SHULMAN, Glasgow, Scotland, 1947. Guitarist and singer with brothers Phil and Ray in Simon Dupree and the Big Sound, later forming Gentle Giant.

Van Halen

SHOCK THAT ROCKED THE WORLD! Rock legends Buddy Holly, Richie Valens and The Big Bopper (J.P. Richardson) die in a small plane crash outside Mason City, Iowa enroute to a concert date. Holly is only 22 years old. (1959)

1961 **Bob Dylan's** first recording session at the home of friends **Sid** and **Bob Gleason,** East Orange, New Jersey. Dylan sings "San Francisco Bay Blues," "Jesus Met The Woman At The Well" and others.

1969 The **Beatles** hire Allen Klein as manager, against the wishes of **Paul McCartney.**

1978 **Dead Man's Curve**, a made-for-TV movie about singers Jan and Dean, airs on ABC with Jan in a token role.

1979 **Buddy Holly** fans crowd the Surf Ballroom for the 20th anniversary memorial concert to honor Holly and others who died after their final appearance.

Birthdays:

DAVE DAVIES, London, England, 1947. With brother, Ray, the Kinks are born in 1964 and he continues as guitarist.

MELANIE SCHEKERYK, Long Island, New York, 1947. Singer and songwriter from 1970 with hits "Look What They've Done To My Song, Ma" and "Brand New Key."

Also, **JOHNNY "GUITAR" WATSON,** 1935.

Notes:

PLEASED TO MEET YOU! The Beatles bow to Paul's insistence that the Eastman & Eastman law firm be appointed to handle the affairs of The Apple Corp. Eastman is McCartney's father-in-law. (1969)

1971 **Chicago** is awarded a Gold Record for *Chicago 3*.

1974 **John and Yoko** split up, the relationship strained from their immigration ordeal.

1977 *Evita* is released on MCA Records, the follow-up to the **Tim Rice** and **Andrew Lloyd Webber** hit *Jesus Christ Superstar*. Both albums are adapted the London and Broadway stages.

1979 A month-long rock memorabilia auction begins in San Francisco to benefit the Save-The-Whales campaign. Among the items are **John Travolta's** black leather jacket worn in *Grease*, **Alice Cooper's** five-foot boa constrictor, a **Paul Kantner** guitar, and a **Cheech and Chong** bong.

1982 **Alex Harvey** of the **Alex Harvey Band** dies a day before his 47th birthday.

🎵 **RECORD RELEASES** include **Mitch Ryder and The Detroit Wheels** "Sock It To Me Baby" (1967).

Birthdays:

JOHN STEEL, England, 1941. Drummer with the Animals after starting with the Alan Price Combo.

ALICE COOPER, Detroit, Michigan, 1948. Born Vincent Furnier, he's best known for his theatrical rock antics with snakes and the hits "Eighteen," "School's Out," and "Welcome To My Nightmare."

JERRY SHIRLEY, Essex, England, 1952. The original drummer for Humble Pie, and remained so until they disbanded in 1981.

Notes:

FIRST TIME'S A CHARM! The #1 song on the American singles chart is The Shirelles' "Will You Still Love Me Tomorrow," written by Carole King. It returns as a hit ten years later, sung by her. (1960)

1972 **Paul Simon's** "Mother and Child Reunion" and **Neil Young's** "Heart Of Gold" released.

1973 **Elton John** is awarded a Gold Record for the single "Crocodile Rock."

Birthdays:

BOB MARLEY, Middlesex, Jamaica, 1945. Singer and guitarist credited with bringing reggae to the world's rock fans. Formed The Wailers in 1965 and remained with them until his death in 1981.

ALEX HARVEY, Glasgow, Scotland, 1935. Formed The Alex Harvey Big Soul Band in 1958 and evolved to The Sensational Alex Harvey Band in 1972.

NIGEL OLSSON, England, 1949. Drummer with the reformed Spencer Davis Group in the midsixties before joining Elton John in 1970.

CORY WELLS, Buffalo, New York, 1942. Singer with Three Dog Night.

AL KOOPER, Brooklyn, New York, 1944. Singer and keyboard player for Blood, Sweat & Tears, the group he formed in 1967 after playing session dates with Bob Dylan and others.

Bob Marley

HELTER SKELTER REVEALED! A *New York Post* reporter is among the first to discover the connection between lyrics of five tunes on the Beatles' "White Album" and the twisted motivations of Charles Manson in the deaths of actress Sharon Tate and others in Los Angeles. (1970)

1965 **The Righteous Brothers'** "You've Lost That Lovin' Feeling" is #1 in the U.S.

1976 **Vince Guaraldi** dies of a heart attack in San Francisco at age 47. The jazz composer is best remembered for his Grammy-winning "Cast Your Fate To The Wind" and the scoring of the *Peanuts* TV specials.

1981 Geffen Records releases **Yoko's** "Walking On Thin Ice" with **John Lennon** on guitar, the song being mixed in the studio the night Lennon is murdered.

1981 **Paul McCartney** and **Ringo Starr** join **George Harrison** in recording "All Those Years Ago," a tribute to Lennon.

Birthdays:

FABIAN, born Fabiano Forte, Philadelphia, Pennsylvania, 1943. A teenage hearthrob of the fifties, he had a big hit in '59 with "I'm A Man."

Notes:

THE BEATLES HAVE LANDED! Kennedy Airport in New York is swarming with screaming teenagers, as the Beatles step off the plane and set foot on American soil for the first time. The "hysterical airport crowd" scene becomes a regular scenario for Beatles visits. (1964)

1965 **George Harrison** has his tonsils removed at University College Hospital in London.

1966 The premiere issue of *Crawdaddy,* the first rock magazine, is published by **Paul Williams** in New York City.

1979 **Steve Stills** makes the first digitally recorded rock album.

1980 **Pink Floyd's** spectacular new concert "The Wall" debuts in Los Angeles before moving on to New York for a second and final series of American performances. The elaborate stage includes a 120-foot-long wall, which is destroyed at the concert's climax.

🎵 **RECORD RELEASES** include the **Beatles** "Nowhere Man" (1966) . . . **Badfinger** "Come and Get It" and **Simon & Garfunkel** "Bridge Over Troubled Water" (1970).

Birthdays:

JIMMY GREENSPOON born in 1948. Keyboardist with Three Dog Night, his credits also include session work with Kim Fowley and Beck, Bogert and Appice.

Notes:

_____

_____

_____

_____

_____

_____

_____

_____

I AM A DJ, THAT'S WHAT I AM! Congressional investigators question what it's worth as they open hearings into payola in the radio and record industries. Among the accused, DJs Alan Freed and Dick Clark. (1960)

1971 **Bob Dylan's** protest documentary film *Eat The Document* premieres at the New York Academy of Music. ABC buys it, then rejects the project when the network discovers the film isn't a Dylan concert, as promised.

1972 **Frank Zappa's** concert at Royal Albert Hall in London is canceled because of "obscene lyrics" in the score of "200 Motels," the composition to be premiered that night. Four thousand fans demonstrate to little avail.

1972 The **Beatles** Fan Club goes out of business for good, nearly two years after the band breaks up.

1973 **Max Yasgur** dies of a heart attack in Florida. His dairy farm in upstate New York became the concert site of the Woodstock celebration in 1969.

RECORD RELEASES include the **Zombies** "Time of the Season" and the **Classics IV** "Traces" (1969) . . . the **Beatles** "I Saw Her Standing There" (1964) . . . the **Ozark Mountain Daredevils** "Jackie Blue," **Ringo Starr** "No, No Song," and **Queen** "Killer Queen" (1975).

Birthdays:

TOM RUSH, Portsmouth, New Hampshire, 1941. Singer, songwriter and guitarist of the sixties folk era.

ADOLPHO DE LA PARRA, Mexico City, 1946. Original drummer for blues-boogie band Canned Heat.

Notes:

LADIEEZH 'N GENNLEMEN! The Beatles debut on *The Ed Sullivan Show,* opening with "I Wanna Hold Your Hand" which is barely audible over the screams from the audience. (1964).

1970   John Lennon's "Instant Karma" is released, his first collaboration with producer **Phil Spector.**

1972   Paul McCartney appears live for the first time since the Beatles disbanded in a concert at Nottingham University in London. "Without planning any gigs or anything . . . one of our fellows went in and asked 'Do you want Paul McCartney and **Wings** to play here?' . . . the fellow luckily said 'yes.'"—Paul.

1974   Paul McCartney releases "Jet."

1981   Bill Haley dies of a heart attack in Harlingen, Texas. Haley and his group, **The Comets,** carved out a niche in rock history with the song that would become the rock 'n' roll anthem, "Rock Around The Clock."

1982   George Harrison presents an $8.8 million check to UNICEF Chairman Hugh Downs as settlement for the proceeds from the 1971 Concert for Bangla Desh. The money had remained inaccessible for eleven years because of legal entanglements.

Birthdays:

CAROLE KING, born Carole Klein, Brooklyn, New York, 1941. Singer and songwriter who penned hits for various artists in the late fifties and sixties, until her solo career in 1971. Best known for her hugely successful LP *Tapestry.*

TED TURNER, England, 1950. Guitarist with Wishbone Ash, he left the group in 1974 to pursue solo ventures.

George Harrison

A DAY FOR DANCIN'! Three singles released on this day would put America's rock fans' feet in motion, with Sly and The Family Stone's release of "Dance To The Music," Kenny Rogers and The First Edition's "Just Dropped In (To See What Condition My Condition Was In)," 1968 . . . and the Dire Straits debut, "Sultans of Swing," 1979.

1974   Phil Spector is seriously burned in an auto accident. Spector's "wall of music" concept has given birth to a dynamic new trend in rock, with R & B overtones and hits from **The Ronettes, Shirelles** and others.

1981   Elvis Costello makes a rare TV appearance on NBC's *Tomorrow Show* with Tom Snyder.

Birthdays:

ROBERTA FLACK, Asheville, North Carolina, 1940. Singer and pianist with a strong solo career and duet history with Donny Hathaway, best known for "Killing Me Softly With His Song," soundtrack theme from Clint Eastwood's *Play Misty For Me.*

Elvis Costello

GO EAST, YOUNG WOMAN! Janis Joplin plays four sold-out shows at New York's Fillmore East, to an audience that includes reporter Mike Wallace. Janis later confesses she doesn't remember Wallace or her interview for CBS's *60 Minutes.* (1969)

1963   *Introducing The Beatles* is recorded.

1965   **Ringo Starr** marries **Maureen Cox** in London. It lasts ten years.

1978   **Jackson Browne** releases *Running On Empty,* a unique LP of all his own material, recorded live during August and September concerts, 1977.

♫ **RECORD RELEASES** this day include **Herman's Hermits** "There's A Kind Of Hush" . . . **Tommy James and the Shondells** "I Think We're Alone Now" . . . **The Lovin' Spoonful** "Darlin' Be Home Soon" . . . and the **Turtles** "Happy Together" (1967).

Birthdays:

GENE VINCENT, born Vincent Eugene Craddock, Norfolk, Virginia; 1935. Noted contemporary of Elvis Presley and one of the first "grease and leather" rockers.

ALAN RUBIN of the Blues Brothers Band, 1953. A one-time member of Blood, Sweat and Tears, he also did session work for Johnny Winter, Lou Reed and others. Trumpeter.

Notes:

WHERE NO BAND HAS GONE BEFORE! The Beatles cap off a successful first American tour with a concert at the prestigious Carnegie Hall in New York City, most often reserved for virtuoso performances. (1964)

1967 **Keith Richards, Mick Jagger** and **Marianne Faithful** busted for drug possession at Keith's home in West Wittering, England, the first of a highly publicized chain of drug busts involving the **Rolling Stones** members.

1968 **Jimi Hendrix** is awarded an honorary high school diploma from Garfield High in Seattle, Washington. He was a drop-out at age 14.

1976 **Sal Mineo** is found murdered in Los Angeles at age 37. He's best known for acting in films after a Top Ten hit with "Start Movin'" in 1957.

♫ **GOLD RECORDS** awarded to **Elton John** for *Don't Shoot Me, I'm Only The Piano Player* (1973) . . . and to **Bob Dylan** for "Blood On The Tracks" (1975).

♫ **RECORD RELEASES** include **Simon & Garfunkel** "Homeward Bound" (1966) . . . **Yes** "Roundabout" (1972) . . . and **Paul McCartney's** live version of "Maybe I'm Amazed" (1977).

Birthdays:

RAY MANZAREK, Chicago, Illinois, 1935. Keyboard player for the Doors.

STANLEY KNIGHT, Little Rock, Arkansas, 1949. Original guitarist and founding member of Black Oak Arkansas.

STEVE HACKETT England, 1950. Guitarist with Genesis from 1970, and various solo project since his departure in 1977.

Notes:

Ray Manzarek

BACK IN THE FIFTIES AGAIN! *Grease* opens to mild reviews at the off-Broadway Theater in New York City. The fifties rock Martin Eden musical is soon to move uptown and become the longest running song-and-dance show on Broadway. (1972)

1966 **The Rolling Stones** appear on *The Ed Sullivan Show.*

1974 **Bob Dylan** caps off his triumphant U.S. Tour with the **Band** at the Fabulous Forum in Los Angeles. It's here where most of the songs on *Before the Flood* are recorded.

🎵 **RECORD RELEASES** include **Jr. Walker and the Allstars** "Shotgun" (1965) . . . and **Cat Stevens** "Wild World" (1971).

Birthdays:

PETER TORK, Washington, D.C., 1944. Guitarist with The Monkees until 1969 when he left the made-for-TV rock group to form The Release, and later, The New Monks.

ED GAGLIARDI, New York City, 1952. Original member and bassist with Foreigner in 1976.

Notes:

_____

_____

_____

_____

_____

_____

_____

_____

VALENTINES TO REMEMBER! John and Yoko begin a week-long stint as co-hosts on the *Mike Douglas Show,* during which John reveals his much publicized riff with Paul McCartney is ending. (1972)

1960 **Mark Denning's** "Teen Angel" is #1 on American singles charts.

1972 **Mayor Sam Yorty** declares "Steppenwolf Day" in Los Angeles, just days after the band announces its retirement.

1973 **David Bowie** opens his midnight Valentine's Day concert at New York's Radio City Music Hall by dropping to the stage in a glass-domed "space capsule." His exit is marred by a fan charging the stage, knocking Bowie to the floor.

1974 **Janis Joplin's** manager sues a San Francisco life insurance company for refusing to pay a $200,000 policy claim. The company says Janis' death was suicide.

1977 In "At Seventeen," **Janis Ian** claims she never received Valentine's cards while a teen, but fans make up for it by sending 461 cards this Valentine's Day.

Birthdays:

TIM BUCKLEY, Washington, 1947. A songwriter of considerable talent, he died tragically in 1975 of a drug overdose.

ERIC ANDERSEN, Pittsburgh, Pa., 1943. An accomplished folk guitarist, Brian Epstein was on the verge of signing him when Brian died.

Notes:

_____

_____

_____

_____

_____

_____

_____

F-A-K-E-O-U-T! A Florida hairdresser is jailed for staging a phony Aretha Franklin concert at a Fort Meyer nightclub. The "Aretha" impersonator, Vickie Jones, is so convincing nobody asks for a refund. (1969)

1958 "Get A Job" by **The Silhouettes** is #1.

1964 **The Beach Boys** "Fun, Fun, Fun" and "Glad All Over" by **The Dave Clark Five** released.

1967 An anti-bootlegging law goes into effect as an attempt to curb the pirating of records.

1976 **Bette Midler** bails out seven members of her entourage following a bust for cocaine and pot possession.

1977 **Glen Matlock** is fired from **The Sex Pistols,** to be replaced by the notorious **Sid Vicious.**

1981 **Mike Bloomfield** dies in his car in San Francisco. The blues guitarist came to national prominence in the mid-sixties for performances with **Paul Butterfield** and **Bob Dylan,** then formed **The Electric Flag.** Best known for his *Super Session* LP recording in 1968 with **Steve Stills** and **Al Kooper.**

Birthdays:

BRIAN HOLLAND, Detroit, Michigan, 1941. Super songwriter and producer of The Motown Sound in the sixties, with brother Eddie and partner Lamont Dozier.

MICK AVORY, London, 1944. Former drummer for The Kinks.

MELISSA MANCHESTER, Bronx, New York, 1951. Singer and songwriter with an early background in The Harlettes, then success as a solo performer.

Michael Bloomfield

AIMS TO PLEASE! The Beatles "Please Please Me" moves to the top of the British rock charts only a month after its release. This is the first in an unbroken chain of #1 Beatles hits throughout the sixties. (1963)

1963 **Paul Anka** marries **Ann Dezogheb** in Paris.

1974 **Elton John's** "Bennie and the Jets" is released.

Birthdays:

SONNY BONO. born Salvatore Bono, Detroit, Michigan, 1935. Singer and songwriter in partnership with wife Cher for "I Got You Babe" in 1964, and later with "The Beat Goes On." Sonny and Cher host a weekly TV show in the early seventies before splitting up both personally and professionally in 1974 to pursue solo careers.

PETE WILLIS of Def Leppard born.

Elton John

A BEATLES' DOZEN! The Beatles' "All My Lovin'" is released to mark the third of a dozen Beatles singles to chart during the year. (1964)

1965 **The Rolling Stones** re-record vocals for "The Last Time" at RCA Studios in London, displeased with the original version.

1969 **Bob Dylan** and **Johnny Cash** record together in Nashville, but the LP will not be released.

1970 **Joni Mitchell** announces retirement from live concert performances after an appearance at Royal Albert Hall in London. In 1974 she returns with the double-live LP *Miles of Aisles.*

1973 "Dueling Banjos" is #1 in U.S., from the film *Deliverance*

1975 **John Lennon's** *Rock and Roll* LP is released.

1976 *Rockabye Hamlet* opens on Broadway, an attempt to fuse Shakespeare and rock music, it fails only days later.

1979 **Blondie's** "Heart of Glass" single released.

1982 Jazz great, **Thelonius Monk,** dies of a stroke in Englewood, New Jersey.

Birthdays:

GENE PITNEY, Hartford, Connecticut, 1941. Pop singer and songwriter in the mid-sixties, best known for "Town Without Pity."

BOBBY LEWIS, Indianapolis, Indiana, 1933. Sixties pop star known for "Tossin' and Turnin'."

Joni Mitchell

FEBRUARY 18

NOW OR NEVER! Dr. Hook and The Medicine Show takes its name during a small club date in Union City, New Jersey when the club owner demands the band members come up with a name by concert time. Guitarist Ray Sawyer's eyepatch gives way to the visual of "Dr. Hook" and "The Medicine Show" is what follows. (1969)

1968 **David Gilmore** joins **Pink Floyd** replacing guitarist **Syd Barrett.**

1974 **Kiss'** debut album released, the first LP on Casablanca Records.

1981 **Mick Fleetwood** performs benefit concert for local musicians union in Accra, Ghana and begins recording *The Visitor* LP.

Birthdays:

YOKO ONO LENNON, Tokyo, Japan, 1933. Meets John Lennon and is married in 1969, with various recordings with Lennon after Beatles breakup in 1970.

ROBBIE BACHMAN, Winnipeg, Canada, 1953. Joins brothers Randy and Tim in 1970 in Brave Belt, evolving into Bachman-Turner Overdrive.

Yoko Ono

IT'S PAUL-ITICS! Paul McCartney's "Give Ireland Back To The Irish" is promptly banned in England under a law that prohibits artists from commenting on issues under a Crown investigation. The ex-Beatle's outrage over Britain's "Bloody Sunday" killings hits #1 in Ireland (1972)

1972 **Harry Nilsson's** "Without You" is #1 in the U.S., just as **America's** debut single, "Horse With No Name," enters the charts.

1972 **Elton John** is awarded a Gold Record for his *Madman Across The Water* LP.

1974 **Dick Clark's** *American Music Awards* debuts on ABC-TV. The show is set up to reflect the tastes of the record-buying public rather than those of the record industry, as in the Grammy Award.

1974 **Kiss** makes its debut television appearance on Don Kirshner's "In Concert."

1976 Tower of Power singer **Rick Stevens** surrenders to San Jose police in triple-murder case.

1980 **AC/DC** singer **Bon Scott** dies of alcohol poisoning in London.

1981 **George Harrison** is ordered to pay $587,000 to ABKCO Music for "subconscious plagiarism" because of musical similarities between Harrison's "My Sweet Lord" and ABKCO's copyright on "He's So Fine."

Birthdays:

WILLIAM "SMOKEY" ROBINSON, Detroit, Michigan, 1940. Singer, songwriter and founder of The Miracles from 1957 through the seventies.

TOMMY IOMMI, Birmingham, England, 1948. The guitarist's beginnings in Earth evolved into Black Sabbath in '69.

ANDY POWELL, England, 1950. Guitarist with Wishbone Ash, a founding member.

LOU CHRISTIE, Glen Willard, Pennsylvania, 1943. Falsetto pop singer noted for #1 single "Lightning Strikes."

Notes:

Kiss

RINGO STARS! Although not the male lead in this film adaptation of *Candy*. Ringo Starr is prominently featured in the part of a Mexican gardener at the premiere of this X-Rated feature film. (1969)

1973 **Rolling Stones** fans riot in Adelaide, Australia when they can't get tickets to a sold-out concert. Local police fight with the 4,000 fans for nearly an hour before arresting forty.

1974 **Cher** files for separation after ten years of marriage to **Sonny Bono.**

1974 **Yes** sells out Madison Square Garden in New York City without a stitch of advertising. Word-of-mouth alone clears the box office of tickets.

1976 Members of **Kiss** plant their footprints alongside the famous at Grauman's Theater in Los Angeles.

1976 Pharmacist, **Joe Fuchs,** pleads guilty to conspiracy for the sale of drugs to **Greg Allman** via group roadie **Scooter Herring.**

1982 **Pat Benatar** marries guitarist-producer, **Neil Geraldo,** in the Hawaiian island of Maui. This just four days before winning her second Grammy.

RECORD RELEASES include the **Beatles** "Eight Days A Week," **The Moody Blues** "Go Now," and **The Supremes** "Stop In The Name of Love," (1965) . . . **Marvin Gaye** "What's Going On" and **Santana** "Oye Como Va" (1971).

Birthdays:

RANDY CALIFORNIA, Los Angeles, 1946. Guitarist with Jimi Hendrix and other noted musicians before forming Red Rover in '65, which evolved into Spirit.

J. GEILS, 1946. Guitarist who weathered the Boston club scene for years with the J. Geils Band, before reaching stardom with the *Freeze Frame* LP in 1982.

Notes:

BALLAD OF A SUPREME! Florence Ballard dies a pauper in Detroit at age 32. One of the original Supremes, she quits the group in 1967 after a string of #1 hits. Ballard never receives any royalties for her work. (1976)

1976   Peter Frampton's "Show Me The Way" is released as a single from mega-LP *Frampton Comes Alive.*

1981   REO Speedwagon's *Hi Infidelity* LP is #1 following the band's ten-year climb to national prominence. The LP sells 6 million copies the first year.

1982   Murray The K dies of cancer in Los Angeles. The New York DJ, known for his close association with the **Beatles** during their early American tours.

Birthdays:

DAVID GEFFEN, born 1943. Formed Geffen Records in the early eighties and signs John Lennon and Elton John as its first artists.

Notes:

TOP OF THE POPS! Elvis Presley gets his first national record exposure with the inclusion of "Heartbreak Hotel" in the U.S. charts, the first Presley single of many to hit #1. (1956)

1965 Filming begins in the Bahamas on the second **Beatles'** movie *Help*

1968 The debut single from **Genesis,** "The Silent Sun" is released on Decca Records.

1973 **Roberta Flack** is awarded a Gold Record for "Killing Me Softly," a song inspired by **Don McLean.**

1980 **Rolling Stones** guitarist, **Ron Wood,** and a girlfriend are arrested in St. Maarten when police find five grams of cocaine in the couple's rented apartment. No charges are filed.

🎵 **RECORD RELEASES** include **Leo Sayer** "Long Tall Glasses" (1975).

Ron Wood

WHERE EAGLES DARE! The Grammy Award for "Record of the Year" is won by The Eagles for "Hotel California," but the band members choose not to attend the "pretentious" ceremony. (1978)

1979   **Dire Straits** begins their first American tour in Boston.

🎵 **RECORD RELEASES** include **Buddy Holly's** "It Doesn't Matter Anymore" (1959). . . **The Chiffons** "He's So Fine" (1963). . . **Billy Joel** "Piano Man" and **Maria Muldaur** "Midnight At The Oasis" (1974).

Birthdays:

JOHNNY WINTER, Leland, Mississippi, 1944. Guitarist with delta blues background who has collaborated often with brother Edgar Winter.

RUSTY YOUNG, Long Beach, California, 1946. Pedal steel guitarist with Poco from the band's inception in 1968.

BRAD WHITFORD, Boston, Massachusettes, 1952. Guitarist and founding member of Aerosmith until the band dissolved in late seventies, then co-founded the Whitford-St. Holmes Band in '81.

STEVE PRIEST, Middlesex, U.K., 1950. Bassist with Sweet until he left to pursue a solo career.

Eagles

SIGN OF THE TIMES! The Bee Gees sign with manager-promoter Robert Stigwood, who tells reporters it's "impossible to overstate their international potential both as performers and composers." He's never proved wrong. (1967)

1968   Jimi Hendrix's *Axis: Bold As Love* LP enters the American Top Twenty.

1981   Rockpile, one of the most promising bands of the eighties, disbands over personality riff between group co-leaders, **Dave Edmunds** and **Nick Lowe.**

♫ **RECORD RELEASES** include **Dobie Gray** "Drift Away" (1973) . . . and the **Police** "Roxanne" (1979).

Birthdays:

NICKY HOPKINS, London, England, 1944. Keyboard player for Screaming Lord Sutch's Savages and the Cyril Davies' All-Stars, evolving as guest performer with The Who, Rolling Stones, John Lennon, Jeff Beck and others.

PAUL JONES, Portsmouth, England, 1944. Original singer for Manfred Mann's Earth Band through the early seventies.

Bee Gees with manager Robert Stigwood

A BRAND NEW DAY! Buddy Holly travels to Norman Petty's studio in Clovis, New Mexico, to record "That'll Be The Day" with his new back-up band The Crickets. Twenty years later, Linda Ronstadt will have success with a cover version of the song. (1957)

1968 *The New York Times* hails **Jimi Hendrix** as "the black Elvis."

1975 **Led Zeppelin's** *Physical Graffiti* LP is released on the band's own Swan Song label. The sixth Zeppelin album boasts one of the costliest sleeves ever produced for a rock album.

1977 **The Jam** is signed by Polydor Records, the label's first new wave act.

1981 **Christopher Cross** sweeps the Grammy Awards at New York's Radio City Music Hall with his debut LP. The Texas born ex-roadie for the **Doobie Brothers** takes five top honors.

🎵 **RECORD RELEASES** include the **Beatles** "Penny Lane-Strawberry Fields" and the **Mamas and the Papas** "Dedicated To The One I Love" (1967) . . . and **Eddie Money** "Baby Hold On" (1978).

Birthdays:

GEORGE HARRISON, Liverpool, England, 1943. Guitarist with the Beatles, he met John Lennon and Paul McCartney in 1960. Continued success as a solo artist following the Beatles' break-up ten years later.

STUART WOOD, Edinburgh, Scotland, 1957. Guitarist for the Bay City Rollers, later to be called the Rollers.

Notes:

Christopher Cross

ONE ON ONE! A momentous day for the Beatles when they are awarded a Gold Record for "Hey Jude," the same day the song is released on Apple Records. (1970)

1966   The **Beach Boys**' "Barbara Ann" enters British rock charts to reach #3.

1977   Bluesman, **Booker T. Washington,** ("Bukka" White) dies.

🎵 **RECORD RELEASES** include the **Lovin' Spoonful** "Day Dream" and **The Rolling Stones** "19th Nervous Breakdown" (1966) . . . the **Eagles** "Hotel California" and **Leo Sayer** "When I Need You" (1977).

Birthdays:

ANTOINE "FATS" DOMINO, New Orleans, Louisiana, 1928. Legendary singer and piano player who influenced many rock styles of the fifties and sixties with his upbeat keyboard work. Best known for his hits "Blueberry Hill," "Josephine," "Walking' To New Orleans."

JOHNNY CASH, Dyess, Arkansas, 1932. Singer and guitarist with early recordings on the Sun label, including "I Walk The Line," later a major country star of TV and films.

PAUL COTTON, 1943. Guitarist for Poco as replacement for Jim Messina in 1975.

BOB "THE BEAR" HITE, Torrance, California 1945. Singer with Canned Heat.

Johnny Cash

FEBRUARY 27

ONE GOOD TURN DESERVES ANOTHER! Jerry Lee Lewis fathers a son, Steve Allen Lewis, named for TV comedian-host, Steve Allen. Allen gave Jerry Lee one of the early breaks in his career. (1959).

1962 **Gene Chandler's** "Duke of Earl" is #1 in U.S.

1967 **Pink Floyd** records "Arnold Layne," their first single.

1970 **The Jefferson Airplane,** is fined $1,000 for singing the "ultimate" profanity while on stage in Oklahoma City. City fathers enforce the ordinance prohibiting obscene language on stage, drawn up a year earlier when **Doors'** singer, **Jim Morrison,** fondled himself at a Miami concert date.

1976 **Mick Jagger** is admitted to a New York City hospital suffering a respiratory infection, earlier rumored to be a drug overdose. Jagger and girlfriend sign the hospital register "Mercedes" and "Benz."

1977 **Keith Richards** is busted in a Toronto hotel by Canadian Mounties who uncover an ounce of heroin. The sentence Keith draws is to include a benefit Rolling Stone concert.

Birthdays:

STEVE HARLEY, born Steven Nice in South London, 1951. Formed his band The Cockney Rebel in the fall of '74.

Notes:

Brian Jones

FEBRUARY 28

SO IT GOES! The Cavern Club in Liverpool, once the hangout of the Beatles and scores of their fans, closes its doors because the club owners can't meet their debts. (1966)

1969   **Elton John** is the first artist to sign with "This Record Company" label.

1970   **Norman Greenbaum's** "Spirit In The Sky" and "Celebrate" by **Three Dog Night** released.

1972   A New York magazine accuses former **Beatles** manager **Allen Klein,** of skimming profits from the sales of **George Harrison's** *Concert For Bangla Desh* LP. Klein responds with a $150 million damage suit against the magazine.

1972   The "French Connection" drug bust occurs at the port of Marseilles, as authorities seize 937 pounds of pure heroin valued at $100 million.

1974   Singer, **Bobby Bloom,** dies of self-inflicted gunshot wounds in a West Hollywood motel.

1975   Guitarist/singer/composer, **Russ Ballard,** of Argent forms his own band to begin an American tour.

1978   **Bob Dylan** records his Budokan concert in Tokyo, Japan.

1980   Sam Goody, Inc. and two of the record chain's top executives are charged with trafficking counterfeit records and tapes, including titles by **Billy Joel, The Bee Gees, Eric Clapton, Paul McCartney** and others.

Birthdays:

BRIAN JONES, Cheltenham Spa, England, 1942. Guitarist for The Rolling Stones until he exited the band in June, 1969. He drowns a month later.

JOE SOUTH, born 1942. Best known for his hit "Games People Play."

FEBRUARY 29

ODD MAN OUT! John Lennon's U.S. immigration visa expires, setting off his four-year fight to gain permanent residency in the United States. (1972)

PEOPLE ARE STRANGE! Jim Morrison arrested during a concert at the Dinner Key Auditorium in Miami, charged with lewd and lascivious behavior, open profanity, indecent exposure and public drunkenness. "It was real hot and Jim was real drunk, but as far as I can see he didn't drop his pants."—John Densmore, Doors drummer. (1969)

1952 "Drivin' Slow" by **Johnny London** is the first single released on Sun Records, one of the first rock 'n' roll labels. **Elvis Presley, Jerry Lee Lewis, Johnny Cash** and others would grace Sun in the years ahead.

1973 **The Robert Joffrey Dance Company** opens in New York City with "Deuce Coupe Ballet," featuring **Beach Boys** music and local graffiti artists.

1976 **Jackson Browne** begins his first recording session for the *Pretender* album.

1977 **Sara Dylan** files for divorce after twelve years of marriage to Bob.

1980 **Patti Smith** marries **Fred Smith,** former **MC 5** guitarist, in a civil ceremony in Detroit. The bride wears ballet slippers.

♫ **RECORD RELEASES** include **Blood Sweat and Tears** "You've Made Me So Very Happy" . . . and **Steppenwolf** "Rock Me" (1969).

Birthdays:

ROGER DALTRY, London, England, 1944. Lead singer and founding member of The Who with Pete Townshend, Keith Moon, and John Entwistle. His solo career includes film roles in *Tommy* and *McVicar*.

MIKE D'ABO, singer first with Band of Angels, then as replacement for Paul Jones in Manfred Mann's Earth Band.

Notes:

Jim Morrison

COMES IN LIKE A LION! Four major singles are released on the same day and all will become hits. Blue Cheer's "Summertime Blues," The Box Tops "Cry Like A Baby," Simon and Garfunkel's "Scarborough Fair" and "Young Girl" by Gary Puckett and The Union Gap. (1968)

1969   *The Ed Sullivan Show* is again first to present the **Beatles,** this time the film clip from the final Beatles' project "Let It Be," when the song is first heard in the U.S.

1969   Side One of **John Lennon's** "Life With The Lions" is recorded live at Lady Mitchell Hall, Cambridge, England.

1974   Five Grammy's are awarded to **Stevie Wonder** for the LP *Innervisions* and singles "You Are The Sunshine Of My Life" and "Superstition."

1975   **Linda McCartney** is busted when Los Angeles police stop the car carrying Linda and Paul and catch a whiff of marijuana. A quick search yields eight ounces of pot in Linda's purse.

Birthdays:

LOU REED, New York City, 1944. Singer and guitarist with John Cale, then formed The Velvet Underground in the mid-sixties and later pursued a solo career. Best known for "Walk On The Wild Side" and "Sweet Jane."

GEORGE BENSON, Pittsburgh, Pennsylvania, 1943. Jazz guitarist and vocalist with successes in the seventies for "This Masquerade" and "On Broadway."

RORY GALLAGHER, Ballyshannon, Ireland, 1949. Blues guitarist for Taste in 1968, with prominent rock solo career following.

WILLIE CHAMBERS, Flora, Mississippi, 1938. R&B guitarist after early gospel and choir career, then formed The Chambers Brothers in the sixties.

KAREN CARPENTER, New Haven, Connecticut, 1950. She and Brother Richard impressed Herb Alpert with demo, and were signed on his A&M label in the late sixties.

Notes:

George Benson

THERE'S SOMETHIN' HAPPENIN' HERE! Buffalo Springfield forms in Los Angeles when Steve Stills and Richie Furay meet Canadian folk singer Neil Young in a traffic jam. The trio is later joined by Dewey Martin and Bruce Palmer, and the band evolves into a supergroup in the mid-sixties with the release of "For What It's Worth." (1966)

1955 **Elvis Presley** makes his first ever TV appearance on a local sing-along show called *Louisiana Hayride*.

1972 **Harry Nilsson** is awarded a Gold Records for "Without You."

Birthdays:

JANCE GARFAT, California, 1944. Bassist for Dr. Hook and the Medicine Show.

Janis Joplin

FROM THE COLLECTION OF NEAL PETERS

SIX DAY TRIPPER! A second scandal for the radio and record industry breaks when it's revealed that Federal Communications Commission chairman, John Doerfer, has taken a six-day junket to Florida, courtesy of the Storer Broadcasting Company. Doerfer resigns his post within the week. (1960)

1970   Janis Joplin is fined $200 and court costs for using obscene language on stage in Tampa, Florida.

1977   Santana performs at Roseland Dance City in New York, advertised only in Spanish-language publications.

1977   The Rolling Stones record the *Love You Live* LP in concert at Toronto's El Macombo Club.

1978   Atlanta Rhythm Section's "Imaginary Lover" released.

1978   The Bee Gees set a new record when the single "How Deep Is Your Love" stays in the Top Ten for 17 weeks on *Billboard's* Hot 100.

🎵 **GOLD RECORDS** awarded to **The Foundations** for "Build Me Up Buttercup" (1969) . . . and **Badfinger** for "Day After Day" (1972).

Birthdays:

MARY WILSON, Detroit, Michigan, 1944. Founding member of The Supremes with Diana Ross and Flo Ballard.

BOBBY WOMACK, Cleveland, Ohio, 1944. Singer and composer with the Valentino's until 1964, then various projects with Aretha Franklin, Janis Joplin, Wilson Pickett, J. Geils and The Rolling Stones.

CHRIS SQUIRE, London, England, 1948. Bassist for Yes and co-founder of the group until their breakup in 1981. Expected to form new supergroup in 1982-83.

Notes:

_____

_____

_____

_____

_____

_____

_____

HOME IS WHERE IT IS! Elvis Presley is discharged from the Army in one of the most publicized returns of a soldier since General Douglas MacArthur. (1960)

1966 **Sergeant Barry Sadler's** "Ballad Of The Green Berets" is #1 in the U.S.

1968 *Catch My Soul* opens in Hollywood, touted as a musical R&B version of Shakespeare's "Othello" with **Jerry Lee Lewis** as Iago.

1969 *Creem Magazine* premieres at the newsstands.

1971 The Federal Communications Commission warns owners of progressive FM stations not to air "One Toke Over The Line," "White Rabbit," "Puff The Magic Dragon," "Lucy In The Sky With Diamonds" and other songs with possible drug references.

1973 **Mike Jeffrey,** manager for Jimi Hendrix, dies in a plane crash in France.

1975 **Rod Stewart** and actress **Britt Ekland** begin a highly publicized romance after meeting at a party given by **Joni Mitchell** in Los Angeles.

1979 ABC Records cites declining profits and goes out of business.

1982 **John Belushi** dies of respiratory failure at a rented bungalow in Los Angeles. A regular player on "The National Lampoon Radio Show" and later on *Saturday Night Live,* Belushi branched into film work with *Animal House, 1941, The Blues Brothers* and *Continental Divide.* His death attributed to a drug overdose.

1982 The reformed **Mamas & Papas** perform for the first time in the eighties at Princeton University, with originals **John Phillips** and **Denny Doherty** and two new "Mamas," **Spanky McFarlane** and **McKenzie Phillips,** John's daughter.

Birthdays:

ANDY GIBB, Brisbane, Australia, 1958. Youngest brother of The Bee Gees members, a solo artist with many successes, including co-host of the weekly TV series *Solid Gold.*

Notes:

A DAY IN THE LI*E! Awareness Records releases LP of songs by Charles Manson titled *Lie*, the album jacket a reproduction of the *Life* magazine cover photo of the convicted murderer, with magazine logo altered to read "Lie" instead of *Life*. Proceeds from the record sales are to be used to finance Manson's defense for the murders of Sharon Tate and others in Los Angeles. (1970)

1972 **John Lennon's** temporary visa is revoked by the U.S. Department of Immigration.

1975 **Led Zeppelin** is awarded a Gold Record for the *Physical Graffiti* LP and **Average White Band** for the single "Pick Up The Pieces."

1976 All 22 **Beatles** singles are released by Britain's EMI Records, starting with "Got To Get You Into My Life."

1978 **Billy Joel** is awarded a Platinum Record for his single "Just The Way You Are."

🎵 **RECORD RELEASES** include **Del Shannon** "Runaway" (1961) . . . **Paul McCartney** "Just Another Day" (1971) . . . **Elvin Bishop** "Fooled Around And Fell In Love" and **Fleetwood Mac** "Rhiannon" (1976).

Birthdays:

DAVID GILMOUR, Cambridge, England, 1947. Guitarist for Pink Floyd at the invitation of founder Syd Barrett.

KIKI DEE, born Pauline Matthews, Bradford, England, 1947. Moderately successful as a singer until joining Elton John's Rocket Records in 1973, with the hit single "Don't Go Breakin' My Heart" in 1976.

HUGH GRUNDY, Winchester, England, 1945. Drummer and founding member of The Zombies.

Billy Joel

ALL THAT JAZZ, AND MORE! "The Dixie Jazz Band One Step," the first jazz record in America, is released by Nick LaRocca's Original Dixieland Jazz Band. (1917)

1964   **Jan & Dean's** "Dead Man's Curve" and "Needles and Pins," by **The Searchers,** released.

1965   **The Rolling Stones** perform at the Palace Theater in Manchester, England.

1973   **Loggins & Messina** awarded a Gold Record for "Your Mama Don't Dance."

1975   **David Bowie's** *Young Americans* LP is released, featuring the title hit and "Fame," with **John Lennon** on backup vocals and guitar.

1976   **Elton John** becomes the first rock celebrity since the **Beatles** to be immortalized in wax at Madame Tussaud's waxworks museum in London. "Mine is the only one that talks."—Elton.

Birthdays:

PETER WOLF, 1946. Singer for The J. Geils Band after an early career with the Hallucinations.

CHRIS TAYLOR WHITE, Barnet, England, 1943. Bassist for The Zombies with Rod Argent, Paul Atkinson, Hugh Grundy and Colin Blunstone.

MATTHEW FISHER, 1946. Keyboards for Procol Harum through the band's third LP, *Salty Dog.*

Notes:

SOMEONE ELSE'S TURN! The Beatles perform for the first time on the BBC, the 5 PM radio show "Teenager's Turn," where John, Paul, George and Pete Best play the Roy Orbison hit "Dream Baby." (1962)

1965 **The Rolling Stones** enter the Top Ten in the U.S. with "The Last Time."

1968 Promoter **Bill Graham's** celebrated rock club, The Fillmore East, opens in New York City.

1971 Radio Hanoi opens its first American rock broadcast with the **Jimi Hendrix** version of "The Star Spangled Banner," heard by U.S. soldiers throughout Vietnam. The music provided on tapes sent to Hanoi by **Abbie Hoffman, John Gabree and John Giorno.**

1973 **Paul McCartney** is busted for growing pot on his farm in Campbeltown, Scotland.

1973 **Ron "Pigpen" McKernan** dies of a stomach hemorrhage at his home in Corte Madera, California. The Keyboard player, vocalist and founding member of **The Grateful Dead** is 27.

1975 "How Long" by **Ace** and **Elton John's** "Philadelphia Freedom" released.

1976 **Gary Wright** is awarded a Gold Record for his *Dream Weaver* LP.

1977 **The Hollies** play a rare London concert at the Royal Albert Hall.

Birthdays:

RANDY MEISNER, Scottsbluff, Nebraska, 1946. Bass and vocals for The Eagles, after early associations with Rick Nelson and Poco. His solo career began in 1977 after he left the Eagles.

Notes:

NOT FOR SALE! Lawyers for Jimi Hendrix attempt to stop Capitol Records from selling the Curtis Knight LP *Get That Feeling* featuring a picture of Hendrix and his name on the cover. Hendrix thinks it deceitful because he appears on the album merely as a session player. (1968)

1972 **Allen Klein** presents UNICEF with the first check from the proceeds of **George Harrison's** Bangla Desh concert and LP, $1.2 million. Nearly $9 million more will be held up in legal entanglements until 1982.

1974 **Bad Company** debuts in concert in Newcastle, England.

1976 **Keith Moon** collapses on stage at the start of **The Who** concert at Boston Garden, suffering from the "flu," according to singer **Roger Daltry.**

1976 **Queen** is awarded a Gold Record for *A Night At The Opera* LP.

♫ **RECORD RELEASES** include the **Monkees** "Valeri" (1968) . . . **Badfinger's** debut LP (1974).

Birthdays:

MICKEY DOLENZ, Los Angeles, California, 1945. Drummer and vocalist for the made-for-TV band, The Monkees, which he later reformed with singer, Davy Jones.

ROBIN TROWER, London, England, 1945. Original member of Procol Harum, then Jude and evolving into a solo career as guitarist. Best known for LP *Bridge of Sighs.*

JIMMY FADDEN, Long Beach, California, 1949. Cofounder of The Nitty Gritty Dirt Band with a film appearance in *Paint Your Wagon*

Also, **TREVOR BURTON,** 1949. Guitarist and drummer for The Move.

Queen

MARCH 10

YOU DON'T GIVE ME YOUR MONEY A London court appoints an independent receiver to handle the assets of the Beatles and bars manager, Allen Klein, from any further meddling in their affairs. (1971)

1972 **America** is awarded a Gold Record for their debut LP, featuring "Horse With No Name."

1973 **Steely Dan's** "Reelin' In The Years" and **The Edgar Winter Group's** "Frankenstein" released.

1975 Carnegie Hall overflows with **Moody Blues** fans who turn out to hear the debut performance of ex-band favorites, **Justin Hayward** and **John Lodge,** now **The Blue Jays.**

Birthdays:

DEAN TORRANCE, Los Angeles, California, 1940. With Jan Berry formed Jan & Dean, sixties surf-pop duo.

TOM SCHOLZ, 1947. Guitarist and keyboard player credited with masterminding the success of the group, Boston, and the phenomenally successful debut LP.

Notes:

75

PLAYING FOR KEEPS! Less than a month after Janis Joplin's manager sued for a settlement, a San Francisco insurance company paid $112,000 on the singer's life insurance policy, the court agreeing with a coroner's report that Janis died from an accidental drug overdose, not suicide. (1974)

1976 **Paul Simon** is awarded a Gold Record for the single "50 Ways To Leave Your Lover."

Birthdays:

MARK STEIN, Bayonne, New Jersey, 1947. Singer and keyboards for Vanilla Fudge, which evolved from The Pigeons.

MIKE HUGG, Hampshire, England, 1940. Drummer with Manfred Mann after the Mann-Hugg Blues Brothers was dissolved.

HARVEY MANDEL, Detroit, Michigan, 1945. Session guitarist for many, including Canned Heat, John Mayall.

Notes:

FOR PAUL, THAT'S ALL! Paul McCartney marries freelance photographer, Linda Eastman, in a small civil ceremony in London. The wedding news is all but overshadowed by another Beatle event the same day. (1969)

1969 **George Harrison** and wife **Patti** are arrested at their home and charged with possession of 120 joints of marijuana. Harrison claims "frame-up" and says the raid is timed to coincide with Paul's wedding.

1974 **John Lennon** and **Harry Nilsson** are bounced out of The Troubador in Hollywood for causing a disturbance. "We were just waiting for the Smothers Brothers to come on and we were singing a little bit, having a good time." — Nilsson.

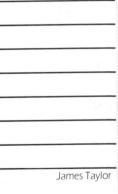RECORD RELEASES . . . **The Young Rascals,** "Good Lovin' " and the debut LP from **Love** (1966) . . . **John Lennon** "Power To The People" (1971) . . . "Lido Shuffle" by **Boz Scaggs** (1977).

Birthdays:

JAMES TAYLOR, Boston, Massachusetts, 1948. Singer and songwriter who joined with Danny Korchmar to form The Flying Machine in 1966. His solo successes have been numerous since "Sweet Baby James" in 1968.

Notes:

_____

_____

_____

_____

_____

_____

_____

James Taylor

BOOGIE 'TIL IT BENDS! The Fillmore East is packed with fans of The Allman Brothers Band, who record a decisively successful live album during the concert. The two-record set will launch the band to new heights with versions of "Whipping Post" and "In Memory of Elizabeth Reed." (1971)

1965 The Temptations top American singles charts with "My Girl."

♫ **RECORD RELEASES** include **The Kinks** "Tired Of Waiting" and **Freddie and the Dreamers** "I'm Telling You Now" (1965) . . . **Emerson, Lake and Palmer** "Lucky Man" and **Ocean** "Put Your Hand In The Hand" (1971) . . . and **Electric Light Orchestra** "Strange Magic" (1976).

Birthdays:

NEIL SEDAKA, New York City, 1939. Singer and concert pianist as a child, a songwriter for other artists until recording "Oh! Carol!" in 1959 and enjoying a successful solo career.

DONALD YORK, Boise, Idaho, 1949. Singer with Sha Na Na, an original member of the fifties nostalgia band.

Notes:

THE DOZEN PLUS TWO! Presenting Gold Records to the Beatles has become almost a given, so the Fab Four add number Fourteen to their collection for "Yellow Submarine." (1969)

1971 **The Rolling Stones** play a farewell concert at The Roadhouse in London before moving to France to escape high English taxes.

1981 **Eric Clapton** is hospitalized in St. Paul, Minnesota, with severe stomach ulcers. He's forced to cancel a four-month U.S. tour and ironically, his new single "I Can't Stand It" is doing well on the charts.

RECORD RELEASES include the **Beatles** "Twist and Shout" (1964) . . . **Marmalade** "Reflections Of My Life" and **Rare Earth** "Get Ready" (1970) . . . and **Three Dog Night** "Joy To The World" (1971).

Birthdays:

WALTER PARAZAIDER, Chicago, Illinois, 1948. Founding member of Chicago, he continues as sax and clarinet player.

Notes:

THE SIGHS OF MARCH! *Life* magazine hails Jimi Hendrix as "the most spectacular guitarist in the world" and Jimi throws a wild party at New York's Waldorf-Astoria to celebrate. (1968)

1974   The Emerson, Lake & Palmer film, *Pictures At An Exhibition,* premieres in Los Angeles.

1975   Marc Bolan and **Mickey Finn** disband T. Rex, best known for "Bang A Gong."

Birthdays:

PHIL LESH, Berkeley, California, 1940. Bassist for The Grateful Dead after starting with the band Warlocks in 1965.

MIKE LOVE, Los Angeles, California, 1941. With cousins Brian, Carl and Dennis Wilson, he forms Carl & The Passions, then Kenny & The Cadets, before making history as The Beach Boys lead singer.

SLY STONE, born Sylvester Stewart, Dallas, Texas, 1944. Formed Sly and The Family Stone after beginning with the Viscanes. Career highlights include Woodstock.

RY COODER, Los Angeles, California, 1947. Guitarist with Rising Sun and Taj Mahal,then with Captain Beefheart's Magic Band.Currently pursues a solo career and occasional session work.

Notes:

Ry Cooder

CATCH AS CATCH CAN! Fifties DJ, Alan Freed, is charged with income tax evasion by a Federal Grand Jury probing into radio and record company payola, less than two years after he admitted guilt in the same investigation. (1964)

1968 **Tammi Terrell** dies of a brain tumor. Best known for her duets with Marvin Gaye, the end is signaled some months earlier when she collapses into Gaye's arms during a concert.

1968 **Otis Redding's** "Sittin' On The Dock Of The Bay" is #1 in the U.S.

1970 **Randy Bachman** records his first LP since leaving **The Guess Who,** at RCA Studios in Chicago.

1971 **Bob Dylan** and **Leon Russell** team to record Dylan's "Watchin' The River Flow."

1975 The Rainbow Theater in London closes.

🎵 **RECORD RELEASES** include **Peter, Paul & Mary** "Puff The Magic Dragon" (1963) . . . The **Beatles** "Can't Buy Me Love" (1964) . . . **Joni Mitchell** "Help, Me" **Cat Stevens** "Oh, Very Young" and **Three Dog Night** "The Show Must Go On" (1974).

Birthdays:

JERRY JEFF WALKER, New York City, 1942. Singer and guitarist noted for work with Circus Maximus and the rendition of his own "Mr. Bojangles."

NANCY WILSON, Vancouver, B.C., 1954. With sister Ann develops Heart into major act in the seventies winning hit status the first time on record with "Magic Man."

Notes:

_____

_____

_____

_____

_____

_____

_____

_____

A FEW STONES YET UNTURNED! Blues Incorporated performs for the first time at the Ealing Club in London with a line-up that includes Mick Jagger, Charlie Watts, Cyril Davies and Jack Bruce. From this group emerges the nucleus of The Rolling Stones. (1962)

1971 **Creedence Clearwater Revival** awarded a Gold Record for the single "Have You Ever Seen The Rain."

1976 **Rubin "Hurricane" Carter** is granted a retrial, in part because his murder case is championed by **Bob Dylan** in the song "Hurricane."

1978 *American Hot Wax* premieres as Hollywood's portrait of the fifties rock 'n' roll radio and record industry, starring **Tim McIntire** as DJ **Alan Freed,** and **Larraine Newman** as a Carole King character.

♫ **RECORD RELEASES** include **Bad Company** "Rock 'n' Roll Fantasy" . . . and **Styx** "Renegade" (1979).

Birthdays:

PAUL KANTNER, San Francisco, California 1942 Singer, guitarist and founding member of The Jefferson Airplane, then Jefferson Starship. A variety of other music projects including "Blows Against The Empire."

JOHN SEBASTIAN, New York City, 1944. Singer and guitarist best known for work with the Lovin' Spoonful and his theme to the hit TV show, "Welcome Back Kotter."

Notes:

_____

_____

_____

_____

_____

_____

_____

A POUND OF FLESH, OR SO! The Rolling Stones earn their "bad boys" reputation when the group members are fined five pounds each for urinating in front of a public filling station after a concert in Essex. (1965)

1968 **Steve Miller's** first single "Sittin' In A Circle" is released, featuring **Boz Scaggs** on guitar.

1970 **Country Joe McDonald** is convicted of obscenity for leading his famous "FISH" cheer during a Worcester, Massachusetts concert. "Gimme an F . . . gimme a U . . . gimme a C . . . !"

1978 California Jam II draws 250,000 fans to the Ontario Motor Speedway near Los Angeles to hear **Ted Nugent, Aerosmith, Foreigner** and others. The event televised for an ABC prime time special and later released as a double-live LP on Columbia Records.

1982 **Teddy Pendergrass** is paralyzed when his car hits a road divider and crashes into a tree in Philadelphia.

GOLD RECORDS awarded to **Chicago** for *Chicago VII* (1974) . . . *Tommy,* the original film soundtrack (1975).

🎵 **RECORD RELEASES** include **The Easybeats** "Friday On My Mind," **The Hollies** "On A Carousel," and **Simon & Garfunkel** "At The Zoo" (1967) . . . **Jackson Browne** "Doctor My Eyes" (1972) . . . and **Meatloaf** "Two Out of Three Ain't Bad" (1978).

Birthdays:

WILSON PICKETT, Pratville, Alabama, 1941. Sixties R&B singer best known for "In The Midnight Hour," "Mustang Sally" and others.

BARRY WILSON, Middlesex, England, 1947. Drummer with The Paramounts, evolving with Robin Trower and Gary Brooker to form Procol Harum in 1966.

Notes:

ALMOST THE SAME OLD SONG! *Rolling Stone* magazine reveals that John Lennon's opening lyrics to "Come Together" were written by Chuck Berry for "You Can't Catch Me" . . . "Here come old flat top, he come groovin' up slowly." (1970)

1971   The group **Mountain** is close to tragedy as the Lear jet carrying the band to a concert date in Cleveland develops engine trouble mid-flight and is forced to dump fuel and make an emergency landing.

1976   **Paul Kossoff** dies of a heart attack in his sleep enroute to New York from Los Angeles. This is the guitarist's second "death" in a year, after doctors pronounce him clinically dead in 1975, when his heart fails for 35 minutes before he can be revived. His band **Free** splits up after his death.

1976   Former **Uriah Heep** bassist **Gary Thain** dies from a drug overdose in his apartment.

1982   **Randy Rhodes,** lead guitarist for **Ozzy Osbourne,** is killed in a small plane crash near Orlando, Florida, when the plane swoops low and explodes in a grove of pine trees.

🎵 **RECORD RELEASES** include **Paul Revere and The Raiders** "Kicks" . . . **Johnny Rivers** "Secret Agent Man" . . . **Shadows Of Knight** "Gloria" . . . and the **Yardbirds** "Shape of Things" (1966).

Birthdays:

PAUL ATKINSON, Herfordshire, England, 1946. Guitarist and founding member of The Zombies.

DEREK LONGMUIR, Edinburgh, Scotland,1955. Drummer for the early seventies pop group, Bay City Rollers.

Notes:

RIGHT PLACE, WRONG TIME! Eric Clapton, Neil Young, Richie Furay and Jim Messina are arrested at a private home in Los Angeles and charged with "being in a place where it is suspected marijuana is being used." (1968)

1969 **John Lennon** marries **Yoko Ono** at the Rock of Gibraltar, a site John says is "quiet, friendly and British."

1970 **David Bowie** marries **Mary Angela Barnetty** in a civil ceremony in England.

1971 **Janis Joplin's** "Me and Bobby McGee" is #1 in the U.S.

1976 **Bad Company's** "Young Blood" is released.

1980 **Radio Caroline,** the original British pirate radio station, sinks.

Birthdays:

CARL PALMER, Bournemouth, England, 1950. Drummer with The Crazy World of Arthur Brown until he formed Atomic Rooster and Emerson, Lake & Palmer. In 1982, new success with the supergroup, Asia.

A FIRST TIME FOR EVERYTHING! The Beatles make their debut appearance at Liverpool's The Cavern Club and within several months have a regular Wednesday night gig. (1961)

1969 **John and Yoko** begin their first of two "Bed-Ins for Peace" at the Amsterdam Hilton Hotel. It's Yoko's idea of the perfect way to illustrate their message, even though the couple is honeymooning.

1970 **The Guess Who's** "American Woman" is released.

1976 **David Bowie** and **Iggy Pop** are busted in a hotel room in Rochester, New York, and charged with possession of six ounces of pot.

1982 **REO Speedwagon's** *Hi Infidelity* LP and "Keep On Lovin' You" single are #1 in the U.S.

Notes:

UP-RUTTING THE MYTH! Monty Python's Eric Idle creates "Ruttle-mania" when his film *All You Need Is Cash* is televised. *Cash* is a satirical "documentary" of the "famous" four-man Liverpool rock group, The Ruttles. Mick Jagger, Paul Simon, John Belushi and George Harrison all make guest appearances. (1978)

1970 The Electric Circus, New York's famous rock club, is damaged by a bomb.

1974 **Ten Years After** performs their last concert at The Rainbow Theater in London, before group leader, **Alvin Lee,** forms his own band to begin a solo career.

1977 Comedienne, **Lily Tomlin,** makes her Broadway debut *Lily Tomlin On Stage,* later to be released as an LP.

Birthdays:

KEITH RELF, Surrey, England, 1943. Singer and harmonica with the Yardbirds until 1969, then formed the duo Together, and finally Renaissance.

ANDREW LLOYD WEBBER, London, England, 1948. Composer of *Jesus Christ Superstar* and *Evita.*

Notes:

_____

_____

_____

_____

_____

_____

_____

_____

THE WRITE THING TO DO! John Lennon's first book is published. *In His Own Write* is a collection of Lennon poetry and prose and will later be adapted for the theater. (1964)

1969   Thirty Thousand attend "The Rally for Decency" at the Orange Bowl in Miami in response to **Jim Morrison's** "indecent" pants-dropping incident three weeks earlier.

1973   The U.S. Board of Immigration rules that **John Lennon** is an "overstay" in America and he is judged to be deportable. John and Yoko reply by asking for permanent residency.

🎵 **RECORD RELEASES** include the **Beach Boys** "Surfin' U.S.A." (1963) . . . and **The Beatles** "Lady Madonna" (1968).

THE PRIVATE LIFE BEGINS! Elvis Presley is sworn into the U.S. Army as Private Presley, US 53310761. Elvis' new job costs the U.S. government $500,000 a year in lost taxes from Presley earnings. (1958)

1972   **America** is awarded a Gold Record for the single "A Horse With No Name."

1973   **Lou Reed** suffers a bite on the butt by an excited fan during a concert in Buffalo, New York.

1980   The **Beatles'** *Rarities* is released by Capitol Records. The collection of rare versions of previously released songs includes a stereo version of "Penny Lane," "She Loves You" in German, and an inner groove sound effect from *Sgt. Pepper* not included on the LP released in the U.S.

♪ **RECORD RELEASES** include **The Shirelles** "Soldier Boy" (1962) . . . and **Supertramp** "The Logical Song" (1979).

Birthdays:

LEE OSKAR, Copenhagen, Denmark, 1946. Harmonica player friend of Eric Burdon of The Animals, the two teamed in the band, Night Shift, and then in 1970, in War.

MIKE KELLIE, Birmingham, England, 1947. Drummer with Spooky Tooth after an early start with the band V.I.P.

Notes:

_____

_____

_____

_____

_____

_____

_____

_____

JUST YOU AND ME! "Happy Together" becomes The Turtles #1 single in the U.S. The song marks a high point in the career of group leaders, Mark Volman and Howard Kaylan, who later record and perform as Flo and Eddie. (1967)

1967 The **Jefferson Airplane's** *Surrealistic Pillow* and the debut LP from **The Doors,** featuring "Light My Fire," enter the American LP charts.

1976 **Jackson Browne's** wife, **Phyllis Major,** commits suicide. Much of the music on his *Pretender* LP, which he is recording at the time, reflects his emotional distress.

🎵 **RECORD RELEASES** include **The Monkees** "A Little Bit Me, A Little Bit You" and **The Spencer Davis Group** "I'm A Man" (1967) . . . and **Paul McCartney** "With A Little Luck" (1978).

Birthdays:

ARETHA FRANKLIN, Detroit, Michigan, 1943. The daughter of a Baptist minister, Aretha got her first record deal at 18 and has since enjoyed success.

ELTON JOHN, born Reginald Kenneth Dwight, Middlesex, England, 1947. Singer and pianist first with Bluesology in the early sixties, then successful as a solo artist with superstar status in the seventies.

JOHNNY BURNETTE, Memphis, Tennesee, 1934. Singer and guitarist who got his professional start on *The Steve Allen* TV show in the mid-fifties. He and brother, Dorsey, wrote a number of hit songs. Billy and Rocky Burnette carry on the musical tradition.

Notes:

MARCH 26

UPS AND DOWNS! Peter Yarrow pleads guilty to charges of "taking immoral liberties" with a girl of 14, shortly after Peter, Paul and Mary win a Grammy for Best Children's Recording. (1970)

1971 **Emerson, Lake & Palmer** record *Pictures At An Exhibition* live at New Castle City Hall in England, a performance based on the stage version of the Moussorgsky classical work.

1972 **David Bowie** talks **Mott The Hoople** out of disbanding and introduces the group to his own manager. Bowie then offers the band the song "All The Young Dudes," which becomes Mott The Hoople's first hit.

1974 **Ike Turner** is arrested at his recording studio in Inglewood, California, for using an illegal "blue box" to make free long distance telephone calls.

1974 **Mike Oldfield** is awarded a Gold Record for the LP *Tubular Bells.*

1975 *Tommy,* the **Ken Russell** film based on the rock opera by **The Who,** premieres in London.

1977 **Foreigner's** debut single, "Feels Like The First Time," is released.

1980 **Gilda Radner** of *Saturday Night Live* marries **G.E. Smith,** guitarist for **Hall & Oates.**

Birthdays:

DIANA ROSS, Detroit, Michigan, 1944. Original member and leader of The Supremes from 1961 until her solo career began in 1969.

STEVEN TYLER, Boston, Massachusetts, 1948. Lead singer with Aerosmith.

RICHARD TANDY, England, 1948. Guitarist and keyboard player for Electric Light Orchestra.

FRAN SHEEHAN, 1949. Bassist for Boston.

Notes:

END OF THE TRACK! Terry Knight is fired as manager for Grand Funk Railroad after leading the group through six Gold Records and countless sold-out tours. John Eastman, Paul McCartney's father-in-law, is signed as a replacement. (1972)

1966 **The Yardbirds'** "For Your Love" is #1 in England.

1973 **The First Edition** is awarded a Gold Record for their *Greatest Hits* LP.

1973 **Jerry Garcia** of **The Grateful Dead** is busted for speeding on the New Jersey Turnpike, but the $15 speeding ticket turns into $2,000 bail when the police find pot, cocaine and LSD in Garcia's car. He spends three hours in jail.

RECORD RELEASES include **The Seekers** "I'll Never Find Another You" and **The Who** "I Can't Explain" (1965) . . . and **John Sebastian** "Welcome Back" (1976).

Birthdays:

WALLY STOCKER, London, England, 1954. Guitarist with The Baby's until they disband in 1980.

Notes:

_____

_____

_____

_____

_____

_____

_____

_____

ROCK THE BOAT! The first pirate radio station begins broadcasting off the coast of England. "Radio Caroline" plays a variety of rock music mixed with DJ chatter, all out of the reach of British authorities. (1964)

1969   **Joe Cocker** plays his first American concert at The Fillmore East in New York.

1974   **Arthur "Big Boy" Cruddup** dies of a stroke in Virginia. The alleged "father of rock 'n' roll" composed many hits, including "That's Alright Mama," recorded by **Elvis Presley.**

1979   **Eric Clapton** marries **Patti Boyd,** former wife of **George Harrison,** in Tuscon, Arizona. Clapton says Patti inspired him to write "Layla".

1981   **Blondie's** "Rapture" is the #1 single in the U.S.

1982   **David Crosby** is busted for possession of Quaaludes and drug paraphenalia, driving under the influence of cocaine and carrying a concealed .45 caliber pistol. Crosby's reply when asked why he carried the pistol—"John Lennon."

🎵 **RECORD RELEASES** include **Crosby, Stills, Nash & Young** "Woodstock" (1970) . . . and **Bread** "If" (1971).

Birthdays:

JOHN EVANS, Blackpole, England, 1948. Keyboardist with Jethro Tull.

CHARLES PORTZ, Los Angeles, California, 1945. Bassist for Crossfires, which later became The Turtles.

Notes:

_____

_____

_____

_____

_____

_____

_____

_____

FINALLY A PHOTO! " . . . when you git your picture on the cover of the Rolling Stone." Dr. Hook finally gets a group picture on the cover of the rock magazine. The magazine confirms, true to the song's lyrics, that group members did buy five copies for their mothers. (1973)

1969 **Blood, Sweat and Tears'** first LP *The Child Is Father To The Man* is #1 in the U.S.

1969 Two thousand turn out to hear the first performance of the new band, **Southside Fuzz,** whose members are four Chicago police officers.

1973 *Hommy,* the Puerto Rican version of **The Who's** rock opera *Tommy,* opens at Carnegie Hall in New York.

Birthdays:

BOBBY KIMBAL, born in 1947. Lead singer with Toto and hits "Hold The Line" and "Rosanna."

Notes:

_____

_____

_____

_____

_____

_____

_____

_____

MARCH 30

ONCE AND FUTURE PAST! Little did The Chiffons know that their #1 single "He's So Fine" would someday subliminally influence Beatle, George Harrison, sued 13 years later for plagiarism for his version of "My Sweet Lord." (1963)

1968 The Yardbirds record live at the Anderson Theater in New York, a work that is later released as *Live Yardbirds* and recalled on the insistence of the band members, who are now pursuing careers with other bands.

🎵 **RECORD RELEASES** include **Archie Bell and The Drells** "Tighten Up" (1968) . . . and the **Genesis** LP *Selling England By The Pound* (1974).

Birthdays:

ERIC CLAPTON, Surrey, England, 1945. Guitarist with an early career in John Mayall's Bluesbreakers, The Yardbirds, Cream, Blind Faith and Derek & The Dominoes before settling down to solo work.

GRAEME EDGE, Staffordshire, England, 1942. Drummer with the Moody Blues since 1961.

JIM DANDY, born James Mangrum, Black Oak, Arkansas, 1948. Lead singer for hometown group, Black Oak Arkansas.

DAVE BALL, Los Angeles, California, 1946. Guitarist for The Turtles.

TONY BROCK, England, 1954. Drummer with The Babys until they disbanded in 1980.

Notes:

94

THE FAB FIVE! The Beatles hold the top five spots on *Billboard*'s Hot 100 chart with "Can't Buy Me Love," "Twist and Shout," "She Loves You," "I Wanna Hold Your Hand," and "Please Please Me." Seven other Beatles songs are also on the chart the same day. (1964)

1967 **Jimi Hendrix** begins a major British tour at Finsbury Park with **The Walker Brothers, Cat Stevens** and **Engelbert Humperdinck** also on the bill.

1969 **John Lennon's** *Rape (Film No. 6)* world premieres on Australian National Television.

1975 **Chicago** is awarded a Gold Record for *Chicago VIII.*

♪ **RECORD RELEASES** include **Chuck Berry** "Johnny B. Goode" (1958).

Birthdays:

MICK RALPHS, Hereford, England, 1948. Guitarist first with Mott The Hoople in '69, then Bad Company.

HERB ALPERT, Los Angeles, California, 1935. Trumpet player with the Tijuana Brass on A&M Records, the company he founded with Jerry Moss in '62.

RICHARD HUGHES, Trenton, New Jersey, 1950. Drummer with Johnny Winter.

Notes:

_____

_____

_____

_____

_____

_____

_____

_____

NO FOOLIN'! THE WHO SELL OUT! Eighty Thousand seats for four Who concerts in New York sell out in just 60 hours, setting a new record for "the most concert tickets sold in the shortest period of time." Many of the tickets are bought by fans who attend all four shows! (1974)

1927 **HMV (His Master's Voice),** through its German Branch **Electrola** introduces the world's first automatic record changer as part of its new radio-phonograph combination.

1966 **David Bowie's** first single as a solo artist, "Do Anything You Say," is released.

1969 **The Beach Boys** sue **Capitol Records** for more than $2 million, claiming the label owes that much in unpaid royalty and producer fees.

1978 The Philadelphia Fury soccer team plays its first game with co-owners **Paul Simon, Peter Frampton, Rick Wakeman, James Taylor, Peter Wolf, Gilda Radner** and **Bill Murray** as spectators. The Fury loses 3-0 to Washington Diplomats.

1979 **The Who's** *The Kids Are Alright* soundtrack LP is released.

♫ **RECORD RELEASES** include **Jefferson Airplane** "Somebody To Love" (1967) . . . **Dr. Hook** "Sylvia's Mother" (1972) . . . **Cat Stevens** "Morning Has Broken" (1972) . . . and **Jimmy Buffet** "Margaritaville" (1976).

Birthdays:

RONNIE LANE, born in London, England, 1948. Bassist for Small Faces, then the Faces with Rod Stewart before soloing with Ronnie Lane's Slim Chance.

RUDOLPH ISLEY, Cinncinnati, Ohio, 1939. Singer with The Isley Brothers.

Notes:

The Beach Boys

EASY ENOUGH! Ringo Starr's first single "It Don't Come Easy" is released, produced by George Harrison. The song is to become a Top Ten hit. (1971)

1974   The Doobie Brothers awarded a Gold Record for the LP *What Were Once Vices Are Now Habits*

🎵 **RECORD RELEASES** include **The Beach Boys** "Sloop John B." (1966) . . . and **Stevie Wonder** "Sir Duke" (1977)

Birthdays:

MARVIN GAYE, Washington, D.C., 1939. Singer and multi-instrumentalist son of a minister, known for his sixties hit singles and LPs, including "I Heard It Through The Grapevine."

LEON RUSSELL, Lawton, Oklahoma, 1941. Singer and keyboard player with a history of playing with Jerry Lee Lewis, Joe Cocker, The Byrds, The Rolling Stones and George Harrison before forming his own Shelter Records in 1969.

EMMYLOU HARRIS, Birmingham, Alabama, 1948. Singer and guitarist, popular for her associations with Gram Parsons, Linda Ronstadt, Little Feat, John Sebastian and Bob Dylan, as well as numerous solo works.

LARRY CORYELL, Galveston, Texas, 1943. Jazz guitarist known for his work with the Gary Burton Quartet.

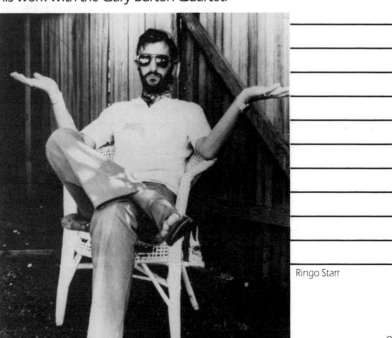

Ringo Starr

IN THROUGH THE OUT DOOR! Jim Morrison surrenders to the FBI in Los Angeles to answer charges of lewd conduct in public during a performance a month earlier in Miami. The FBI wants The Doors lead singer for interstate flight to avoid prosecution by Florida authorities. (1969)

1956 **Elvis Presley** makes an appearance on *The Milton Berle Show,* live from the flight deck of the U.S.S. *Hancock.*

1964 **Bob Dylan** enters the British pop charts for the first time with "The Times They Are A Changin'."

1969 **Billy Preston** becomes one of the first to sign with **Apple Records,** after previously appearing on the label as backing keyboardist for the **Beatles'** "Get Back."

♫ **RECORD RELEASES** include **Sam The Sham** and **The Pharoahs** "Wooly Bully" (1965) . . . and **Diana Ross** "Love Hangover" (1976).

Birthdays:

JAN BERRY, Los Angeles, California, 1941. Singing partner with Dean Torrance in the sixties pop-surf duo Jan & Dean.

RICHARD MANUEL, Stratford, Ontario, 1943. Keyboard player for The Band.

DEE MURRAY, 1946. Bassist for The Spencer Davis Group, then with Elton John.

Notes:

THESE ARE THE BEST OF TIMES! Styx finally makes the mark as the top band in the U.S. when the LP *Paradise Theater* reaches #1 on the LP charts. The band typifies the hard-working rock group that starts in the small clubs and finally plays the sold-out arenas, and *Paradise Theater* is one of the most profitable rock tours ever. (1981)

1964   The **Beatles'** "Can't Buy Me Love" is #1 in the U.S.

1973   **Dr. Hook** is awarded a Gold Record for "Cover Of The Rolling Stone."

♬ **RECORD RELEASES** include **The Dave Clark Five** "Bits and Pieces" (1964) . . . **Chicago** "Make Me Smile" and **Mountain** "Mississippi Queen" (1970).

Birthdays:

MUDDY WATERS, born McKinley Morganfield, Rolling Fork, Mississippi, 1915. Blues singer and guitarist who began a recording career in 1941 and is a major influence to many of today's rock musicians.

BERRY OAKLEY, Chicago, Illinois, 1948. Bassist with The Allman Brothers Band, an original member until his death in 1972.

DAVE HILL, Devon, England, 1952. Guitarist with Slade.

CHRISTOPH FRANKE, Germany, 1942. Drummer and keyboard player with Tangerine Dream, co-founder of the band with Edgar Froese in 1967.

Styx

MUSIC FOR THE DEEP! One hundred and fifteen American musicians and environmentalists take part in the four concerts in Tokyo as "Japan Celebrates The Whale and Dolphin." Appearances by Jackson Browne, John Sebastian, J.D. Souther, Richie Havens, Country Joe McDonald and others raise $150,000 in three days. (1977)

1981   **Bob "The Bear" Hite** dies of a heart attack in Venice, California, after years as the lead singer for **Canned Heat.**

1982   The highly respected record industry trade publication, *Record World,* files for bankruptcy after eight years in business.

🎵 **RECORD RELEASES** include **Donovan** "Atlantis," **The Who** "Pinball Wizard," and **The Guess Who** "These Eyes" (1969). . . **America** "Sister Golden Hair" and **Alice Cooper** "Only Women Bleed" (1975).

Birthdays:

TOMMY WILLIAMS, Roselle, New Jersey, 1928. Lead singer with The Platters until pursuing a solo career in 1961.

ALLAN CLARKE, Lancashire, England, 1942. Singer for The Hollies.

AGNETHA "ANNA" ULVAEUS, Stockholm, Sweden, 1950. Singer with hugely successful Abba.

JANE ASHER, 1946. Sister of singer-producer Peter Asher, and one-time fiancee of Paul McCartney.

DAVE SWARBRICK, 1941. Fiddler with Fairport Convention until '76.

Notes:

DARK SIDE OF THE MOOD! Syd Barrett, lead guitarist and founder of Pink Floyd, quits the band when his interest in LSD outweighs his commitment to the music. (1968)

1970 Twenty-four hundred fans gather for an **Animals-Zombies** concert in Duluth, Minnesota, only to realize that neither group has any of the original members.

1971 **Rolling Stones Records** is formed with the unveiling of the now-famous "lips" label logo.

1974 *Ladies and Gentlemen: The Rolling Stones* premieres at the Ziegfeld Theater in New York as the first concert film with a true quadraphonic soundtrack.

1974 **The Eagles, Emerson, Lake & Palmer, Deep Purple, Black Sabbath** and others perform for *California Jam,* the first made-for-TV rock festival.

1977 **Allen Klein** is indicted for income tax evasion after allegedly earning $200,000 from selling promotional LPs.

1979 **Rod Stewart** and **Alana Hamilton** are married in the Beverly Hills home of Tina Sinatra.

🎵 **RECORD RELEASES** includes **Elvis Presley** "All Shook Up" (1957) . . . **The Mamas and The Papas** "Monday Monday" (1966) . . . and **Tommy James and The Shondells** "Mony Mony" (1968).

Birthdays:

MICHELLE PHILLIPS, born Michelle Gilliam, Long Beach, California. Singer with The Mamas and The Papas, and one-time wife of Papa, John Phillips.

Notes:

Rod Stewart

FUTURE SHOCK! Lysergic acid diethylamide is first synthesized by Albert Hofmann in a laboratory in Switzerland. LSD is later to play a major role in the evolution of music and culture in the 1960s. (1943)

1962 **Mick Jagger** and **Keith Richards** first meet **Brian Jones,** then known as Elmo Lewis, at the Ealing Club in London.

1977 **The Clash** release their debut LP.

1981 **Humble Pie** guitarist, **Steve Marriott,** suffers crushed fingers when he catches his hand in a closing door in Chicago. Rumors that Marriott will never play again prove unfounded.

♫ **RECORD RELEASES** include **The Platters** "Twilight Time" (1958) . . . **Little Richard** "Long Tall Sally" (1956) . . . and **Elton John** "Daniel" (1973).

Birthdays:

BILLIE HOLIDAY, Baltimore, Maryland, 1915. Blues singer considered to be the greatest female vocalist of the genre, characterized in film by Diana Ross in *Lady Sings The Blues.*

SPENCER DRYDEN, New York City, 1943. Drummer with The Jefferson Airplane, replacing Skip Spence in 1966 and exiting in 1970.

JOHN OATES, New York City, 1949. Guitarist and singing partner with Daryl Hall in Hall & Oates.

JANIS IAN, New York City, 1951. Singer and songwriter who recorded her first hit at age 15 and continues to perform as a solo artist.

RAVI SHANKAR, India, 1920. Sitarist and mentor to George Harrison.

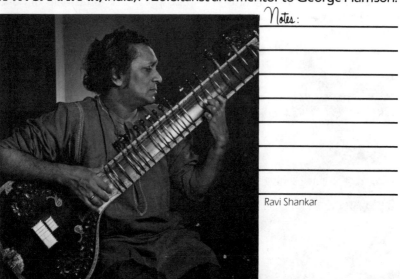

Ravi Shankar

Notes:

FRAMED IN ROCK! Neil Young's first film *Journey Through The Past,* premieres to warm reviews at the U.S. Film Festival in Dallas, Texas. (1973)

1974   Elton John is awarded a Gold Record for "Bennie and The Jets."

1976   Nazareth is awarded a Gold Record for "Love Hurts."

1976   Phil Ochs hangs himself at his sister's home in Queens, New York. The folk singer and political activist best known for anti-Vietnam war anthem "I Ain't Marching Anymore" takes his life following a period of deep depression fueled by the inability to write meaningful lyrics.

🎵 **RECORD RELEASES** include **The Supremes** "The Happening" (1967) . . . and **Todd Rundgren** "I Saw The Light" (1972).

Birthdays:

STEVE HOWE, London, England, 1947. Guitarist for Yes from 1971 until its demise in '81, then joined supergroup Asia.

MEL SCHACHER, Owosso, Michigan, 1951. Bassist for Grand Funk Railroad.

JULIAN LENNON, Liverpool, England, 1963. Son of John Lennon and drummer on the final track of the *Walls and Bridges* LP.

Notes:

Julian Lennon

103

A CROWNING TOUCH! The Speakeasy Club in London is the venue for the first concert by King Crimson with Robert Fripp, Ian McDonald and Greg Lake. (1969)

1971 **Three Dog Night** is awarded a Gold Record for "Joy To The World."

1975 **Country Joe McDonald** performs a free lunchtime concert at the University of California at Berkeley to support his mother's campaign for city auditor.

1981 The **Sam Goody** record store chain and one of its top executives are convicted of trafficking in pirated tapes. Singer, **Billy Joel,** testifies he can't tell the difference between the bogus tape and an authorized one, even though his *The Stranger* LP is part of the evidence.

♫ **RECORD RELEASES** include **Percy Sledge** "When A Man Loves A Woman" and **Jr. Walker and The All Stars** "(I'm A) Roadrunner" (1966).

Birthdays:

GENE PARSON, Florida, 1944. Drummer for The Byrds, replacing Mike Clarke in 1966 and later, co-founder of The Flying Burrito Brothers.

TERRY KNIGHT, Flint, Michigan, 1943. Singer for Terry Knight and The Pack before managing Grand Funk Railroad and founding his own Brown Bag Records label.

CARL PERKINS, Tipton County, Tennessee, 1932. Singer and songwriter of "Blue Suede Shoes" and other hits, both rock and country.

Notes:

WE'RE SORRY BUT IT'S TIME TO GO! Paul McCartney announces he's quitting the Beatles, ending the decade-long reign of the most influential rock band in history. (1970)

1962   Stu Sutcliffe, the original bassist with John Lennon's Silver Beatles, dies of a brain hemorrhage in Hamburg, Germany, opening the way for **Paul McCartney** to join the group.

1970   Doors' singer, **Jim Morrison,** is dragged off stage by keyboardist **Ray Manzarek** during a concert in Boston, when Morrison screams to the audience, "Would you like to see my genitals?" Boston police, fearing another "Miami incident," immediately powers down the Doors' sound system, but Jim is not arrested.

1971   The Cafe Extrordinaire in Minneapolis is nearly demolished by irate customers angry at a **Buddy Miles** imposter. The damage is estimated to be $50,000.

1971   Thirty tons of record pirating equipment is confiscated when Federal marshals raid the **National Manufacturing Company** in Phoenix, Arizona.

1973   Led Zeppelin is awarded a Gold Record for the *Houses of the Holy* LP.

1981   Pretenders guitarist, **James Honeyman-Scott,** marries model, **Peggy Sue Fender,** in London.

♪ RECORD RELEASES include the **Doors** "Love Her Madly" (1971) . . . and **Paul McCartney** "Silly Love Song" (1976).

Birthdays:
BOBBY HATFIELD, Beaver Dam, Wisconsin, 1940. Singing partner of Bill Medley in The Righteous Brothers.

Notes:
_____
_____
_____
_____
_____
_____
_____
_____

COURT OF THE KING! Elvis Presley uses the Jordanaires as a back-up vocal group for the first time during the recording of "I Want You, I Need You, I Love You" at a session in Nashville. (1956)

1961 **Bob Dylan** performs for the first time professionally at Gerde's Folk City in Greenwich Village, singing "Blowin' In The Wind," "Song To Woody" and several others.

1969 **The Zombies** are awarded a Gold Record for "Time Of The Season."

1981 "Kiss On My List" by **Hall & Oates** is #1 in the U.S.

1981 Guitarist, **Eddie Van Halen,** marries actress, **Valerie Bertinelli** of television's *One Day At A Time* in Los Angeles.

Notes:

_____

_____

_____

_____

_____

_____

_____

Daryl Hall and John Oates

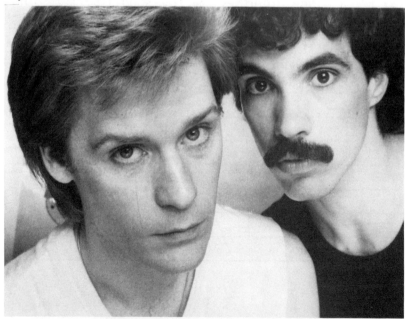

THE CLOCK STRIKES ALMOST! Bill Haley and The Comets record the classic rock 'n' roll anthem, "Rock Around The Clock," but find they have to wait an entire year for the song to become a hit. (1954)

1962 Bob Dylan's Town Hall concert in New York is recorded by Columbia Records, which later releases one song, "Tomorrow Is A Long Time."

1966   Jan Berry of **Jan & Dean** barely survives the crash of his white Corvette in Los Angeles, causing severe paralysis for more than a year. "I got a letter saying I was drafted, so I jumped in my car and turned a corner, and there was this truck. I didn't see it."—Jan

🎵 **RECORD RELEASES** include **Joe Turner** "Shake Rattle and Roll" (1954) . . . **Simon and Garfunkel** "The Boxer" (1969) . . . **Linda Ronstadt** "When Will I Be Loved" (1975) . . . and **Marshall Tucker Band** "Heard It In A Love Song" (1977).

Birthdays:

JOHN KAY, East Germany, 1944. Singer, songwriter and guitarist for Steppenwolf, a band he formed and reformed at various intervals during the sixties, seventies, and eighties.

DAVID CASSIDY, New York City, 1950. Singer and actor best recognized from the TV series *The Partridge Family* and various solo LPs.

PAT TRAVERS, Toronto, Canada, 1954. Singer and featured solo guitarist in the band that bears his name.

Notes:

JUST THE BOYS! Roger Daltry's first solo project away from The Who is finally recorded. The LP features Leo Sayer's writing on eight of the ten tracks. (1973)

1973 Network censors snip a line from the lyrics of **The J. Geils Band's** "Give It To Me" before allowing the song on a segment of ABC-TV's *In Concert.* The line cut is "get it up!"

1979 **David Lee Roth** collapses on stage at a **Van Halen** concert in Spokane, Washington and is rushed to a hospital where he's treated for a stomach virus, then cautioned to "calm down."

1980 *Grease,* Broadway's longest running musical, closes after eight years, 3388 performances and an $8 million gross.

1982 **David Crosby** is arrested on drug and weapons charges for the second time in two weeks when police find the singer "preparing" cocaine in his dressing room, a pistol stashed nearby.

🎵 **GOLD RECORDS** awarded to **The Allman Brothers Band** for *Eat A Peach* and to the **Beatles** for two double-disc compilations, *1962-1966* and *1967-1970.*

Birthdays:

JACK CASADY, Washington, D.C., 1944. Bassist and founding member of The Jefferson Airplane and then Hot Tuna.

LESTER CHAMBERS, Flora, Mississippi, 1940. Percussionist with the Chambers Brothers.

ROY LONEY, San Francisco, 1946. Singer-songwriter with the Flaming Groovies.

JIM PONS, Santa Monica, California, 1946. Bassist for the Turtles and the Mothers of Invention.

Notes:

_____

_____

_____

_____

_____

_____

_____

OVER HERE. OVER THERE! Pink Floyd demonstrates the Azimuth Coordinator, a device for projecting sound from anywhere in the concert hall, during the performance of "More Furious Madness From The Massed Gadgets of Auzimenes" at London Festival Hall. (1968)

1970 **Steve Stills** breaks his wrist when his car crashes into a parked car while Steve is watching a Los Angeles police cruiser in his rear-view mirror.

1980 **Pete Townsend's** *Empty Glass* LP, featuring "Rough Boys," is released.

1980 The first rock video casette, a **Gary Numan** concert, is re- leased and is followed shortly by **Blondie's** video version of *Eat To The Beat*.

🎵**RECORD RELEASES** include **Paul McCartney** "My Love" 1973 . . . and **Dr. Hook** "When You're In Love With A Beautiful Woman" (1979).

Birthdays:
RITCHIE BLACKMORE, England, 1945. Guitarist and founder of Deep Purple in 1967, then with Elf in 1975, evolving to Rainbow.

Notes:

_____

_____

_____

_____

_____

_____

_____

_____

APRIL 15

FACE THE MUSIC! Guitarist, Ron Wood, makes his record debut with The Rolling Stones with the release of the *Black and Blue* LP, an album that later causes controversy because of sexist overtones and promotional billboards dipicting violence against women. (1976)

1977 "In The City," the debut single from **The Jam,** is released.

1982 **Billy Joel** suffers serious injuries to his wrist and left thumb in a motorcycle crash near his Long Island home. Surgeons at Columbia Presbyterian Hospital work through the night to repair the damage.

♬ **RECORD RELEASES** include **The Who** "Happy Jack" (1967) . . . and **Gary Wright** "Love Is Alive" (1976).

Birthdays:

DAVE EDMUNDS, Cardiff, Wales, 1944. Singer and guitarist with Love Sculpture in the mid-seventies, but best known for his teaming with Nick Lowe in Rockpile and various solo projects.

Notes:

THE ROCKY BOTTOM! Elektra Records dumps the MC 5 from the label when the group takes out a local newspaper ad slamming a record store for not carrying MC 5 records. (1969)

1973 **Paul McCartney's** first TV special airs. "James Paul McCartney" features a slick video version of Wings' *Live And Let Die.*

♪ **RECORD RELEASES** include **Bob Dylan** "Rainy Day Woman #12 and #35," **The Walker Brothers** "The Sun Ain't Gonna Shine Anymore," **Wayne Fontana** and **The Mindbenders** "Groovy Kind Of Love" (1966) . . . **Pablo Cruise** "Watcha Gonna Do?" and **Fleetwood Mac** "Dreams" (1977).

Birthdays:

DUSTY SPRINGFIELD, West Hampstead, England, 1939. Singer and founder of The Springfields in 1960, then a solo artist after 1963.

BOBBY VINTON, Cannonsburg, Pennsylvania 1935. Fifties and sixties pop singer best known for "Roses Are Red" and "Blue Velvet."

JIMMY OSMOND, 1963. Youngest of the Osmond Brothers and Osmond Family Singers.

Notes:

END OF THE ROAD! Eddie Cochran dies and Gene Vincent seriously injured when Cochran's car blows a tire and crashes at Chippenham, England. The two fifties rockers were in the midst of a major British tour. (1960)

1964 **The Rolling Stones** debut LP is released on Decca Records in England, featuring only one original Stones composition, ''Tell Me,'' by Mick and Keith.

1969 **The Band,** previously known as **Bob Dylan's** back-up group, **The Hawks,** make their concert debut at Winterland in San Francisco.

1970 *McCartney* is released on Apple Records. It's the first true solo endeavor by **Paul** since the **Beatles'** breakup, with Paul playing all the instruments himself.

1974 **Vinnie Taylor,** guitarist for **Sha Na Na,** dies from a heroin overdose in a Charlottesville, Virginia, hotel.

1977 **Led Zeppelin** fans storm the Orange Bowl in Miami, causing major damage in the quest for tickets.

1981 **Eric Clapton** is released from United Hospitals in St. Paul, Minnesota, following treatment for stomach ulcers.

🎵 **RECORD RELEASES** include **The Beach Boys** ''Help Me Rhonda,'' **Beau Brummels** ''Just A Little,'' **Herman's Hermits** ''Mrs. Brown You've Got A Lovely Daughter'' (1965) . . . and **Carly Simon** ''That's The Way I've Always Heard It Should Be'' (1971).

Birthdays:

BILL KREUTZMANN, Palo Alto, California, 1946. Drummer with The Grateful Dead from their earliest stage when the band was known as The Warlocks.

Notes:

_____

_____

_____

_____

_____

_____

_____

_____

WHEN THE MUSIC'S OVER! The supergroup, Yes, calls it quits after 13 years and eleven LPs when drummer, Alan White, and bassist, Chris Squire, join former Led Zeppelin members Robert Plant and Jimmy Page in rehearsals for a new group. Yes was formed in 1968 during a chance meeting in a London pub when Squire and Jon Anderson decided to team up. (1981)

1975   Aerosmith awarded a Gold Record for *Get Your Wings* LP.

1975   Alice Cooper's first TV special *Welcome To My Nightmare: The Making of a Record Album* is aired.

1982   Mike Oldfield, famous for "Tubular Bells," makes his U.S. concert debut at The Ritz in New York City.

Birthdays:
MIKE VICKERS, Southampton, England, 1942. Guitarist and sax player with Manfred Mann.

Notes:

_____

_____

_____

_____

_____

_____

_____

The Beach Boys

COME TOGETHER! John Lennon, Paul McCartney, George Harrison and Ringo Starr form a legal partnership called the Beatles Company. Three years later the Fab Four would engage in a bitter court battle to end the business relationship. (1967)

1975 **Elton John** fires bassist **Dee Murray** and drummer **Nigel Olsson** on the eve of the release of "Captain Fantastic and The Brown Dirt Cowboy." The pair would perform occasional gigs with Elton before being re-hired in 1982.

1978 More than 40 rock musicians, including **James Taylor, Carly Simon, Bonnie Raitt** and **John Hall,** petition President Carter to halt America's commitment to the use of nuclear power.

Birthdays:

ALAN PRICE, Newcastle, England, 1942. Keyboard player in The Alan Price Combo, which evolved into The Animals in 1964.

MARK VOLMAN, Los Angeles, California, 1942. Singer with The Turtles until 1970 when Volman and Howard Kaylan left to join The Mothers Of Invention, then formed Flo and Eddie.

ALEXIS KORNER, Paris, France, 1928. Singer and songwriter often mentioned as a major influence in blues and jazz circles. Founder of Blues Incorporated, the band that featured Mick Jagger, Charlie Watts, Ginger Baker, Cyril Davies and others.

John Hall, Graham Nash, James Taylor, Jackson Browne, Bonnie Raitt, and Carly Simon join voices to bring the Madison Square Garden crowd to their feet in Warner Bros.' "No Nukes."

PAPA TAKES THE HIGH ROAD! John Phillips is jailed after pleading guilty to charges of pill pushing. The judge suspends all but 30 days of his sentence and orders the founder of The Mamas and The Papas to join a drug abuse program and perform 250 hours of community service. Phillips later reforms the group with original Denny Doherty and new "Mamas" Spanky McFarlane and McKenzie Phillips, John's daughter. (1981)

1969 One hundred and seventeen people are arrested and dozens injured when violence erupts at a free festival in Venice, California.

RECORD RELEASES include **Spanky and Our Gang** "I'd Like To Get To Know You" (1968) . . . **The Hollies** "Air That I Breathe" and **Paul McCartney** "Band On The Run" (1974).

Birthdays:
CRAIG FROST, Flint, Michigan, 1948. Keyboadist with Grand Funk Railroad.

Notes:

GOOD TO MEET YOU, HOPE YOU KNOW MY NAME! The Beatles and The Rolling Stones meet for the first time during a Stones appearance at The Crawdaddy Club in Richmond, England. "We were playing there one Sunday and suddenly looked up and there were four sort of silhouetted guys with black leather overcoats . . . all dressed exactly the same. And we said to ourselves, 'Shit, that's the Beatles!' and got all nervous. But then we had a chat with them afterwards and stayed up all night rappin' and we became really good mates."—Bill Wyman. (1963)

1969   **Janis Joplin** makes her London concert debut at Royal Albert Hall, a performance considered one of the finest of her career.

1971   *Sticky Fingers* is released as the first album on Rolling Stones Records.

1972   **Neil Young** is awarded a Gold Record for "Heart Of Gold."

1977   **Jesse Winchester** performs his first concert in the U.S. since moving to Canada ten years earlier to avoid the draft.

1978   **Sandy Denny** dies of a brain hemorrhage after falling down a flight of stairs. Her days as lead singer for Fairport Convention were followed by a successful solo career in Britain.

🎵 **RECORD RELEASES** include **Jim Croce,** "Bad, Bad, Leroy Brown" and **The Doobie Brothers** "Long Train Runnin' " (1973).

Birthdays:

IGGY POP, born James Jewel Osterburg, Ann Arbor, Michigan, 1947. Founding member of The Stooges in the late sixties with various appearances on David Bowie tours, remembered mostly for his outrageous stage antics.

Notes:

_____

_____

_____

_____

_____

_____

_____

APRIL 22

ONO FOR TWO! John Lennon officially changes his middle name from Winston to Ono in a ceremony on the rooftop of the Beatles' Apple headquarters in London. (1969)

1965 **Bob Dylan's** *Blonde On Blonde* LP is released, his first double album.

1966 "Wild Thing" by **The Troggs** is released on both Atco and Fontana Records, a contractual mix-up. The song is recorded in one take.

1978 **Bob Marley** headlines the "One Love" peace concert in West Kingston, Jamaica, to raise money for unemployed ghetto youths. Thirty thousand fans gather to see and hear the largest contingent of reggae talent in the world.

1979 **The Rolling Stones** perform two free benefit concerts for the blind in Toronto to fulfill the terms of **Keith Richards** sentence for heroin trafficking.

1981 **Eric Clapton** is hospitalized again, this time for bruised ribs and scuffed shins suffered in a car accident in Seattle. Clapton had only been out of the hospital in St. Paul for two days when the accident occurred.

🎵 **RECORD RELEASES** include **The Rascals** "Groovin' " (1967) . . . and **Gerry Rafferty** "Baker Street" (1978).

Birthdays:

PETER FRAMPTON, Kent, England, 1950. Guitarist, singer and founding member of Humble Pie with Steve Marriot in 1969, then left to form Frampton's Camel. He achieved a short-lived superstardom with the release of the double live LP *Frampton Comes Alive* in 1975.

Notes:

DAY AFTER DAY! Vocalist and guitarist for Badfinger, Peter Ham, hangs himself in the garage of his London home only days after quitting the successful group. Ham was presumably despondent and depressed over financial problems. (1975)

1969   The famous **Ash Grove** in Los Angeles burns to the ground. The club was well known for its folk and blues acts and was the first to book **Canned Heat, Taj Mahal, The Chambers Brothers** and others.

1975   **Elton John** is awarded a Gold Record for "Philadelphia Freedom."

🎵 **RECORD RELEASES** include **Sam and Dave** "Hold On, I'm Coming" . . . **The Standells** "Dirty Water" . . . **The Swingin' Medallions** "Double Shot Of My Baby's Love" (1966).

Birthdays:

ROY ORBISON, Vernon, Texas, 1936. Singer, songwriter and guitarist best known for his hits "Oh! Pretty Woman" and "Only The Lonely."

Notes:

_____

_____

_____

_____

_____

_____

_____

_____

IF IT FITS, PLAY IT! "There Goes My Baby" by The Drifters is released and is noted to be the first rock 'n' roll song to utilize a string section, an "innovation" that will be expanded upon in the future to include the use of entire symphony orchestras. (1959)

1972 Anxious fans stampede into the lobby of the Nassau Coliseum on Long Island as tickets go on sale for a **Jethro Tull** concert. A hundred police are sent in to control the melee, but not before a dozen girls faint and several other fans are injured.

1972 **John Lennon** is the guest on **The Dick Cavett Show,** the same day his single, "Woman Is The Nigger Of The World," is released.

1974 **Grand Funk Railroad** is awarded a Gold Record for "Loco-Motion."

🎵 **RECORD RELEASES** include **Elvis Presley** "Crying In The Chapel" and **Soupy Sales** "The Mouse" (1965).

Birthdays:

DOUG CLIFFORD, Palo Alto, California, 1945. Drummer with Creedence Clearwater Revival.

GLEN CORNICK, Lancashire, England, 1947. Original bassist with Jethro Tull until 1971 when he formed Wild Turkey, then bassist with Bob Welch's Paris.

Notes:

_____

_____

_____

_____

_____

_____

_____

_____

THE KING MAKES GOOD! Elvis Presley's "Heartbreak Hotel" is the #1 single in the U.S. and the first hit for The King. (1956)

1964   Peter and Gordon's version of "World Without Love," a **Paul McCartney** tune, is #1 in England.

1970   Pacific Gas and Electric Company is forced off stage at a bar in Raleigh, North Carolina, when rednecks in the audience pelt the group with beer cans, then fire shots at their rented car when the group drives away.

1974   Pamela Morrison, wife of the legendary lead singer for **The Doors,** dies of a heroin overdose.

1979   The FBI confiscates $1 million in illegal 8-track tapes during a four-state raid against record pirates.

1981   Wings disbands when guitarist, **Denny Laine,** announces he will pursue a solo career. **Paul McCartney** says he, too, will return to recording under his own name.

🎵 **RECORD RELEASES** include **Melanie** "Lay Down" . . . and **Freda Payne** "Band Of Gold" (1970).

Birthdays:

BJORN ULVAEUS, Stockholm, Sweden, 1945. Originally with The Hootenanny Singers, he co-founded Abba in 1966.

STEVE FERRONE, England, 1950. Drummer with The Average White Band after stints with Brian Auger's Oblivion Express and Bloodstone.

Also, **ALBERT KING,** 1923. Noted Chicago blues great.

Notes:
_____
_____
_____
_____
_____
_____
_____
_____

A SPOTLIGHT ON THE STARR! Ringo stars in his first TV special, an updated version of Mark Twain's *The Prince and The Pauper,* for which he sings new versions of "Act Naturally," "Yellow Submarine," "With A Little Help From My Friends" and "You're 16." (1978)

1982   Rod Stewart is mugged and robbed of his $50,000 Porsche by a gunman in broad daylight while Rod is walking his three-year-old daughter on Sunset Blvd. in Hollywood.

Birthdays:

PETE HAM, Swansea, Wales, 1947. Singer and guitarist with Badfinger.

DUANE EDDY, Corning, New York, 1938. Guitarist and songwriter noted for pop-rock instrumentals "Rebel Rouser" and "Peter Gunn" in the fifties.

GARY WRIGHT, Englewood, New Jersey, 1945. Singer and keyboard player, original member of Spooky Tooth and later successful as a solo artist with "Dream Weaver."

Notes:

_____

_____

_____

_____

_____

_____

_____

_____

APRIL 27

STONED GOLD! The Rolling Stones are awarded a Gold Record for a collection of their best songs on *Big Hits—High Tide and Green Grass, Volume 1,* the first of a series of "best of" LPs to be released by the Stones. (1966)

1967 **Traffic's** debut LP *Mr. Fantasy* enters the U.S. charts.

1972 **Blue Oyster Cult** manager, **Phil King,** is murdered by a gambling partner in New York City.

1975 Five hundred and eleven pot smokers are busted over the course of a five-night series of concerts by **Pink Floyd** at the Sports Arena in Los Angeles. The concert promoters accuse the LAPD of harassment.

1976 **David Bowie's** collection of Nazi books and mementos is confiscated by guards at the Russia-Poland border. Bowie tells customs officials that Britain would benefit from a fascist leader.

1977 **Southside Johnny** and **The Asbury Jukes** make their movie debut in *Behind The Lines,* the story of a struggling underground newspaper attempting to stave off being purchased by a conglomerate.

1981 **Ringo Starr** marries actress, **Barbara Bach,** at London's Marylebone Registry Office. The **McCartney's, George Harrison** and **Harry Nilsson** are in attendance.

🎵 **RECORD RELEASES** include **Lloyd Price** "Personality" (1959) . . . and **Simon and Garfunkel** "Mrs. Robinson" (1968).

Birthdays:
PAUL "ACE" FREHLY, Bronx, New York, 1951. Guitarist with Kiss.

Notes:

DIALING UP THE MOVIES! *FM,* a film depicting the beginning of progressive FM radio, premieres to dismal reviews in New York and Los Angeles. "The whole idea was really 'right on' and it got blown in the editing room. They took out the story to make a double album!"— *FM* star, Michael Brandon. (1978)

1980 Tommy Caldwell, bassist for the **Marshall Tucker Band,** dies from head injuries received in a car crash near his hometown of Spartanburg, South Carolina.

🎵 **RECORD RELEASES** include **Cheap Trick** "I Want You To Want Me" . . . and **Van Halen** "Dance The Night Away" (1979).

APRIL 29

THE DAWN OF A NEW DREAM! Pink Floyd headlines the Fourteen House Technicolour Dream Festival for the underground newspaper *International Times,* at Alexander Palace, North London. The Floyd appear in concert at the break of dawn. (1967)

1968 Hair premieres on Broadway after a successful run at **Joe Papp's Public Theater** in Greenwich Village. It marks the first time actors appear nude in a Broadway musical.

1971 Bill Graham announces he will close both the **Fillmore East** in New York and **Fillmore West** in San Francisco.

🎵 **RECORD RELEASES** include **Aretha Franklin** "Respect" . . . and **The Mamas and The Papas** "Creeque Alley" (1967).

Birthdays:

TOMMY JAMES, Dayton, Ohio, 1947. Singer, guitarist and founder of The Shondells.

Notes:

_____

_____

_____

_____

_____

_____

_____

APRIL 30

END OF THE BEGINNING! Folk singer and author, Richard Farina, is killed in a motorcycle accident following a party to celebrate the publication of his novel, *Been Down So Long It Looks Like Up To Me.* Farina was a popular fixture in Greenwich Village folk circles with his wife, Mimi, sister of Joan Baez. (1966)

1968 **Frankie Lymon** dies of a heroin overdose, ending a singing career that began at age 14 when he recorded "Why Do Fools Fall in Love."

1970 **Twiggs Lyndon,** road manager for **The Allman Brothers Band,** is booked on murder charges after the stabbing death of a New York nightclub owner.

♫ **GOLD RECORDS** awarded to the **Fifth Dimension** for "Aquarius/Let The Sun Shine In" (1969) . . . to **The Edgar Winter Group** for the LP *They Only Come Out At Night* (1973) . . . and to the **Beach Boys** for their *Spirit of America* hits compilation (1975).

♫ **RECORD RELEASES** include **The Supremes** "Love Is Like An Itching In My Heart" (1966) . . . and the **Steve Miller Band** "Jet Airliner" (1977).

Birthdays:

BOBBY VEE, Fargo, North Dakota, 1943. Pop singer best known for "Take Good Care Of My Baby" and "Blue On Blue."

JOHNNY HORTON, Rusk, Texas, 1927. Singer of note in the fifties for his historic ballads, "Battle Of New Orleans," "Sink The Bismark" and "North To Alaska."

Notes:

MAY 1

A WEDDING FIT FOR A QUEEN! Elvis Presley marries Priscilla Beaulieu, his long-time sweetheart, at The Aladdin Hotel in Las Vegas. The wedding cake alone cost $3,500.! (1967)

1969 **Bob Dylan** and **Johnny Cash** tape a TV special for ABC-TV at The Grand Ole Opry in Nashville, Tennessee.

1970 **Elton John's** first American album, *Elton John,* is released. It marks the first union of Elton, lyricist **Bernie Taupin,** producer **Gus Dudgeon** and arranger **Paul Buckmaster.** The LP renders the classic "Your Song."

1973 *BTO I* is released, featuring the first **Bachman-Turner Overdrive** hit single "Let It Ride."

1976 **Frank Zappa** is awarded a Gold Record for *Apostrophe.*

1979 **Kenny Jones** performs for the first time at a Who concert to a sold-out crowd at London's Rainbow Theater. Jones, formerly with the Faces, replaced **Keith Moon** as drummer.

RECORD RELEASES include **The Supremes** "Back In My Arms Again" (1965) . . . **The Rolling Stones** "Brown Sugar" and **Ringo Starr** "It Don't Come Easy" (1971).

Birthdays:

JUDY COLLINS, Seattle, Washington, 1939. Singer and songwriter instrumental in the discovery of Joni Mitchell and Randy Newman; the object of affection in "Suite: Judy Blue Eyes" by Crosby, Stills & Nash. Best known for the hits "Both Sides Now" and "Someday Soon."

LITTLE WALTER, born Marion Walter Jacobs, Alexandria, Louisiana, 1930. Harmonica player signed to Chess Records noted for his blues playing with Jimmy Rogers and Muddy Waters and cited as a major influence on the music of The Rolling Stones.

RITA COOLIDGE, Nashville, Tennessee, 1945. Singer and pianist with Delaney & Bonnie and Joe Cocker's Mad Dogs & Englishmen tours before pursuing a solo career.

Notes:

125

THE SECOND TIME'S A CHARM! Despite his vow never to have the Rolling Stones perform on his TV show again, Ed Sullivan reconsiders, and the band makes a second appearance. The group is locked in the studio twelve hours before airtime to avoid a disturbance by fans outside the theater. (1965)

1980   **Sheena Easton** is #1 in the U.S. with "Morning Train (9 to 5)."

1982   The Solar Lobby Radio-thon begins a week long campaign to alert the public to the advantages of free, safe solar energy. Among the more active supporters is **Styx** guitarist, **James Young.**

🎵 **RECORD RELEASES** include **The Rolling Stones** "Not Fade Away" (1964) . . . and **The Moody Blues** "Question" (1970).

Birthdays:

LOU GRAMM, Rochester, New York, 1950. Lead singer with Foreigner, an original member of the supergroup discovered singing in local clubs by Foreigner founder, Mick Jones.

JOHN VERITY, England, 1944. Guitarist and singer with Argent, replacing Russ Ballard in 1974.

ROBERT HENRIT, Herts, England, 1946. Drummer and founding member of Argent.

GOLDY McJOHN, 1945. Keyboards with Steppenwolf.

Notes:

The Rolling Stones

AND WHAT AN IMPACT IT WAS! Andrew Loog Oldham and Eric Easton sign The Rolling Stones to an exclusive management deal that includes the formation of Impact Sound, which supervises the group's recording sessions. (1963)

1969 **Jimi Hendrix** is busted by Canadian Mounties at Toronto International Airport when they find several ounces of heroin in a travel bag.

1971 A disappointing turnout at **Grand Funk Railroad's** first American press conference. Only six reporters attend.

1972 **Stone The Crows** guitarist, **Les Harvey,** is electrocuted on stage in Swansea, Wales, when a poorly grounded microphone wire shorts out. Harvey is literally thrown into the air by the shock as his girlfriend and group vocalist, **Maggie Bell,** watches in horror.

1972 **Deeds Music Company** in Elk Hills, Maryland, is raided by police who haul away nearly 60,000 bootleg tapes, estimated to be merely a one-day supply.

1976 The first "Wings Over America" tour date thrills fans in Fort Worth, Texas. **Paul McCartney** ends the tour seven weeks later with a three-night stand at The Forum in Los Angeles.

1977 **Paul Simon** and **Phoebe Snow** perform at a special concert at Madison Square Garden to benefit the debt-ridden New York Public Library. Fifteen thousand fans pay up to $250 a ticket.

Birthdays:

BOB SEGER, Ann Arbor, Michigan, 1945. Superstar singer, guitarist and keyboard player who formed the Bob Seger System in 1968, with an enormous resurgence in popularity in the late seventies with The Silver Bullet Band and the hit LP *Night Moves.*

PETE SEEGER, New York City, 1919. Noted as father of the early sixties folk and environmental movement, with more than fifty LPs recorded during his career.

FRANKIE VALLI, born Frank Castelluccio, Newark, New Jersey, 1937. Lead singer and founder of The Four Seasons.

JAMES BROWN, Macon, Georgia, 1928. Singer and songwriter celebrated as the "King of Rhythm, Blues and Funk" for his dynamic, but outrageous stage performances with The Famous Flames.

Also, **MARY HOPKIN,** Wales, 1952. Sixties singer signed to Apple Records by Paul McCartney.

MAY 4

"BE BOP" BEGINS! Gene Vincent and The Blue Caps record a song Vincent has written only three days before a Capitol Record talent search audition. "Be Bop A Lula" rockets into the Top Ten and becomes one of the all-time classics of rock. (1956)

1963   **The Beach Boys** make their debut on the U.S. LP charts with *Surfin' U.S.A.*

1968   "Days of Future Past" enters the U.S. charts and signals a new era for rock music because of the lush arrangements and heady lyrics of **The Moody Blues.**

1970   Four students die in a barrage of gunfire from National Guard rifles at Kent State University in Ohio. The incident inspires the **Crosby, Stills, Nash & Young** anti-war anthem, "Ohio."

1976   **Kiss** performs their first concert in New York City.

🎵 **RECORD RELEASES** include **The Ohio Express** "Yummy, Yummy, Yummy" . . . and **Merilee Rush** "Angel Of The Morning" (1968).

Birthdays:

ED CASSIDY, Bakersfield, California, 1931. Prominent jazz drummer before joining Spirit in 1967 as an original member with Randy California and John Locke.

JACKIE JACKSON, Gary, Indiana, 1951. Singer with The Jacksons.

Also, **RONNIE BOND,** 1944. Drummer with The Troggs.

Notes:

GO WEST, IF YOU'RE NOT ALREADY THERE! Scott McKenzie's "San Francisco (Be Sure To Wear Flowers In Your Hair)" debuts in the U.S. singles charts. The song helps activate an exodus of young people from all over the country who aspire to be part of the "flower generation" in San Francisco's Haight-Ashbury. (1967)

1968   **Buffalo Springfield** disbands because of internal conflicts, extreme fatigue and the absence of sustained national success. **Steve Stills** and **Neil Young** form supergroup with **David Crosby** and **Graham Nash. Jim Messina** joins with **Kenny Loggins.**

1972   Actor, **Warren Beatty,** gathers thirty top rock stars together for a concert benefit to support presidential hopeful, **George McGovern.** Four hundred thousand dollars is raised by the performances of **Judy Collins, Paul Simon, Carole King, James Taylor, Chicago,** and **Quincy Jones.**

1973   **Paul McCartney's** "Red Rose Speedway," featuring the #1 single, "My Love," is released to coincide with Wings' first major British tour.

🎵 **RECORD RELEASES** include **Creedence Clearwater Revival** "Bad Moon Rising" . . . **Elvis Presley** "In The Ghetto" . . . and **Three Dog Night** "One." (1969)

Birthdays:

BILL WARD, Birmingham, England, 1948. Drummer and founding member of Earth, which evolved into Black Sabbath.

JOHNNY TAYLOR, Crawfordsville, Arkansas, 1938. Singer best known for his million-selling single "Who's Making Love?"

Notes:

_____

_____

_____

_____

_____

_____

_____

_____

MAY 7

SONG FOR THE WORKING CLASS! The Mamas and The Papas tap into the working class consciousness with the song that is to become the group's first million-seller, as "Monday, Monday" hits #1 in the U.S. (1966)

1966 "Gloria" by **Them** moves into the Top Ten and becomes a most-played favorite of bar bands everywhere.

1971 **Dan Peek,** guitarist with **America,** suffers severe cuts when he falls through a plate glass window.

1972 *Exile On Main Street* by **The Rolling Stones,** later touted as one of their most imaginative recordings, is released as a double LP.

🎵 **RECORD RELEASES** include **Simon & Garfunkel** "I Am A Rock" and **The Lovin' Spoonful** "Did You Ever Have To Make Up Your Mind" (1966) . . . and **Stephen Bishop** "On And On." (1977).

Birthdays:

JIMMY RUFFIN, Carlinsville, Mississippi, 1939. Singer and songwriter with a string of hit singles in the early sixties and seventies including "What Becomes Of The Broken Hearted."

DEREK TAYLOR, England. Publicist and record executive responsible for the first press images of the Beatles and later a top executive with Warner/Elektra/Asylum Records.

Notes:

LAST BUT NOT FORGOTTEN! The Beatles' final release, *Let It Be,* is issued on Apple Records. Not truly a group effort, the LP is little more than a compilation of previously unreleased songs packaged by producer, Phil Spector. (1970)

1972   Billy Preston's long-time dream is finally realized when he is the first rock star to headline Radio City Music Hall in New York. Preston's dream is not the concert, but the chance to play Radio City's mighty Wurtlitzer organ.

1974   Graham Bond, a founding father of British rock 'n' roll, dies under the wheels of a tube train at Finbury Park Station, London. The latter part of his career was marked by frequent depressions due to drug addiction and his obsession with the occult.

1975   Bad Company is awarded a Gold Record for the LP *Straight Shooter.*

1982   Neil Bogart dies of cancer at age 39. The effervescent record company executive created numerous trends in his rollercoaster career, from his productions of "bubblegum" hits to the development of Casablanca Records, where he was responsible for the "disco explosion" led by **Donna Summer** and **The Village People** and "theater rock" stars, **Kiss.** Bogart's Casablanca Filmworks produced *The Deep* and other movies, with his final venture, Boardwalk Entertainment, developing hit songstress, **Joan Jett.**

🎵 **RECORD RELEASES** include **Carole King,** "It's Too Late" (1971) . . . **The Steve Miller Band** "Take The Money And Run" and **The Starland Vocal Band** "Afternoon Delight" (1976).

Birthdays:

RICK NELSON, born Eric Nelson, Teaneck, New Jersey, 1940. Singer, songwriter, TV actor with his family in "Ozzie and Harriet," selling more than 20 million records in the fifties and sixties.

PAUL SAMWELL-SMITH, England, 1943. Bassist with the Yardbirds until 1966, when he joined Renaissance. More recently a producer for, among others, Jethro Tull.

GARY GLITTER, born Paul Gadd, Oxfordshire, England, 1944. Singer best known in the early seventies for "Rock and Roll, Parts 1 & 2."

Notes:

MUSIC IS BUSINESS FIRST! The Beatles sign their first record contract with EMI Parlophone and George Martin is hired to be the group's producer. (1962)

1963 **Paul McCartney** meets his future fiancée—**Jane Asher,** sister of **Peter Asher,** then of singing duo **Peter and Gordon.** The couple end their relationship before marriage.

1973 **Mick Jagger** makes the official donation of $350,000 to aid the victims of the Nicaraguan earthquake, adding $150,000 of his own money to the receipts from the **Stones'** benefit concert at The Forum in Los Angeles.

1978 **Fee Waybill,** lead singer with **The Tubes,** falls off the stage in Leicester, England, and breaks his leg.

🎵 **RECORD RELEASES** include **Peter and Gordon** "A World Without Love" (1964) . . . and **The Blues Image** "Ride, Captain, Ride" (1970).

Birthdays:

DAVE PRATTER, Ocilla, Georgia, 1937. Partner with Sam Moore in the soul duo, Sam & Dave, consistent hit makers with "Soul Man," "Hold On, I'm Comin' " and others.

RICHIE FURAY, Dayton, Ohio, 1944. Guitarist and founding member of Buffalo Springfield in 1966, then formed Poco in 1968 and The Souther/Hillman/Furay Band in 1974, before pursuing a solo career.

STEVE KATZ, New York City, 1945. Guitar and harmonica player with the Even Dozen Jug Band and then The Blues Project, before forming Blood, Sweat & Tears with Al Kooper in 1967, then American Flyer in the mid seventies.

Notes:

THE FIRST, BUT NOT THE BEST! The Rolling Stones begin their first recording session at Olympic Studios in London. The band's first single, "Come On," is the only track released from the session, although other songs occasionally are heard on a bootleg titled "Bright Lights, Big City." (1963)

1965 **Bob Dylan** ends his first British tour with a concert at Royal Albert Hall in London.

1967 **Mick Jagger, Keith Richards** and **Brian Jones** are all defending themselves in separate drug-related cases.

1969 **The Turtles** and **The Temptations** perform at The White House for **Tricia Nixon's** Masque Ball. **Mark Volman** and **Howard Kaylan** later deny popular reports that they snorted cocaine at Abe Lincoln's desk, but add "we were much younger then."

1975 The **Beatles'** Apple Records is dissolved.

1975 **Stevie Wonder** draws 125,000 at an unannounced and unsolicited free concert near the Washington Monument to celebrate Human Kindness Day.

1976 **Elton John's** first live-in-concert LP *Here And There* is released.

1977 Lawyers for **The Eagles** sue former manager **David Geffen** for anti-trust violations, claiming Geffen signed the group to both Asylum Records and his own Companion Music company.

Birthdays:

GRAHAM GOULDMAN, Manchester, England, 1946. Bassist for 10cc.

JAY FERGUSON, Los Angeles, 1947. Singer and original member of Spirit, then Jo Jo Gunne and finally a solo career in 1975.

DAVE MASON, Worcester, England, 1945. Singer and guitarist with various groups before joining Traffic in 1968. His solo career has been punctuated with a number of hits.

DONOVAN, born Donovan Leitch, Glasgow, Scotland, 1946. Guitarist, songwriter and singer in the mold of Bob Dylan, best known for "Catch The Wind," "Mellow Yellow" and "Sunshine Superman."

SID VICIOUS, England, 1957. Bassist with the Sex Pistols as replacement for Glen Matlock in 1977. Arrested and tried for the murder of his girlfriend before taking his own life.

LONG LIVE RASTA! Bob Marley, the "King of Jamaican Reggae," dies in his sleep just forty hours after entering a Miami hospital where he was being treated for lung, liver and brain cancer. Marley is responsible for bringing reggae music and the Rastafarian doctrine to all corners of the globe and is mourned by tens of thousands of followers in his homeland. (1981)

1956 **Elvis Presley** first enters the British music charts with "Heartbreak Hotel." It reaches #2.

1972 **John and Yoko** make a surprise appearance on **The Dick Cavett Show** to talk about the upcoming deportation hearing and to plug Lennon's new record "Woman Is The Nigger Of The World." John is angered that only five radio stations report playing the song.

1980 *McVicar,* starring Who vocalist, **Roger Daltry,** premieres at the Cannes Film Festival.

🎵 **RECORD RELEASES** include **Richard Harris** "MacArthur Park" (1968) . . . and **Steely Dan** "Rikki, Don't Lose That Number" (1974).

Birthdays:

ERIC BURDON, Walker-on-Tyne, England, 1941. Founder and lead singer with The Animals until 1966 when he formed a new Eric Burdon and The Animals. He re-emerged in 1970 with War, then again in the mid-seventies with the original Animals for one LP.

BUTCH TRUCKS, born Claude Hudson Trucks, Jacksonville, Florida, 1947. Drummer with the Allman Brothers Band.

CARLA BLEY, Oakland, California, 1938. Singer and songwriter with The Jazz Composers Orchestra, with various backing performances for Linda Ronstadt, Jack Bruce and John McLaughlin.

Notes:

Bob Marley

OH, WHAT A DAY! Mick Jagger marries Bianca Perez Morena de Macias in a Roman Catholic ceremony in St. Tropez. The British press has a field day reminding the world of Jagger's "bad boy" image, particularly on the occasion of a full-blown church wedding to a woman of social stature and grace. (1971)

1960 **Frank Sinatra** stars in the musical variety show "Welcome Home, Elvis," televised on ABC to usher The King back from his two-year tour-of-duty in the army.

1967 **Pink Floyd** performs "Games For May" at Queen Elizabeth Hall in London. The title is later changed to "See Emily Play" and released as their second single.

1973 **Led Zeppelin's** *Houses Of The Holy* LP is #1 in the U.S.

1977 **Pink Floyd** performs the first quadrophonic concert at Portland Coliseum in Portland, Oregon. The sound system is specially rigged to surround the audience on all four sides.

Birthdays:

STEVE WINWOOD, Birmingham, England, 1948. Singer, producer, multi-instrumentalist who joined The Spencer Davis Group at age 15, writing and singing "I'm A Man" and "Gimme Some Lovin'." He founded Traffic in two incarnations with a stop-over in Blind Faith with Eric Clapton in between. A short career with the band GO in 1976 before evolving with a successful solo career in the eighties and the hit LP *Arc Of A Diver.*

IAN McLAGAN, England, 1946. Keyboardist for Small Faces, then Faces, until its demise in 1978. A well known soloist and session player.

Notes:

Frank Sinatra

From the collection of Ted Allan

YOU SAY YES! I SAY NO! The Beatles shock the world when they refuse an invitation to entertain the Queen at London Palladium. "It's better to say 'no' to all, then 'yes' to one and 'no' to 99 others!"— Ringo. (1968)

1970   The **Beatles** are awarded a Gold Record for the LP *Let It Be.*

1971   **Grace Slick** is seriously injured when her Mercedes rams into a concrete wall near the Golden Gate Bridge in San Francisco, the accident forcing postponement of a **Jefferson Airplane** recording session.

1977   The **Beatles** *Live At The Hollywood Bowl* LP is released. Producer **George Martin** says that resurrecting the tapes from the band's two classic Hollywood Bowl performances is "a labor of love."

1979   Singer, **Mickey Thomas,** and drummer, **Aynsley Dunbar,** both make their debut with **The Jefferson Starship** at a free concert in San Francisco's Golden Gate Park. Thomas was vocalist for **The Elvin Bishop Group** and Dunbar the drummer with **Journey.**

🎵 **RECORD RELEASES** include **The Turtles** "She'd Rather Be With Me" (1967) . . . and **Bob Seger** "Still The Same" (1978).

Birthdays:

RICHIE VALENS, born Richard Valenzuela, Pacoima, California, 1941. Singer and songwriter and early contemporary of Buddy Holly and The Big Bopper, best known for "La Bamba" and "Donna."

STEVIE WONDER, born Steveland Morris Hardaway, Detroit, Michigan, 1950. Singer, songwriter and multi-instrumentalist already well known before his teens for his singing and harmonica talents. Wonder's prolific career has produced scores of hits and Grammy awards, including "You Are The Sunshine Of My Life" and "Superstition."

MAGIC DICK, born Richard Salwitz, 1945. Harmonicas with the J. Geils Band since it formed in 1971.

PETER GABRIEL, London, England, 1950. Singer, producer, multi-instrumentalist and songwriter, founder of Genesis in 1969 as theatrical lead singer. Solo successes after his departure from Genesis in 1975, most notably "Solsbury Hill."

Also, **PETER "OVEREND" WATTS,** England, 1949. Bassist with Mott The Hoople.

Notes:

NEVER AGAIN. UNTIL TOMORROW! Crosby, Stills, Nash & Young announce that the band is breaking up, prior to a concert perform-ance in Chicago. The following day they reform for a concert in Los Angeles, but not before firing bassist, Greg Reeves, and drummer, Dallas Taylor. (1970)

1976   Singer, **Keith Relf,** of **The Yardbirds** fame is electrocuted at his West London home while tuning an electric guitar.

🎵 **RECORD RELEASES** include the **Rolling Stones** "Paint It Black" (1966).

Birthdays:

JACK BRUCE, Glasgow, Scotland, 1943. Bassist and singer first with Alexis Korner and John Mayall before forming Cream with Eric Clap-ton in 1966. Bruce formed Bruce, West and Laing in between various solo projects.

BOBBY DARIN, born Robert Cassotto, New York City, 1936. Teen idol of the late fifties and early sixties with pop hits "Splish Splash" and particularly, "Mack The Knife."

GENE CORNISH, Ottawa, Canada, 1945. Guitarist with The Rascals after a beginning with Joey Dee and the Starlighters and The Young Rascals. Cornish performed with Fotomaker in the late seventies.

Notes:

HOW LOUD WAS IT? Pink Floyd performs a 2¹/₂ hour set at Crystal Palace Garden, U.K., complete with fireworks and a fifty foot inflatable octopus. The concert was so loud that fish died in a nearby lake. (1970)

1971 **John Lennon's** *Apothesis* and **Yoko Ono's** *Fly* are screened at The Filmakers' Fortnight Festival in Cannes, France.

1972 The computer designed to handle ticket distribution for **The Rolling Stones** concert in San Francisco overloads and shuts down, forcing thousands of fans who've waited all night to leave the ticket line and go home.

1974 **Ahmet Rodan**, a son, born to **Frank Zappa**.

1974 *Monkey Grip,* the first solo LP from Rolling Stones' bassist **Bill Wyman,** is released.

1981 **Public Image Ltd.** is forced to flee from rioting fans at The Ritz in New York City when the group substitutes their regular set with an "experiment in noise." The crowd does not approve.

🎵 **RECORD RELEASES** include **The Byrds** "Mr. Tambourine Man," **The Yardbirds** "For Your Love," and **The Four Tops** "I Can't Help Myself" (1965) . . . and **Thin Lizzy** "The Boys Are Back In Town" (1976).

Birthdays:

BRIAN ENO, England, 1948. Singer, songwriter and multi-instrumentalist noted for co-founding Roxy Music, which he left after the second LP to form his own Obscure Records. Eno has close associations with David Bowie, Robert Fripp, John Cale and the Talking Heads.

MIKE OLDFIELD, Essex, England, 1953. A multi-instrumentalist, he is famous for *The Exorcist,* soundtrack. As a one — man orchestra, Oldfield plays all the instruments on all 15 tracks   *Tubular Bells,* the symphonic rock composition from which the popular movie theme was taken.

Notes:

SAY WHAT TO THE WHO! Pete Townshend spends a night in jail in New York City for assaulting a man at The Fillmore East. What Townshend didn't know was that the man who jumped onto the stage during a Who set was a plainclothes policeman trying to grab Townshend's microphone to warn the audience that a fire had broken out. (1969).

1970   **Randy Bachman** quits **The Guess Who** during a time of personal and musical differences within the group.

1972   *Fillmore,* the film documentary of the final days of **Bill Graham's** legendary Fillmore West rock club, premieres in New York. The producers lose the fight to have the film rating changed from ''R'' to ''PG.''

1974   **Neil Young** makes an unannounced appearance at The Bottom Line in New York and plays a set of tunes from his newly released LP *On The Beach.*

1976   **Patti Smith** makes her British debut with a supporting act, **The Stranglers.**

1980   **Dr. George Nickopoulas** is indicted on fourteen counts of overprescribing drugs to **Elvis Presley, Jerry Lee Lewis,** and nine others.

1980   **Rick Wakeman** and **Jon Anderson** quit Yes to pursue solo careers. **Geoff Downes** replaces Wakeman on keyboards and fellow **Buggles** member, **Trevor Horn,** becomes the lead vocalist for Yes.

1981   ''Bette Davis Eyes,'' the **Kim Carnes'** version of the **Jackie DeShannon** song, begins a nine-week reign at #1 on the U.S. singles charts.

1981   **Martin Chambers** of **The Pretenders** marries **Tracy Atkinson** in Los Angeles.

Birthdays:

BILLY COBHAM Panama, 1944. Percussionist and arranger with an early history in the New York Jazz Sextets, then with Miles Davis for three LPs. He currently records with his own Glass Menagerie and Grateful Dead member Bob Weir's group, Bobby and The Midnights.

Notes:

ABSOLUTELY FANTASTIC! Elton John is awarded a Platinum Record for sales of a million copies of the LP *Captain Fantastic and The Brown Dirt Cowboy*, highly unusual because the album is the first in the history of the recording industry to be certified Platinum on the day of its release. A million copies sold in one day! (1975)

1969 *Chicago Transit Authority*, the highly acclaimed double album debut from **Chicago**, enters the U.S. LP charts.

1975 **Mick Jagger** is hospitalized with a severe gash requiring twenty stitches after he smashes his fist through a plate glass window at a Long Island restaurant.

🎵 **RECORD RELEASES** include **Stevie Wonder** "You Are The Sunshine Of My Life" (1973) . . . and **10cc** "I'm Not In Love" (1975).

Birthdays:

TAJ MAHAL, New York City, 1942. Singer, songwriter, producer and multi-instrumentalist who started with The Rising Sons, a band that included Ry Cooder. Taj recorded numerous LP's for Columbia Records in the sixties and early seventies and has film credits that include *Sounder*, which he scored.

JESSE WINCHESTER, Shreveport, Louisiana, 1944. Singer, songwriter and guitarist who moved to Canada to avoid the draft. He carved a niche as a country rock balladeer and is best known for his LP *Third Down, 110 To Go*, produced by Todd Rundgren.

BILL BRUFORD, Birmingham, England, 1950. Drummer and original member of Yes until 1972 when he joined King Crimson. He played in Gong, Pavlov's Dog and Genesis before emerging with a new version of King Crimson in 1981.

Notes:

A TECHNICOLOR ROCK JAM! Eight thousand fans turn out for the Northern California Rock Festival in Santa Clara to spend the day with the cream of the rock crop. Among the groups performing are The Steve Miller Blues Band, The Grateful Dead, Big Brother and The Holding Company, The Jefferson Airplane and The Doors. (1968)

🎵 **RECORD RELEASES** include **Tiny Tim** "Tiptoe Through The Tulips" (1968) . . . **Paul Simon** "Kodachrome" (1973) . . . and **Bachman-Turner Overdrive** "Taking Care Of Business" (1974).

Birthdays:

RICK WAKEMAN, West London, England, 1949. Keyboardist on sessions with Cat Stevens, David Bowie and T. Rex before joining The Strawbs in 1970 and Yes in 1971 as replacement for Tony Kaye. Wakeman's first solo LP *The Six Wives Of Henry VIII,* released while still a member of Yes, earned high critical praise. He interrupted a solo career to rejoin Yes in 1977, only to quit again in 1981.

Notes:

3/4ths OF A DREAM COME TRUE! Paul McCartney, George Harrison and Ringo Starr reunite for an impromptu jam at a "welcome home" party for Eric Clapton and his new bride, Patti Boyd Harrison. Some 200 other rock musicians were also at the party. (1979)

1958 **Bobby Darin's,** "Splish Splash" is released and is the first 8-track recording ever pressed to vinyl.

1960 DJ **Alan Freed,** and eight others are charged by a Federal Grand Jury for commercial bribery, better known as payola. Freed refuses to testify in the investigation and becomes, some say, the scapegoat for many others.

1976 **Keith Richards** is busted when he slams his car into the center divider on a highway 60 miles north of London and police discover a silver cylinder containing cocaine.

🎵 **RECORD RELEASES** include **George Harrison** "Give Me Love" and **Three Dog Night** "Shambala" (1973).

Birthdays:

PETER TOWNSHEND, London, England, 1945. Singer, guitarist and composer with The Who, a band that evolved from The Detours and the High Numbers in the early sixties. Townshend, along with Roger Daltry, John Entwistle, Keith Moon and Kenny Jones, has had a profound influence on rock both with The Who and through his solo compositions.

JOEY RAMONE, New York City, 1952. Singer and founding member of The Ramones.

JERRY HYMAN, New York City, 1947. Trombone player with Blood, Sweat & Tears as an original member until departing in 1970.

GREG HERBERT, 1947. Saxophonist with Blood, Sweat and Tears.

Notes:

143

AN EXPERIENCE THAT PAYS OFF! Reprise Records signs The Jimi Hendrix Experience to the label after agents listen to a number of Hendrix songs and watch him play in small clubs. The debut LP *Are You Experienced* is released soon after the signing. (1967)

1967   **The Young Rascals,** "Groovin' " is #1 in the U.S.

1971   **Peter Cetera,** singer and bassist for **Chicago,** undergoes five hours of emergency surgery after losing four teeth in a fight at a Dodgers - Cubs baseball game. Cetera is beaten by four rednecks who object to the length of his hair.

1975   Drug possession charges against **Linda McCartney** are dropped, but a Los Angeles court directs her to attend drug counseling, write an essay on the evils of drugs and asks her to promise not to get busted again. At least not in L.A.

1975   *Bongo Fury,* the LP that reunited **Frank Zappa** and **Captain Beefheart,** is recorded live at Armadillo World Headquarters in Austin, Texas.

1975   **Blondie** performs their first concert in Britain.

1978   *The Buddy Holly Story,* starring **Gary Busey,** premieres in Holly's hometown of Lubbock, Texas. Busey is nominated for an Academy Award for his portrayal of the fifties rocker.

1980   **Peter Criss** quits **Kiss.** The drummer wrote the group's biggest hit "Beth."

🎵 **RECORD RELEASES** include **Spanky & Our Gang** "Sunday Will Never Be The Same" (1967) . . . and **Frankie Valli** "Can't Take My Eyes Off You" (1968).

Birthdays:

JOE COCKER, Sheffield, England, 1944. Singer and drummer best known for his gutsy vocals and spastic gestures. Cocker rose to fame with the Grease Band, then with Leon Russell in the massive Mad Dogs & Englishmen tour. His solo career has been punctuated with bouts of alcoholism, but he marks a return in 1982 with a highly acclaimed LP *Sheffield Steel.*

CHER born Cherilyn Sakasian LaPierre, El Centro, California, 1946. Singer and songwriter who began as background vocalist with Phil Spector before marrying Sonny Bono and making hit history as Sonny and Cher. The pair skyrocketed to success in the early seventies with a TV variety show and later her solo career.

REGGIE ROCKS THE RUSSIANS! Elton John performs the first of eight concerts in the Soviet Union, making him the first Western rock star to be invited behind the Iron Curtain. Nearly 4,000 people pack Leningrad concert hall to hear the 2½ hour show, some paying 100 rubles ($150) for black market tickets. Elton closes the show with the Beatles' "Back In The U.S.S.R."

1963 "Little" **Stevie Wonder,** 13 years old, records "Fingertips," the song that becomes his first hit record.

1965 **The Who** release "Anyway, Anyhow, Anywhere," a song that becomes the theme for the rock TV show *Ready Steady Go*

1968 **Pete Townshend** marries **Karen Astley,** a dress designer who created some of his more outlandish outfits in the later sixties.

1971 **Paul McCartney's** second solo LP *Ram* is released.

🎵 **RECORD RELEASES** include **The Cyrkle** "Red Rubber Ball" (1966) . . . and **Blood, Sweat & Tears** "Spinning Wheel" (1969).

Birthdays:

LEO SAYER, born Gerard Sayer, Sussex, England, 1948. Singer and songwriter who began with early blues rockers Alexis Korner, Mike Chapman and Mike Cooper before fronting his own band Patches in 1972. He co-wrote songs for Roger Daltry's first solo LP before a successful solo career of his own.

RONALD ISLEY, Cincinnati, Ohio, 1941. Singer with The Isley Brothers.

HILTON VALENTINE, North Shields, England, 1943. Guitarist and original member of The Animals.

Notes:

145

MAY 22

APOCALYPSE ROCKS! The first full-blown rock festival in Army history is held at Fort Campbell, Kentucky. Forty thousand GI's spend the day like any concert crowd . . . drinking beer, throwing frisbees, smoking pot and listening to Joe Cocker, Pure Prairie League and two other bands as they perform for the 101st Airborne. (1975)

1954 **Robert Zimmerman (Bob Dylan)** celebrates his bar mitzvah.

1980 Electric Ladyland Studios in New York is robbed of five Gold Records awarded to **Jimi Hendrix.** The sentimental and historical value is much higher than the $70 per disc replacement cost.

🎵 **RECORD RELEASES** include **Ian Whitcomb** "You Turn Me On" (1965) . . . and **Queen** "You're My Best Friend" (1976).

Birthdays:

BERNIE TAUPIN, Lincoln, England, 1950. Singer and songwriter who first teamed with Elton John in a talent competition in 1967 and went on to pen numerous hits in the seventies including "Your Song," "Honky Cat," and "Goodbye Yellow Brick Road."

Notes:

NOT SO GOOD VIBRATIONS! Thousands of excited Beach Boys fans fail to realize their foot-stomping rhythms in time with their favorite songs is causing the entire second tier of the Anaheim Stadium to sway. Nervous stadium authorities can only look on and hold their breath while hoping the tier does not collapse. (1975)

1958 **The Coasters'** "Yakety Yak" is #1 in the U.S.

1963 Blues great **Elmore James** dies. The distinctive guitarist is a great influence on the music of **Eric Clapton** and **George Harrison,** among others.

1977 **The Jefferson Starship** is barred from giving a free concert at Golden Gate Park when San Francisco authorities pass a resolution banning electrically amplified instruments from being played there.

1979 **Tom Petty** files a petition for bankruptcy and asks to be released from his contract with ABC Records so he can pursue a more lucrative deal with another label.

🎵 **RECORD RELEASES** include **The Beach Boys** "I Get Around" and **Gerry and The Pacemakers** "Don't Let The Sun Catch You Crying" (1964) . . . the **Beatles** "Paperback Writer" (1966) . . . **The Temptations** "Ball Of Confusion" and **Three Dog Night** "Mama Told Me (Not To Come)" (1970).

Birthdays:

ROBERT MOOG, 1934. Inventor of the Moog Electronic Music Synthesizer, a staple of nearly all rock bands.

Notes:

_____

_____

_____

_____

_____

_____

_____

_____

THE BIRTH OF A LEGEND! A man who singlehandedly diverted the course of modern music is born Robert Allen Zimmerman in Duluth, Minnesota. While in college he takes a new name, Bob Dylan, in honor of a boyhood hero, Dylan Thomas, the poet. The early years as a musician are spent on the streets and in the coffeehouses of Greenwich Village, where he's discovered by Columbia Records executive, John Hammond, and records his first and most famous song "Blowin' In The Wind." When Dylan decides to "go electric," folk fans agonize and desert him, only to become part of the legions of new converts who are drawn to "Like A Rolling Stone," "Lay Lady Lay," and later, "Hurricane." Dylan's religious conversion to "born again" finds him recording Christian songs in the late seventies, but his role in music is not diminished. (1941)

1968 **Mick Jagger** and **Marianne Faithful** are busted for drug possession at their London home on the same day "Jumpin' Jack Flash" is released by **The Rolling Stones.**

1970 Singer, guitarist and group founder **Peter Green** quits **Fleetwood Mac** to join a religious cult, The Children of God.

1974 *The Divine Miss J.* premieres, a low budget film that bills **Bette Midler** as its star. She actually only appears in the film for twelve minutes.

1974 Big Band leader **Duke Ellington** dies of lung cancer.

1982 *The Cooler,* an eleven minute film featuring **Paul McCartney** and **Ringo Starr,** is shown at the Cannes Film Festival. Ringo plays a prisoner in a jail policed entirely by women, two of whom are **Linda McCartney** and **Barbara Bach.**

Birthdays:

STEVE UPTON, England, 1946. Drummer with Wishbone Ash.

Notes:

_____

_____

_____

_____

_____

_____

_____

MAY 6

DEAD HEADS COME TO LIFE! The Grateful Dead first enter the LP charts with the debut *Grateful Dead* album, recorded in just three days. It allows them to spread their music from the San Francisco area to the rest of the world and eventually become one of the biggest cult bands in rock. (1967)

1969 **Jeff Beck's** "Hi-Ho, Silver Lining" first enters the British rock charts.

1971 **Ike and Tina Turner** awarded a Gold Record for their hit version of the **Creedence Clearwater Revival** hit "Proud Mary."

1972 "Rocket Man" by **Elton John** is released.

1973 **Paul Simon** begins his first concert tour without partner **Art Garfunkel,** using The Jesse Dixon Singers as a back-up group on stage. Simon's extensive tour of America and Europe is recorded and released as *Live Rhymin'.*

MAY 25

THE START OF SOMETHING BIGGER! Carole King's "Sunset Concert" in New York's Central Park draws 100,000 people and is the largest crowd ever to gather there for a rock concert. That mark has been topped numerous times since by The Cars in 1979, Elton John in 1980, Simon & Garfunkel in 1981 and in 1982 by a crowd numbering five times the "Sunset Concert" gathering when Jackson Browne, Linda Ronstandt and others performed during a "No Nukes" rally. (1973)

1978   **The Who** perform a secret date in London to get some extra footage for their nearly completed film *The Kids Are Alright.*

🎵 **RECORD RELEASES** include **The Righteous Brothers** "Rock and Roll Heaven" . . . and **Wet Willie** "Keep on Smilin' " (1974).

Birthdays:

MILES DAVIS, Alton, Illinois, 1926. Trumpeter and true pioneer of the jazz-rock fusion with over 40 LPs in his career.

BRIAN DAVISON, England, 1942. Drummer and original member of The Nice until 1970, then joined Lee Jackson for the short-lived Refugee.

JESSI COLTER, born Miriam Johnson, Phoenix, Arizona, 1947. Singer and songwriter best known for "I'm Not Lisa," written for her husband Waylon Jennings, who called her by the wrong name one night in bed.

Miles Davis

THE BALLAD HAS A SECOND VERSE! John Lennon and Yoko Ono begin the second "Bed-In For Peace" in a 29th floor room at The Queen Elizabeth Hotel in Montreal. On the same day, Lennon's *Life With Lions* LP is released. (1969)

1965   Bob Dylan is admitted to Saint Mary's Hospital in Paddington, England, with a viral infection.

1975   Deep Purple's "Smoke On The Water" is released, to become the group's biggest hit record.

Birthdays:

STEVIE NICKS, born Stephanie Nicks, 1948. Singer and songwriter who teamed with Lindsey Buckingham in the early seventies and later, as a pair, joined Fleetwood Mac at the invitation of Mick Fleetwood. A separate solo career has exploded Stevie Nicks to international stardom with the hits "Stop Draggin' My Heart Around" and "Edge of Seventeen," while she continues recording with Fleetwood Mac.

VERDEN "PHALLY" ALLEN, Hereford, England, 1944. Keyboardist with Mott The Hoople.

LEVON HELM, Marvell, Arkansas, 1943. Drummer with Ronnie Hawkins and The Hawks, then with The Band until its demise in 1976. His solo work continues and his only film credit to date is *Coal Miner's Daughter,* as Loretta Lynn's father.

Notes:

Stevie Nicks

IT'S RIGHT IF YOU THINK TWICE! *The Freewheelin' Bob Dylan* LP appears on Columbia Records, his second release. It contains more classic songs than any Dylan album since, including "Blowin' In The Wind," "A Hard Rain's Gonna Fall," and "Don't Think Twice, It's Alright." (1962)

1957   **Buddy Holly and The Crickets** release their first record, "That'll Be The Day." It reaches #1 in Britain and #3 in the U.S.

1977   **Tom Waits** and a friend are arrested at a local coffee shop in Los Angeles for allegedly "disturbing the peace."

1977   **The Sex Pistols'** outlandish first single "God Save The Queen" is released and races to the top of the British rock charts.

♫ **RECORD RELEASES** include **The Association** "Windy," **The Bee Gees** "New York Mining Disaster," **Janis Ian** "Society's Child," and **Scott McKenzie** "San Francisco (Wear Some Flowers)" (1967). . . **Procol Harum** "Conquistador" (1972) . . . **Frankie Valli** "Grease," **The Rolling Stones** "Miss Ya," and **Steve Martin** "King Tut" (1978).

Birthdays:

RAMSEY LEWIS, Chicago, Illinois, 1935. Jazz pianist with his own trio, best known for several pop hits including "The In Crowd" and "Hang On Sloopy."

PETE SEARS, England, 1948. Bassist on various solo projects with Grace Slick and Paul Kantner before joining The Jefferson Starship in 1974.

Notes:

_____

_____

_____

_____

_____

_____

_____

_____

ON THE CUTTING ROOM FLOOR! *Performance* premieres in New York and stars Mick Jagger in his first dramatic role. The film is re-edited before the New York showing to cut some of the violent scenes that drove half the audience out of the theater in its San Francisco premiere two months earlier. (1970)

1973   Bassist, **Ronnie Lane,** quits **The Faces** after generally poor reception to the group's *Ooh La La* LP, and forms his own group, **Slim Chance,** a name he had wanted to call The Faces.

1976   **The Allman Brothers Band** dissolves when group members decide they can no longer play in the company of **Greg Allman,** who has testified against Allman roadie, **Scooter Herring,** in a drug case.

1977   **Bruce Springsteen** wins a settlement against manager, **Mike Appel,** in which Bruce gets control of his music publishing, master recordings and a concert film made in 1975. Appel receives a five year production deal with CBS and $1 million cash.

1980   **Jefferson Starship** drummer, **Aynsley Dunbar,** files a $3.25 million suit against his old band, **Journey,** claiming he was squeezed out just as the cash started flowing in. Journey denies the claim and contends Dunbar was overpaid by $60,000.

1981   **The Clash** perform the first of seven concert dates at Bonds discoteque in New York. Fire marshalls move in to close the club when tens of thousands of fans stuff themselves inside.

1982   Promoter **Bill Graham** stages a special Vietnam Veterans benefit concert in San Francisco starring **The Jefferson Starship, The Grateful Dead, Santana** and **Country Joe.**

🎵 **RECORD RELEASES** include **The Temptations** "Ain't Too Proud To Beg" (1966) . . . **Peter Frampton** "I'm In You" and **Heart** "Barracuda" (1977).

Birthdays:

PAPA JOHN CREACH, Beaver Falls, Pennsylvania, 1917. Fiddler with Jefferson Starship and Hot Tuna.

JOHN FOGERTY, Berkeley, California, 1945. Guitarist and singer with Creedence Clearwater Revival until 1971, then with The Blue Ridge Rangers.

GLADYS KNIGHT, Atlanta, Georgia, 1944. Singer and songwriter best known for her soul hits with The Pips.

MILLIONS OF VIRGINS! Mike Oldfield's *Tubular Bells* is released on Virgin Records and keeps the label afloat with its subsequent multi-million LP sales. A true solo work, Oldfield composes the melodies and plays all the instruments himself. The haunting opening theme becomes the title music to the movie *The Exorcist.*

1960 **The Everly Brothers'** "Cathy's Clown" is #1 in the U.S.

1973 **Roger McGuinn** performs at the New York Academy of Music, his first solo performance after the breakup of **The Byrds.**

1973 Columbia Records president, **Clive Davis,** is fired for misappropriating company funds. CBS sues Davis for $100,000, including an alleged $20,000 in company money spent on his son's bar mitzvah. Davis moves ahead to form the highly successful Arista Records.

1979 **The Source,** America's first rock radio network, begins broadcasting.

1981 **Bruce Springsteen** performs in London for the first time in six years.

Birthdays:

GARY BROOKER, London, England, 1949. Keyboardist with Procol Harum, formed when he and Robin Trower left the Paramounts in 1965. Brooker departed Procal Harum when it disbanded in the late seventies and released his first solo LP in 1982.

Notes:

_____

_____

_____

_____

_____

MAY 30

WILD IN THEIR SEATS! Unhappy memories for many who attend a Grateful Dead concert in San Francisco when members of the band are accused of distributing LSD-laced apple juice to an unwitting audience. Police shut down the show and rush three dozen people to a nearby Crisis Clinic for treatment. (1971)

1968 The **Beatles** begin recording the *White Album,* a project that will take them nearly five months to complete.

1969 The **Beatles'** "Ballad of John and Yoko" is released.

1972 **The Rolling Stones** awarded a Gold Record for the *Exile On Main Street* double LP.

1980 Bassist, **Carl Radle,** dies of chronic kidney ailment at his home near Tulsa, Oklahoma. Radle is best known for his work with **Eric Clapton** on "Derek and The Dominos" and with **Joe Cocker** on the Mad Dogs and Englishmen tour.

🎵 **RECORD RELEASES** include **The Beach Boys** "Don't Worry Baby" and **Johnny Rivers** "Memphis" (1964) . . . and **Pacific Gas & Electric** "Are You Ready" (1970).

Notes:

THE CHANT HEARD 'ROUND THE WORLD! "Give Peace A Chance" is recorded at The Queen Elizabeth Hotel in Montreal on the final weekend of John and Yoko's second "Bed-In For Peace." Tom and Dick Smothers and Timothy Leary are among the voices in the choral chant during the spontaneous, improvised session. (1969)

1973   **Deep Purple** is awarded a Gold Record for the live LP *Made in Japan.*

1976   **The Who** perform the loudest concert ever at Charlton Athletic Field in London, using a 76,000 watt P.A. system.

1977   The biggest and most expensive rock tour in history begins as **Emerson, Lake & Palmer** embark on a woldwide tour following release of *Works, Volume 1.* The ELP entourage starts with a cast of 125 people, including a 70-piece orchestra, which is soon discarded when the LP fails to sell.

🎵 **RECORD RELEASES** include **Stevie Wonder** "My Cherie Amour" (1969) . . . **The Bee Gees** "Jive Talkin'," **The Eagles** "One Of These Nights," and **Paul McCartney** "Listen To What The Man Said" (1975).

Birthdays:

JOHN "BONZO" BONHAM, Worcestershire, England, 1948. Drummer with Led Zeppelin, creating the driving beat that helped push the band to the heights of rock fame.

PETER YARROW, New York City, 1938. Partner in the sixties folk-pop Peter, Paul and Mary, famous for their versions of "Puff The Magic Dragon," "Blowin' In The Wind" and "Leaving On A Jet Plane."

Notes:

ALL THINGS TO ALL PEOPLE! The Beatles redefine rock music with the release of *Sgt. Pepper's Lonely Hearts Club Band,* an LP heralded as one of the first rock concept albums and for the group, their greatest technical achievement. (1967)

1968   **Eric Burdon and The Animals'** "Sky Pilot" is released.

1968   **Simon and Garfunkel** are No. 1 in the U.S. with "Mrs. Robinson," an achievement due in part to the success of the film *The Graduate.*

1973   James Bond returns in *Live And Let Die,* with the title song by **Paul McCartney and Wings** and musical scoring by **George Martin.**

1975   Guitarist, **Ron Wood,** joins **The Rolling Stones** on tour for the first time, replacing **Mick Taylor,** as the Stones open a string of American dates in Baton Rouge, Louisiana.

1979   **The Knack's** debut LP is released by Capitol Records and the rock press hails the band as the new Messiahs, drawing parallels between *Get The Knack* and The Beatles' first, *Meet The Beatles.*

♫ **GOLD RECORDS** awarded to the **Beatles** for *Sgt. Pepper's Lonely Hearts Club Band,* the day it is released (1967) . . . and to **George Harrison** for "Living In The Material World" (1973).

Birthdays:

RON WOOD, Middlesex, England, 1947. Guitarist with early roots in The Jeff Beck Group and The Faces, then in 1975 with The Rolling Stones as replacement for Mick Taylor.

Notes:

JUNE 2

ABSENCE MAKES THE EARS WONDER! Bruce Springsteen's follow-up to the immensely popular *Born To Run* LP, *Darkness On The Edge Of Town,* is released by Columbia Records. Fan reaction, after a 2½ year lull in Springsteen's recording career, is somewhat less enthusiastic than it had been previously, but the LP does yield the hit "Prove It All Night" and eventually earns a Gold Record. (1978)

1973   **Diana Ross's** "Touch Me In The Morning" is released.

1975   **Paul McCartney and Wings** awarded a Gold Record for "Venus and Mars."

Birthdays:

CHARLIE WATTS, London, England, 1941. Drummer and original member of The Rolling Stones.

Diana Ross

JUNE 3

SATISFACTION COMIN'! The Rolling Stones begin their first American Concert tour. Fans get their money's worth during the 2 ½ weeks of performances, which follow right on the heels of the release of their first LP. (1964)

1969   **Diana Ross's** two pet dogs are inadvertently poisoned by rat bait in a backstage dressing room in Philadelphia.

1974   The live double-LP *Before The Flood* is released by **Asylum Records** and documents **Bob Dylan's** 1974 U.S. tour with **The Band.** Much of the album is recorded during the final concert at The Forum in Los Angeles.

1975   Rock journalist, **Ralph Gleason,** dies. He was a major contributor to *Rolling Stone* magazine and a myriad of rock publications.

1976   **Queen** is awarded a Gold Record for "Bohemian Rhapsody."

🎵   **RECORD RELEASES** include **The Doors** "Light My Fire" (1967) . . . and **The Eagles** "Take It Easy" (1972).

Birthdays:

IAN HUNTER, Shropshire, England, 1946. Singer, songwriter and guitarist with Mott The Hoople until 1974 when he and Mick Ronson formed the Hunter-Ronson Band. A successful solo career followed.

BILLY POWELL, Jacksonville, Florida, 1952. Keyboardist with Lynyrd Skynyrd as an original member, then with The Rossington-Collins Band.

MICHAEL CLARKE, New York City, 1944. Drummer with The Byrds until 1968. Then a solo career.

SUZIE QUATRO, Detroit, Michigan, 1950. Singer from a musical family (her sister was in the all-girl Fanny group). Her solo career has won success in England.

Bob Dylan and Robbie Robertson of The Band

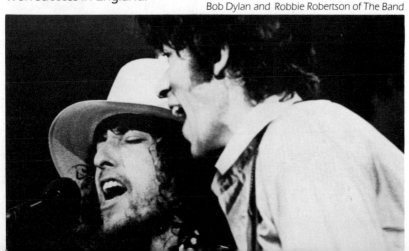

A NEW SPIN FOR AN OLD GAME! Glenn Wallichs launches Capitol Records, initiating a new approach to marketing by being the first company to send copies of record releases to fifty of the most influential DJs around the country. Capitol's most successful years came during the sixties when the Beatles and The Beach Boys boosted company profits from $30 million to $120 million. (1942)

1965 **The Rolling Stones'** "Satisfaction" enters the U.S. charts. From this record on, all Stones singles would feature **Jagger-Richards** compositions on the "A" side.

1969 Keyboardist, **Nicky Hopkins,** quits **The Jeff Beck Group,** disillusioned with the band's poor organization.

1973 **Murray Wilson,** father of **Beach Boys,** Brian, Carl and Dennis, dies of a heart attack at age 55. During the early days of the band, Murray managed the group and produced their first single, as well as co-wrote "Breakaway" with Brian.

1974 **Paul McCartney** is awarded Gold Records for both the single and the LP *Band On The Run.*

1975 **The Rolling Stones** become the first rock band to get record royalties from the Soviet Union.

🎵 **RECORD RELEASES** include **The Association** "Along Comes Mary," **Syndicate of Sound** "Little Girl," and **Tommy James and The Shondells** "Hanky Panky" (1966) . . . and **Supertramp** "Give A Little Bit" (1977).

Birthdays:

GORDON WALLER, 1945. Singing partner with Peter Asher in the sixties pop duo, Peter and Gordon.

ROGER BALL, Dundee, Scotland, 1944. Sax player with The Average White Band, a founding member.

Notes:

LAST DAYS IN THE GREAT WHITE NORTH! Bob Dylan graduates from Hibbing High School in Hibbing, Minnesota. He would soon attend, then quit college, and make his way to New York City to begin a legendary career. "He wore his hair long before anyone else did, and he'd just stand at the piano and bang the hell out of it. A dynamo of energy."—George Peterson, Dylan's English teacher. (1959)

1964 "I Can't Help Thinking About Me," the first record by **Davie Jones and The King Bees,** is released on Pye Records in England. Jones is much better known today as **David Bowie.**

1980 *Urban Cowboy* premieres, starring **John Travolta** and **Debra Winger,** with music by **The Charlie Daniels Band.**

🎵 **RECORD RELEASES Johnny Rivers** "Seventh Son" (1965) ... **Freda Payne** "Bring The Boys Home" and **James Taylor** "You've Got A Friend" (1971).

Birthdays:

BILL HAYES, Harvey, Illinois, 1926. Singer best known for his 1955 hit "The Ballad of Davy Crockett," a single that starts a craze for Crockett "coonskin" hats in the U.S.

Notes:

_____

_____

_____

_____

_____

_____

_____

_____

ROCKIN' TO THE TOP. FINALLY! Bill Haley's version of "Rock Around The Clock" is #1 in the U.S. after a sluggish start nearly a year earlier. Success comes, in part, when the song is used as the theme for the film *The Blackboard Jungle,* a combination of rock 'n' roll and teen wildness that sets many parents on a permanent course against the new trend in music. "Rock Around The Clock" has since sold more than 20 million copies worldwide. (1955)

1962　The **Beatles** audition for EMI Records staff producer, **George Martin.** "I listened to their tapes and they were pretty awful. I understand why other record companies turned them down. But I thought they were interesting and when I met them, I liked them."–George Martin.

1966　**Roy Orbison's** wife, **Claudette,** is killed in a motorcycle accident, touching off a series of personal tragedies in Orbison's life from which his career would not recover.

1971　**John** and **Yoko** join **Frank Zappa** and **The Mothers of Invention** on stage at The Fillmore East in New York.

1972　**David Bowie's** *Ziggy Stardust and the Spiders From Mars* LP is released, and most agree that in concept and execution, it is an album years ahead of its time.

1977　The "**Doobie Brothers** Golf Classic and Concert for The United Way" takes place, the first time a rock group has sponsored an event of this kind.

♫　**RECORD RELEASES** include **Roy Orbison** "Only The Lonely" (1960) . . . **Alive 'N Kickin'** "Tighter and Tighter" and **Crosby, Stills, Nash & Young** "Teach Your Children" (1970).

Birthdays:

GARY U.S. BONDS, born Gary Anderson, Jacksonville, Florida, 1939. Singer and songwriter successful in the early sixties with "New Orleans" and "Quarter To Three," then re-emerging in 1982 with help from Bruce Springsteen and "Miami" Steve Van Zandt.

PETER ALBIN, San Francisco, California, 1944. Bassist and singer with Janis Joplin in Big Brother and The Holding Company.

Notes:

BERRY VERY UNLUCKY! Rock 'n' roll godfather, Chuck Berry, is charged with three counts of income tax evasion by the IRS the day before he's scheduled to perform his most prestigious show ever, a concert for Jimmy and Rosalyn Carter at The White House. (1979)

1963 **The Rolling Stones'** first single "Come On," a **Chuck Berry** song, is released in England on the same day the band makes its first-ever TV appearance on British ITV's *Thank Your Lucky Stars.*

1964 **Dionne Warwick** reaches the Top Ten for the first time with "Walk On By."

1967 Guitarist, **Skip Spence,** and two other members of **Moby Grape** are arrested in San Francisco for contributing to the delinquency of minors. The band members attempt to convince police that the girls in the back seat of the car are "interviewing" the band for a high school newspaper.

1969 **John** and **Yoko** are guests on *The David Frost Show.*

1969 **The Who** rock opera *Tommy* enters the U.S. album charts.

1969 **The Bob Dylan-Johnny Cash** TV special is aired by ABC.

1969 The short-lived supergroup, **Blind Faith,** makes its concert debut with a free performance at London's Hyde Park. One hundred thousand gather to witness the collaboration of **Eric Clapton, Steve Winwood, Ginger Baker** and **Rik Grech** and the *London Daily Mirror* comments that the event is "the most remarkable gathering of young people ever seen in this country."

1970 **The Who** perform *Tommy* live at The Metropolitan Opera House in New York. It is only the second time and will be the last time the band will perform the classic rock opera in its entirety.

♬ **RECORD RELEASES** include **Kenny Rogers and The First Edition** "Ruby, Don't Take Your Love To Town" and **Tommy James and The Shondells** "Crystal Blue Persuasion" (1969).

Birthdays:

CLARENCE WHITE, Lewiston, Maine, 1944. Guitarist with The Byrds when the band reorganized in 1968.

BILL KREUTZMAN, Palo Alto, California, 1946. Drummer and original member of The Grateful Dead.

Notes:

JONES DETHRONES AS A STONE! Guitarist, Brian Jones, quits The Rolling Stones and cites "musical incompatibility" as the reason. Jones joined the band at the beginning using the name Elmo Lewis, and upon his departure, is replaced by Mick Taylor, a former member of John Mayall's Bluesbreakers. (1969)

1965 **Bob Dylan** records a one hour program for the BBC in London.

1974 Keyboardist, **Rick Wakeman,** quits **Yes** to devote full time to his solo career, which began a year earlier with the release of *The Six Wives of Henry VIII.* He rejoins Yes two years later.

🎵 **RECORD RELEASES** include **The Rolling Stones** "Jumpin' Jack Flash" . . . and **Gary Puckett and The Union Gap** "Lady Will Power" (1968).

Birthdays:

BOZ SCAGGS, born William Royce Scaggs, Ohio, 1944. Singer, songwriter and guitarist with The Marksmen with Steve Miller, before going solo in Europe and recording the LP *Boz* in Sweden. Teams with Miller for two Steve Miller Band LPs in the mid-sixties, then solo again with his *Silk Degrees* album boosting him to stardom in 1976.

CHUCK NEGRON, New York City, 1942. Singer and original member of Three Dog Night.

ALEX VAN HALEN, Netherlands, 1950. Drummer with Van Halen, a band formed with brother Eddie in 1976.

Notes:

MUSIC OF HONORARY DEGREES! Bob Dylan accepts an honorary Doctorate of Music degree from Princeton University for "brilliantly distinguishing himself in good works." For the ceremony, Dylan consents to wear the traditional graduation gown, but refuses the mortarboard cap. (1970)

1962   The **Beatles** are given a rousing "welcome home" party on their return to The Cavern Club in Liverpool after a brief booking at The Star Club in Hamburg, Germany.

1971   **Paul McCartney** is awarded a Gold Record for the *Ram* LP.

1980   Comedian, **Richard Pryor,** suffers third degree burns on most of his upper body when a concoction of alcohol and cocaine ignites and explodes. Pryor endures more than two months of painful skin grafting operations, but his body and sense of humor survive.

Birthdays:

LES PAUL, born Lester Polfus, Waukesha, Wisconsin, 1923. Legendary guitarist, best known for his partnership with his wife, Mary Ford, and his association with guitarist, Chet Atkins. The Les Paul line of guitars he developed for Gibson Corporation are standard items in many studios and rock bands.

JACKIE WILSON, Detroit, Michigan, 1934. Singer who dropped a promising career in boxing to replace Clyde McPhatter in The Dominoes, going solo four years later. Wilson is best known for his hit singles *"Lonely Teardrops"* and *"Higher and Higher."*

JON LORD, Leicester, England, 1941. Keyboardist and founding member of Deep Purple in 1968, then with Whitesnake.

MITCH MITCHELL, Ealing, London, 1947. Drummer with The Jimi Hendrix Experience, then with The Jack Bruce Band.

Notes:

JUNE 10

THE BEATLES GET BACKWARDS! The first record to use reversed tape is heard with the release of "Rain" by The Beatles, the "B" side of "Paperback Writer." John Lennon "discovers" the technique after winding his tape recorder the wrong way. (1966)

1966 **The Mamas and The Papas** are awarded three Gold Records . . . one each for the singles "Monday Monday" and "I Saw Her Again," and the third for the LP on which both songs appeared, *If You Can Believe Your Eyes and Ears.*

1967 **Bob Dylan** and **The Band** begin recording *The Basement Tapes* at Big Pink, near Woodstock, New York. The legendary tapes aren't released on record until Dylan resigns with Columbia Records in 1973.

1971 Denver police tear gas **Jethro Tull** and 2,000 fans at the Red Rocks Amphitheater when a mob attempts to climb the barricades to get in free. Crying, the band plays on.

1974 **The Who** begin performing the first of four sold out concerts at Madison Square Garden in New York. All 80,000 tickets for the concert series were sold in 60 hours.

1976 **Paul McCartney and Wings** set a record for the largest gathering of people for an indoor concert, when 67,100 fans pack an arena in Seattle, Washington.

1978 After a five year recording hiatus, **The Moody Blues** release *Octave,* one of the most ambitiously orchestrated rock records ever.

1981 The formation of **Asia** is announced. The band features former **Yes** members, **Steve Howe** and **Geoff Downes, John Wetton** of **Uriah Heep** and **Carl Palmer** of **ELP**.

🎵 **RECORD RELEASES** include **Stevie Wonder** "I Was Made To Love Her" (1967) . . . **Harry Nilsson** "Coconut" (1972) . . . and **Joe Walsh** "Life's Been Good" (1978).

Birthdays:

HOWLIN' WOLF, born Chester Burnett, West Point, Mississippi, 1910. Blues singer and harmonica player most responsible for the blues revival of the sixties, including his work with Eric Clapton, Steve Winwood and The Rolling Stones.

MATTHEW FISHER, England, 1946. Organist and original member of Procol Harum.

SHIRLEY OWENS ALSTON, Passaic, New Jersey, 1941. Singer with The Shirelles.

HOT TIME IN THE STUDIO! Fire breaks out at the Olympic Studios in London where The Rolling Stones are recording for the *Beggars Banquet* LP. Investigators blame a malfunctioning arc lamp used by a photographer filming the session. No one is injured, but the scene is "bloody frightening."–Charlie Watts. (1968)

1966   Roger Daltry is mistakenly reported to be dead by French and German news media, who apparently are confused by a story of Pete Townshend's recent car crash.

1970   The U.S. tour planned for **Ginger Baker's Airforce** is cancelled eight days before it's to begin. Only 3,000 tickets have been sold.

RECORD RELEASES include **Tommy Roe** "Sweet Pea" and **Sam The Sham and The Pharoahs** "Li'l Red Riding Hood" (1966) . . . and **Electric Light Orchestra** "Telephone Line" (1977).

Birthdays:

JOEY DEE, born Joseph Dinicola, Passaic, New Jersey, 1940. Singer and founder of Joey Dee and The Starlighters in 1958. When he landed a residency at The Peppermint Lounge in New York City, fame was his. Best remembered for his million seller "Peppermint Twist."

Notes:

ORDER FOR THE FOURSOME! In the midst of filming their second movie, *Help,* the Beatles get word they've been awarded the prestigious MBE (Member of the Order of the British Empire), an honor previously bestowed to military heroes only. "I didn't think you got MBEs for playing rock and roll," George Harrison quips, not realizing he's reflecting the attitude of many British military men, who promptly return their medals in outrage. (1965)

1972   Creedence Clearwater Revival is awarded a Gold Record for the LP *Mardi Gras.*

1972   John and Yoko's, *Sometime In New York City* is released as a double LP, featuring **Elephants Memory, Plastic Ono Band** and **Frank Zappa** and **The Mothers of Invention.**

1982   Seven hundred and fifty thousand attend the Rally For Nuclear Disarmament in New York's Central Park, the largest assemblage ever to gather for a political rally. The afternoon of music includes performances by **Jackson Browne, James Taylor, Bruce Springsteen, Linda Ronstadt, Gary U.S. Bonds** and others.

RECORD RELEASES include **The Rolling Stones** "Satisfaction" (1965) . . . and the re-release of the **Beatles** "Got To Get You Into My Life" (1976)

Birthdays:

DALE KRANTZ, 1952. Singer with a number of Southern rock bands until approached by Allen Collins to be the lead singer for The Rossington-Collins Band.

BRAD DELP, Boston, Massachusetts, 1951. Guitarist and singer with Boston.

ROY HARPER, Manchester, England, 1941. British "freak poet" with many LP credits, some of which included guest appearances by members of Pink Floyd, Led Zeppelin, The Who and Yes. Harper is the vocalist on Floyd's "Have A Cigar" and Led Zeppelin pays tribute to him on "Hats Off To Harper."

BUN E. CARLOS, 1951. Drummer with Cheap Trick.

Notes:

BAD BOYS, BAD PRESS, BAD LUCK! The Rolling Stones get their first national press exposure in an article that tells of the wild and uncontrollable atmosphere in a station hotel near Richmond, England. Unfortunately, the hotel manager reads the piece and promptly cancels the band's stay. (1963)

1958 **Frank Zappa** graduates from Antelope High School in Lancaster, California. His high school graduation picture adorns the back cover of The Mothers' *Rubin and The Jets* LP.

1969 Guitarist, **Mick Taylor,** officially becomes a member of **The Rolling Stones,** replacing **Brian Jones** who left the group a week earlier because of artistic differences.

1970 **Bread's** "Make It With You" is released.

1970 **The Beatles'** "Long And Winding Road" is #1 in the U.S., but **Paul McCartney** lets it be known that he is "appalled" at producer **Phil Spector's** use of syrupy strings and background chorus.

1972 Singer, **Clyde McPhatter,** a former member of **The Drifters,** dies of a heart attack in Teaneck, New Jersey.

1972 Sixty people are arrested and a dozen others injured when the crowd gets out of hand at a **Rolling Stones** Concert in San Diego, California.

1980 **Billy Joel's** *Glass Houses* LP is #1 in the U.S.

Gary U.S. Bonds

JUNE 14

TELLTALE SIGNS! Elvis Presley graduates from L.C. Humes High School in Memphis, Tennessee. His graduation photo shows Presley to be the only student in his class with a spit curl in the middle of his forehead. It is a trademark that Presley will carry with him throughout his career. (1953)

1965 The *Beatles VI* LP is released in the U.S.

1975 **Janis Ian's** "At Seventeen" is released.

1979 Thousands of fans witness an all-star line-up at a "No Nukes" benefit concert starring **Bruce Springsteen, Gary U.S. Bonds, Bonnie Raitt, Graham Nash** and **Steve Stills.**

Birthdays:

ROD ARGENT, Hertfordshire, England, 1945. Keyboardist and founding member of The Zombies with Paul Atkinson in 1963. In 1969 he formed his own group, Argent, and is best known for the hit single "Hold Your Head Up."

MERVYN "MUFF" WINWOOD, Birmingham, England, 1943. Bassist and older brother of Steve Winwood, with whom he teamed to form The Spencer Davis Group.

Notes:

JUNE 15

HISTORY IN THE MAKING! Bob Dylan's first major "electric" hit is recorded. "Like A Rolling Stone" features Dylan on vocals and harmonica, Mike Bloomfield on guitar and Al Kooper on organ and piano. (1965)

1956   **John Lennon** and **Paul McCartney** first meet at a Woolton Parish Church dinner in Liverpool, where John's group **The Quarrymen** have played. John is 15 and Paul, 13.

1963   **Jan & Dean's** "Surf City," a Brian Wilson tune, is released.

1968   **The Steve Miller Band's** *Children Of The Future* LP is released. The album is not only regarded as one of Miller's finest, but as one of the best examples of progressive rock of the era.

1968   Jazz guitarist, **Wes Montgomery,** dies of a heart attack in Indianapolis at age 45. On the day of his death, Montgomery had three LPs on Billboard's Hot 100 Chart.

1968   **John and Yoko's** "Acorn Event" is held at the National Sculpture Exhibition at Coventry Cathedral. The couple plant acorns in the ground at a preview of a "living-art" sculpture to symbolize the coming together of East and West.

1971   **The Guess Who** is awarded a Gold Record for the LP *Best of The Guess Who.*

1974   **Geoff Britton,** a British karate expert, joins **Wings** as drummer, but only stays with the group a short time before being replaced by **Joe English.**

Birthdays:

HARRY NILSSON, Brooklyn, New York, 1941. Singer and songwriter who broke into the music business with the name Johnny Niles in the early sixties. As Nilsson he wrote songs for The Monkees, The Yardbirds and Blood, Sweat & Tears. Best known for "Everybody's Talking," the theme from *Midnight Cowboy,* "The Point" and his association and work with John Lennon and Ringo Starr.

Notes:

_____

_____

_____

_____

_____

POP IS CULT AND THAT'S HISTORY! Fifty thousand gather for The Monterey Pop Festival at Monterey Fairgrounds in California, a three-day extravaganza of fun and music. The festival introduces Jimi Hendrix and Janis Joplin to the road to fame, and also stars The Who and The Mamas and The Papas. (1967)

1959   Gene Vincent's, "Be Bop A Lula" is released.

1968   **Bill Graham** presents the Matrix benefit concert at The Fillmore Auditorium in San Francisco, starring **Janis Joplin** with **Big Brother and The Holding Company, The Steve Miller Blues Band, Dan Hicks** and **Santana.**

1969   *Feast Of Friends,* a film documentary of **The Doors,** is first screened in Los Angeles.

1978   The film version of the Broadway musical *Grease* opens in New York, starring **John Travolta** and **Olivia Newton-John** in the lead roles. The title theme, "Grease," becomes a hit for **Frankie Valli.**

1980   *The Blues Brothers* movie premieres in Chicago, starring former "Saturday Night Live" cast members **John Belushi** and **Dan Ackroyd** as Jake and Elwood Blues.

1982   **James Honeyman-Scott,** lead guitarist and songwriter with **The Pretenders,** dies at a friend's apartment in London after a benefit concert performance, apparently of natural causes. He is 25-years-old.

1982   Guitarist and singer, **Donny Van Zant,** of **.38 Special** is arrested on stage after a concert in Tulsa, Oklahoma, for public drinking in a dry town.

Birthdays:

LAMONT DOZIER, Detroit, Michigan, 1941. Songwriter who teamed with Brian and Eddie Holland in the early sixties to write hits for Marvin Gaye, The Supremes, The Temptations and The Four Tops, among others.

REG PRESLEY, Hampshire, England, 1944. Singer and founding member of The Troggs.

Notes:

LISTEN, BUT DON'T LOOK! The Beatles' *Yesterday And Today* LP is released in the U.S. and features songs previously only available on the British versions of *Rubber Soul* and *Revolver.* A major problem erupts over the album cover art, which shows the group dressed as butchers holding bloody chunks of meat and decapitated baby dolls. The public outcry is so negative that the photo is changed to the more familiar one of Paul sitting in a trunk. (1966)

1967 "Paper Sun," by **Traffic,** first enters the British rock charts, the group's first single to make it. It eventually climbs to #5.

1968 **The Ohio Express** is awarded a Gold Record for selling a million copies of the ultimate bubblegum hit "Yummy Yummy Yummy."

1977 **Steve Winwood's** first solo LP is released on Island Records, with fellow Traffic drummer, **Jim Capaldi,** co-writing four of the songs. A strong, critically acclaimed attempt, its success pales in comparison to Winwood's 1981 offering, *The Arc Of A Diver.*

♬ **RECORD RELEASES** include **The Hollies** "Carrie Ann" (1967) . . . **The Tremeloes** "Silence is Golden" (1969) . . . **Argent** "Hold Your Head Up" and **Looking Glass** "Brandy (You're A Fine Girl)" (1972).

Steve Winwood

SUCCESSFUL ENOUGH TO BE CALLED J.P.! James Paul McCartney is born in Liverpool, England, to become a larger-than-life figure in contemporary music. McCartney, with John Lennon, George Harrison and Ringo Starr, become the Beatles in 1961 and the course of rock music is permanently altered. Paul bears responsibility for the breakup of the Beatles in 1970, after a decade of fabulous successes, including more #1 hit records than any other musical group. His post-Beatles career has been both as solo artist, with Wings, with Stevie Wonder and occasional interactions with the former Beatles. McCartney has grown to be a devoted family man and collector of others' works, particularly the publishing rights to most of Buddy Holly's material. (1942)

1968 *In His Own Write,* Adrienne Kennedy's theatrical adaptation of **John Lennon's** two books, opens at The National Theater in London. Sir Lawrence Olivier is so impressed, he insists the play be put into the company's regular repetoire.

1976 **Phil May** quits **Pretty Things,** the only original member of the group he and guitarist **Dick Taylor** founded in 1963. Pretty Things is credited with producing the first rock opera, *S.F. Sorrow.*

1977 Singer, **Johnny Rotten,** and drummer, **Paul Cook,** of **The Sex Pistols** are stabbed and beaten by a group of young toughs in the parking lot of a North London pub, causing a delay in the completion of the group's debut LP.

1977 **James Taylor's** "Handy Man" is released.

Notes:

_____

_____

_____

_____

_____

_____

_____

A TIME IN HER LIFE! Carole King dominates the U.S. record charts with "It's Too Late," just one of several hits from her multi-million selling LP *Tapestry*. This will prove to be the height of her career, from beginnings as a songwriter for many successful groups in the mid-sixties. (1971)

1973   The Edgar Winter Group is awarded a Gold Record for "Frankenstein."

1976   Wild Cherry's "Play That Funky Music" is released.

Birthdays:

ANN WILSON, Vancouver, British Columbia, 1950. Singer and founding member of Heart, which her sister Nancy joined shortly thereafter.

SPANKY McFARLANE, born Elaine McFarlane, Peoria, Illinois, 1942. Singer and songwriter for Spanky and Our Gang in the mid-sixties best known for the hits "Sunday Will Never Be The Same" and "Like To Get To Know You." In 1982 she accepts an invitation to join a reformed Mamas and Papas.

Notes:

_____

_____

_____

_____

_____

_____

_____

JUNE 20

SOME STRINGS ATTACHED! Jimi Hendrix receives the highest fee ever paid to a rock act for a single appearance, when he accepts $125,000 for appearing at The Newport Jazz Festival in the San Fernando Valley near Los Angeles. (1969)

1980   **Bob Dylan** dishes out some of that "old time religion" with the release of *Saved,* his first album of all "born again" material.

1981   Two British guitarists quit their respective groups on the same day. **Gerry Cott** departs the **Boomtown Rats** and **Bernie Torme** exits **Gillan.**

♫   **RECORD RELEASES** include **The Four Seasons** "Rag Doll" (1964) . . . and **Neil Young** "Cinammon Girl " (1970).

Birthdays:

BRIAN WILSON, Hawthorne, California, 1942. Singer, songwriter, keyboardist and arranger with his group The Beach Boys. His beginnings are with Carl and The Passions, then Kenny and The Cadets before reaching spectacular success with a string of surf songs and ballads in the sixties as The Beach Boys.

MICHAEL ANTHONY. Bassist with Van Halen, a band he formed with the Van Halen brothers and David Lee Roth in the mid seventies.

CHET ATKINS, Lutrell, Tennessee, 1924. Premiere guitarist who began as a session player before landing a record contract in 1946. Respected and admired as one of the best guitarists ever.

Brian Wilson

IT ALL BEGINS TO SPIN! Columbia Records announces the first mass production of 33-1/3 RPM long-playing discs. Skeptics fail to see the company's wisdom in committing to the LP at a time when the popularity of the 78 RPM is at an all-time high. (1948)

1967   **Billy Preston** is awarded a Gold Record for "Outa Space."

1975   Guitarist, **Ritchie Blackmore,** quits **Deep Purple** to form his own group, **Ritchie Blackmore's Rainbow** (later shortened to Rainbow). He's replaced in Deep Purple by American guitarist, **Tommy Bolin.**

1981   **Steely Dan** disbands, as **Donald Fagan** and **Walter Becker,** the only original members left, reveal that their 14-year partnership is over.

🎵   **RECORD RELEASES** include **Zager & Evans** "In The Year 2525" (1969) . . . and **James Taylor** "How Sweet It Is" (1975).

Birthdays:

RAY DAVIES, London, England, 1944. Singer and guitarist, the founding member of The Kings with brother Dave. The basic dirty two-note guitar hook that made a hit with "You Really Got Me" continues to be the trademark of the band.

JOEY KRAMER, 1956. Drummer with Aerosmith until the group disbanded in 1979, leaving a trail of hits . . . "Dream On," "Walk This Way" and "Back In The Saddle."

Todd Rundgren

ONCE IN A LIFETIME! The first and only LP from Blind Faith is released on Atco Records. The four-man supergroup features Steve Winwood on vocals, Eric Clapton on guitar, Rick Grech on bass and Ginger Baker on drums. The album becomes a standard of FM radio airplay and, to the amazement of most, the four members never attempt to rejoin forces. (1969)

1979 Guitarist, **Mick Taylor,** who once referred to himself as the "only person ever to quit the Rolling Stones and live!," releases his first solo LP, a loose-knit collection of jazz-influenced rock songs.

1981 **Mark David Chapman** pleads guilty to charges of first degree murder for the shooting of **John Lennon** six months earlier.

♫ **RECORD RELEASES** include **Chuck Berry** "Memphis" (1959). . . . **Stevie Wonder** "Fingertips Pt. II" and **The Safaris** "Wipe Out" (1963) . . . **Donovan** "Hurdy Gurdy Man" and **Mason Williams** "Classical Gas" (1968).

Birthdays:

KRIS KRISTOFFERSON, Brownsville, Texas, 1936. Singer, songwriter and actor, a Rhodes scholar with Ph. D. who abandoned his academic career to write songs. His first record contract came on the heels of "Me and Bobby McGee" in 1970, recorded by Janis Joplin. His film credits are numerous.

PETER ASHER, London, England, 1944. Singer, songwriter and producer. Famous as half of Peter and Gordon, then as successful manager and producer for James Taylor and Linda Ronstadt.

TODD RUNDGREN, Upper Darby, Pennsylvania, 1948. Singer, multi-instrumentalist and producer who began with the band Woody's Truckstop, then formed Nazz in 1968. His considerable production credits include work with Janis Joplin, Badfinger, Grand Funk Railroad, Meatloaf and others. He formed Utopia in 1974 and records with them in the eighties.

Notes:

JUNE 23

THE BEAT OF A WELL KNOWN DRUMMER! Ringo Starr begins recording sessions in Nashville with top country session players, Charlie McCoy, Jerry Reed, Charlie Daniels and others. The work is later released as *Beaucoups of Blues* and Ringo begins a series of solo projects. (1970)

1848 **Antoine Joseph Sax** is awarded a patent for his invention, the saxophone.

1967 **Who** bassist, **John Entwistle,** marries **Alison Wise.** "I suspected we would marry. I was already playing in an amateur group and on our first date, Alison carried my amplifier."—John Entwistle.

1981 **Robert Fripp,** keyboardist and group leader, announces the reincarnation of **King Crimson.** The band had been defunct since 1974.

🎵 **RECORD RELEASES** include **The Knack** "My Sherona" and **The Charlie Daniels Band** "Devil Went Down To Georgia" (1979).

Birthdays:

ADAM FAITH, Acton, London, 1940. Singer noted for a pair of hits in Britain, "What Do You Want" in 1959 and "Poor Me" in 1960. Later his career includes TV acting and manager for Leo Sayer.

Ringo Starr

THE BOOM AT THE TOP! Clive Davis and seventeen other top record industry executives are indicted on various charges in a federal crackdown on wrongdoing in the record business. Davis, who faces charges of income tax evasion, was fired as president of Columbia Records two years earlier for encouraging and engaging in the practice of payola. (1975)

1965 **John Lennon's** *A Spaniard In The Works,* his second book, is published.

1966 Counterculture comedian, **Lenny Bruce,** makes his last public appearance at The Fillmore West in San Francisco.

♪ **RECORD RELEASES** include **The Jefferson Airplane** "White Rabbit" and **Procol Harum** "Whiter Shade of Pale" (1967) ... **The Hollies** "Long Cool Woman" and **Helen Reddy** "I Am Woman" (1972).

Birthdays:

JEFF BECK, Surrey, England, 1944. Guitarist who replaced Eric Clapton in The Yardbirds before forming The Jeff Beck Group with Rod Stewart in 1967, then with Beck, Bogert and Appice. A solo LP *Blow By Blow* was recorded in 1975 and his collaborations include work with Jan Hammer.

MICK FLEETWOOD, Cornwall, England, 1947. Drummer and co-founder of Fleetwood Mac, a group that derives its name from Fleetwood and the "Mc" of bassist John McVie.

ARTHUR BROWN, born Arthur Wilton, Yorkshire, England, 1944. Singer, multi-instrumentalist and founder of The Crazy World Of Arthur Brown in the late sixties. His single hit in the U.S. was "Fire."

COLIN BLUNSTONE, England, 1945. Singer and original member of The Zombies.

CHRIS WOOD, Birmingham, England, 1944. Instrumentalist with Traffic, an original member of the group with Steve Winwood.

Notes:

ALL YOU NEED IS FRIENDS! The Beatles' "All You Need Is Love" is recorded during a live worldwide TV broadcast from EMI's London Studios. Mick Jagger, Marianne Faithful and Donovan are among those present who join in on the repetitive chorus, a hypnotic chanting of "All You Need Is Love." (1966)

1965 **The Rolling Stones** classic "Satisfaction" is #1 in the U.S. after only three weeks on the charts.

1966 **The Yardbirds'** "Over Under Sideways Down" is released.

1969 Guitarist, **Mick Taylor,** makes his concert debut with **The Rolling Stones** at the Coliseum in Rome, replacing **Brian Jones** who quit the band two weeks earlier.

1978 **Cream** briefly reforms for one concert at drummer **Ginger Baker's** polo club.

🎵 **GOLD RECORDS** awarded to **The Guess Who** for "These Eyes (1969) . . . and to **Seals and Crofts** for the *Diamond Girl* LP (1973).

Birthdays:

CARLY SIMON, New York City, 1945. Singer and songwriter who helped form The Simon Sisters with sister Lucy, in the early sixties. A solo artist in the early seventies with a number of duets with husband, James Taylor.

IAN McDONALD, London, England, 1946. Guitarist with King Crimson before forming Foreigner with Mick Jones. He left Foreigner in 1980 to pursue a solo career.

Notes:

_____

_____

_____

_____

_____

_____

_____

_____

THE ORIGINAL BEATLES! *A Hard Day's Night,* the first Beatles' LP to feature all original material, is released in the U.S. on United Artists Records. (1964)

1965 **The Byrds'** "Mr. Tambourine Man" is #1 in the U.S. and is the first rock treatment of a **Bob Dylan** song.

1973 **Carole King** is awarded a Gold Record for the LP *Fantasy.*

1975 **Sonny and Cher's** divorce is finalized, leaving her free to marry guitarist, **Greg Allman,** of The Allman Brothers Band, which she does four days later.

1976 The first **Jefferson Starship** LP *Dragon Fly* is released on Grunt Records, reuniting the group with long estranged vocalist, **Marty Balin,** on "Caroline."

1979 **Nigel Olsson, Elton John's** drummer, runs a stop sign in Atlanta and collides with another car, killing the driver. Olsson is charged with unintentional vehicular homocide, a misdemeanor.

🎵 **RECORD RELEASES** include **The Bee Gees** "How Can You Mend A Broken Heart" (1977) . . . and **Peter Frampton** "Baby I Love Your Way" (1976).

Birthdays:

LARRY TAYLOR, New York City, 1942. Bassist with Canned Heat.

GEORGIE FAME, born Clive Powell, Leigh, England, 1943. British pop singer noted for a #1 hit there, "Yeh Yeh."

COLONEL TOM PARKER, 1910. Manager of Elvis Presley and responsible for his meteoric rise to the top.

Bee Gees

THE GHOSTS OF THE GLORY! Rock promoter, Bill Graham, closes the doors to his legendary east side New York City rock club, The Fillmore East, for the last time. During the decade that the Fillmore was open for business, nearly every major rock act that passed through New York played the theater. "I remember hiding behind the speakers because I'd never played or sang before this kind of crowd before."—Rod Stewart. (1971)

1885 **Chichester Bell** and **Charles Tainter** apply for a patent on their invention, the gramophone. The patent is granted May 4, 1886.

1964 **The Rolling Stones** first LP enters the British pop charts, while in the U.S., **Peter and Gordon** are #1 with "World Without Love," a **Paul McCartney** song.

1969 The Denver Pop Festival is held at Mile High Stadium and draws performances from **Jimi Hendrix, Crosby, Stills & Nash, Joe Cocker, Johnny Winter** and others.

1975 **Z Z Top** is awarded a Gold Record for "Fandango."

1981 **Kim Carnes**' *Mistaken Identity* LP is #1 in the U.S. replacing REO Speedwagon's 14 week marathon at the top with *Hi Fidelity*.

♫ **RECORD RELEASES** include **Jan & Dean** "Little Old Lady From Pasadena" (1964) . . . **Stevie Wonder,** "Signed, Sealed, Delivered, I'm Yours" and **Crosby, Stills, Nash & Young** "Ohio" (1970).

Birthdays:

BRUCE JOHNSTON, Chicago, Illinois, 1944. Keyboards and vocals with The Beach Boys, joining the group in 1965 in place of ailing Brian Wilson.

ZZ Top

AN INTERNATIONAL FLAVOR! The debut LP from **Crosby, Stills & Nash** enters the charts in the U.S. The first single released, "Marrakesh Express," becomes a hit on both sides of the Atlantic. (1969)

1973   **Herman's Hermits** and **Gerry and The Pacemakers** headline Richard Nader's "British Re-Invasion show" at Madison Square Garden in New York.

1978   **Kansas** is the first band to be named Deputy Ambassadors of Goodwill by UNICEF, the world charity organization. A cake-cutting ceremony is held backstage at Madison Square Garden in honor of the band.

1980   **Paul McCartney's** "Coming Up" is #1 in the U.S.

♬   **RECORD RELEASES** include The Youngbloods "Get Together" (1969) . . . and **David Bowie** "Fame" (1975).

Birthdays:

DAVID KNIGHTS, London, England, 1945. Bassist with Procol Harum.

Kim Carnes

STONES IN JAIL! Mick Jagger and Keith Richards are both found guilty on drug charges stemming from a February 27, 1967, bust at Keith's home in West Wittering, England. Mick is sentenced to three months in jail and is sent to Brixton Prison. Keith is sentenced to a year. Fans are shocked and outraged. (1967)

1965 The Red Dog Saloon, one of America's earliest important rock clubs, opens in San Francisco.

1966 The **Beatles** are awarded a Gold Record for the LP *Yesterday . . . And Today.*

1968 **Pink Floyd** organizes and headlines a free concert in London's Hyde Park with **Roy Harper** and **Jethro Tull** as opening acts. The same day, **Pink Floyd's** second LP *A Saucerful Of Secrets* is released.

1968 **The Amboy Dukes'** "Journey To The Center Of Your Mind," with **Ted Nugent** on guitar, is released.

1974 **Ted Turner** quits **Wishbone Ash** to form his own group and is replaced by **Laurie Wisefield.**

1975 Singer-songwriter, **Tim Buckley,** dies of a heroin-morphine overdose in a Los Angeles hospital. Ten days later a research assistant at U.C.L.A. is charged with second degree murder for furnishing Buckley with the drugs that caused his death.

1975 **Elton John** makes a surprise appearance at an **Eagles-Doobie Brothers** concert at the Oakland Coliseum in California.

1978 **Peter Frampton** suffers a broken arm, cracked ribs and scalp cuts when his car skids and crashes in the Bahamas.

1979 **Lowell George,** the prolific singer, songwriter, guitarist and founder of **Little Feat,** dies of a heart attack in Washington D.C. while touring with his own new group.

Birthdays:

IAN PAICE, Nottingham, England, 1948. Drummer and founding member of Deep Purple, then Whitesnake.

LITTLE EVA, born Eva Boyd, Belhaven, North Carolina, 1945. Carole King's baby sitter before becoming popular with a recording of King's "Locomotion."

Notes:

FROM VINYL TO INK! Already living cartoons on stage, Kiss makes it official by publishing the *Kiss Book* with Marvel Comics. As a personal touch, each group member drips some of his own blood into the red ink used to print the book. It sells over 500,000 copies. (1977)

1962   **Neil Sedaka's** "Breaking Up Is Hard To Do" is #1 in the U.S., his fourth consecutive hit.

1962   **Ray Stevens** releases his novelty hit "Ahab the Arab."

1975   **The Eagles** are awarded a Gold Record for "One Of These Nights."

1975   Just four days after her divorce from **Sonny Bono, Cher** marries **Greg Allman** of **The Allman Brothers Band,** a marriage that will last only ten days.

1978   **The Sex Pistols** release their version of "My Way" and give a whole new meaning to the song.

1981   **Jerry Lee Lewis** is in critical condition at a Memphis hospital with abdominal pain. Two hours of surgery reveals a two centimeter hole in his stomach and multiple abscesses in his chest.

Birthdays:

GLENN SHORROCK, Sidney, Australia, 1944. Singer and original member of the Little River Band, then solo career in 1982.

FLO BALLARD, Detroit, Michigan, 1943. Along with Diana Ross and Mary Wilson, she formed The Supremes in the late fifties and produced some of the biggest hits of the sixties. She died in poverty never having received royalties for her work.

Kiss

A BUG IN HIS EAR! Consumer advocate, Ralph Nader, warns that amplified rock music can cause hearing damage and should be controlled by government restrictions. Nader says that high db rock is producing a generation of Americans with impaired hearing, and suggests it be classified a public nuisance. (1969)

1956 **Elvis Presley** makes one of his earlier network television appearances on the *Steve Allen Show,* dressed in coat and tails.

1965 The **FCC** rules that AM radio stations be prohibited from duplicating more than 50% of their programming on a sister FM, which paves the way for the creation of progressive FM.

1966 *Three Nights In Tokyo,* a famous **Beatles** bootleg, is recorded during three nights at Budokan Hall.

1967 The **Beatles'** *Sgt. Peppers Lonely Hearts Club Band* is leading LP charts, both in America and Britain.

1968 **John Lennon** publicly announces his love for **Yoko Ono** at the opening of his first art exhibition in London.

1969 **John, Yoko,** and her daughter **Kyoko** are injured in an auto accident in Scotland. All are quickly stitched at a nearby hospital.

1970 **Jimi Hendrix** begins his first recording session at his own Electric Lady Land Studios in New York City.

1973 *Jesus Christ Superstar* closes in New York City after 720 performances.

1975 **King Crimson** records what is believed to be their last concert in New York's Central Park, released as *USA.*

1975 **Ringo Starr** and wife, **Maureen,** divorce.

1976 **Peter Frampton** falls off stage and cracks two ribs at a concert in Hartford, Connecticut.

RECORD RELEASES include **Jim Croce** "Don't Mess Around With Jim" and the **Raspberries** "Go All The Way" (1972). . . and **Foreigner** "Hot Blooded" (1978).

Birthdays:

DEBBIE HARRY, New Jersey, 1946. Former model and Playboy bunny turned singer and mascot of Blondie in the late seventies.

DELANEY BRAMLETT, Pontotoc, Mississippi, 1939. Married Bonnie Lynn and as Delaney and Bonnie, recorded with George Harrison, Eric Clapton and many others. The two divorced in '72.

MAKING MOUNTAIN OUT OF MOLEHILLS! Felix Pappalardi isn't much impressed with The Vagrants, a New York City band he was asked to produce in '68, but he is with their lead guitarist Leslie West, a "fat kid" from Queens. Together they form Mountain, the name taken from the *Leslie West-Mountain* solo LP recorded in '69. "Mississippi Queen" and "Nantucket Sleighride" kept the band in the forefront of rock in the early seventies. (1969)

1956   The first single from **Buddy Holly** is released. "Love Me" on Side A, "Blue Days, Black Night" on the B side.

1956   **Elvis Presley** records "Don't Be Cruel" and "Hound Dog" in New York City, his two all-time top selling singles.

1969   Bassist, **Noel Redding,** and drummer, **Mitch Mitchell,** quit the **Jimi Hendrix Experience** when they learn of Jimi's plans to bring other musicians, writers, and composers into the group.

Buddy Holly

THIS IS THE END! Doors singer, Jim Morrison, dies of a heart attack in the bath of his Paris home. Rumors run rampant of the actual circumstances of his death (mainly that Jim OD'd on drugs), but none are proved. Morrison is buried in a Paris cemetery under the epitaph "James Morrison, poet." (1971)

1960 **Elvis Presley** is heartbroken when father, Vernon, announces his plans to marry Dee Elliott, less than two years after his mother's death.

1969 Guitarist, Brian Jones, recently departed from **The Rolling Stones,** is found floating dead in the swimming pool of his home in Hartfield, England. Brian's is the first in an eerie chain of rock superstar deaths over the next two years, which include **Janis Joplin, Jimi Hendrix,** and **Jim Morrison.**

1969 **The Newport Jazz Festival** includes rock artists for the first time with**Jethro Tull,** the **Mothers of Invention, Ten Years After,** and **Blood Sweat and Tears** among the first.

1973 Gold Record awarded to the **Doobie Brothers** for "The Captain and Me."

1973 **David Bowie** announces his retirement from live performances after a Hammersmith Odeon concert in London. False alarm.

1975 **Chuck Negron,** lead singer for **Three Dog Night,** is busted for drug possession in Louisville when police find a leather pouch with two grams of heroin and a gram of cocaine in his hotel room.

1976 **Brian Wilson** returns to the stage for the first time in twelve years to join **The Beach Boys** at Anaheim Stadium in California. An audience of 74,000 looks on.

1981 Former **Doors** player, **Ray Manzarek, Robbie Krieger** and **John Densmore** join hundreds of fans in a graveside tribute to **Jim Morrison** at Pere Lachaire cemetery in Paris, on the tenth anniversary of his death.

♬ **RECORD RELEASES** include **Billy Joe Royal** "Down In The Boondocks" (1965) . . . and the **Doors** "Riders On The Storm" (1971).

Birthdays:

PAUL BARRERE, 1948. Singer-guitarist and original member of Little Feat, he went solo in 1982.

MIKE CORBY, London, 1945. Guitarist with the Babys.

JULY 4

A KILLA IN MANILA! "Never again," said Beatle, George Harrison, after a harrowing tour of Manila. When the Fab Four's schedule forces them to refuse a last-minute invitation to play the Presidential Palace, they're denied security protection and narrowly escape mobs of fans awaiting them everywhere. (1966)

1964 **The Beach Boys'** "I Get Around" tops American singles charts, their first #1 record.

1967 Philadelphia is named the #1 concert city in America.

1969 **Bob Dylan** joins **The Band** on stage at the Mississippi River Festival at Southern Illinois University.

1971 **Bill Graham** closes the Fillmore West in San Francisco.

1972 Sixty-one fans are arrested when **The Rolling Stones** play Washington, D.C.

1976 **The Ramones** play a dynamic set at the London Roadhouse, their British concert debut.

1976 **Paul Revere** of " . . . and the Raiders" fame, is married on America's Bicentennial at Kings Island Amusement Park in Cincinnati. The entire wedding party dresses in traditional 1776 garb.

1977 **Gary Valentine,** bassist and co-author of *X Offender,* quits **Blondie** citing "artistic integrity."

1980 **Badfinger** reforms after a five-year hiatus, and releases the successful *Say No More* LP in '81.

🎵 **RECORD RELEASES** include the **Rolling Stones** "Tell Me" (1964) . . . the **Bee Gees** "You Should Be Dancing," **Fleetwood Mac** "Say That You Love Me," **Elton John-Kiki Dee** "Don't Go Breaking My Heart," **Cliff Richard** "Devil Woman," and **Boz Scaggs** "Low Down" (1976).

Birthdays:

JOHN WAITE, London, 1952. Bassist and vocalist, he founded the Babys in '76 and released his first solo LP *Ignition* in '82.

BILL WITHERS, Slab Fork, West Virginia, 1938. "Ain't No Sunshine" and "Lean On Me" hit big in the early seventies.

JEREMY SPENCER, West Hartlepool, England, 1948. Early guitarist with Peter Green's Fleetwood Mac, before leaving to join a religious sect. Bob Welch replaced him.

SHAKE, RATTLE & ROLL! After the intially unsuccessful "Rock Around The Clock," Bill Haley and the Comets finally hit the American Top Twenty with a follow-up effort "Shake, Rattle & Roll." It was this record that first put Bill in the spotlight and prompted the producers of the movie *The Blackboard Jungle* to use Haley's earlier "Rock Around the Clock" in the film. The rest, as they say, is history. (1954)

1969 The Rolling Stones give a free concert in Hyde Park in London where **Mick** reads to the assembly of 250,000 an excerpt from a Shelly poem as a memorial to recently departed **Brian Jones.**

🎵 **GOLD RECORDS** awarded to **Dobie Gray** for the single "Drift Away" (1973) . . . and to **Elton John** for the *Caribou* LP (1974).

🎵 **RECORD RELEASES** include **Tony Joe White** "Polk Salad Annie" (1969) . . . and **Bad Company** "Feel Like Making Love" (1975).

Birthdays:

ROBBIE ROBERTSON, born Jamie Robertson in Toronto, Canada, 1944. Guitarist and founding member of The Band, turned movie actor and producer. Good friend of Bob Dylan.

Notes:

THE AIRPLANE TAKES OFF! San Francisco's pride, The Jefferson Airplane is formed by singer, Marty Balin, and guitarist, Paul Kantner, in the Haight Ashbury district, with a line-up which also includes bassist, Jack Cassidy, drummer, Skip Spence and singer, Signe Anderson. (Signe quits to have a baby after release of the debut album in '66 to be permanently replaced by Grace Slick). (1965)

1964   The **Beatles** first film, *A Hard Days's Night,* has a Royal premiere at the London Pavillion, and is later nominated for two Academy Awards.

1967   **Brian Jones** is hospitalized for strain and fatigue.

1969   **Mick Jagger** starts work on his first feature film, the title role in *Ned Kelly.*

1973   "Keep Yourself Alive" is released as the first single from **Queen.**

1974   *Bad Company,* their debut album, is released on Swan Song, the Led Zeppelin-owned label. It's first spin-off single, "Can't Get Enough," soon tops American record charts.

1980   Thirty-six are arrested at a **Ted Nugent** concert in Hollywood, Florida, for pot-smoking, bottle-throwing and other offenses.

🎵 **GOLD RECORDS** awarded to **Simon & Garfunkel** for their *Greatest Hits* album (1972) . . . and to **Paul McCartney** for single "My Love" (1973).

Birthdays:

GENE CHANDLER, Chicago, 1937. Best known for "Duke of Earl."

BILL HALEY, born William Clifton Haley, Highland Park, Michigan, 1925. Released "Crazy Man Crazy," the first rock 'n' roll record to enter U.S. charts, in 1953, and the classic "Rock Around The Clock" in 1954. Haley is often credited with starting the rock 'n' roll movement.

Notes:

Ted Nugent

NO TIME TO HESITATE! The definitive classic from The Doors "Light My Fire" is leading American singles charts. "It was the song of the decade. I played it 2,000 times, but because of its jazz, improvisational nature I never got tired of playing it."—Doors drummer John Densmore. (1967)

1969 **John** and **Yoko Lennon** unveil the **Plastic Ono Band,** on stage for the first time at Chelsea Town Hall in London. The gig is set up to promote their first single "Give Peace A Chance," recorded during the Montreal "Bed-In."

1975 **Stones** guitarist, **Keith Richard,** is arrested in Arkansas, and charged with possession of an offensive weapon and reckless driving.

🎵 **RECORD RELEASES** include **The Platters** "My Prayer" (1956) . . . and **Paul McCartney** "Live and Let Die" (1973).

Birthdays:

RINGO STARR, Liverpool, England, 1940. He joined the Beatles in place of Pete Best in '62, and rode the wave of their legend. Solo recordings include "It Don't Come Easy" and "Photograph". He also acts in the films "The Magic Christian" and "Caveman" with wife, **Barbara Bach.**

JIM RODFORD, Hertfordshire, U.K., 1945. Bassist with Argent, his cousin Rod's band.

LARRY RHEINHARDT, Florida, 1948. Guitarist with Iron Butterfly until the group's demise in '72.

Notes:

The Doors

HAVE FAITH-FUL, MARIANNE! Singer, Marianne Faithful, is found in a coma following a suicide attempt in Australia. Boyfriend, Mick Jagger, surrenders the relationship not long after they return home from the filming of *Ned Kelly* there. (1969)

1969   **Zager & Evans** are awarded a Gold Record for their hit single "In The Year 2525."

1978   "Kiss You All Over" is released by **Exile.**

Birthdays:

JAI JOHNNY JOHANSON, Ocean Springs, Mississippi, 1944. Drummer and original member of the Allman Brothers Band until 1980 when he's replaced by Dan Toller.

Notes:

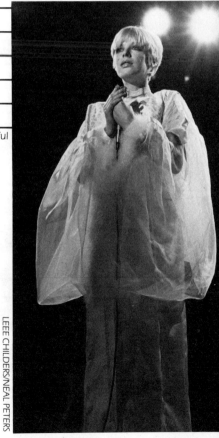

Marianne Faithful

LEEE CHILDERS/NEAL PETERS

JULY 9

BONJOUR, MONSIEUR PAUL! Paul McCartney opens his first scheduled tour with Wings at Chateauvillon, a village in the south of France. Some 2,000 fans witness McCartney's first scheduled stage appearance since the Beatles played Candlestick Park in 1966. (1972)

1969 **Brian Jones** is buried in his home town of Cheltenham Spa six days after the ex-Stones guitarist was found dead in his swimming pool.

🎵**RECORD RELEASES** include the Rolling Stones "Mother's Little Helper" (1966) . . . **Leo Sayer** "How Much Love" and **Fleetwood Mac** "Don't Stop" (1977).

Birthdays:

MITCH MITCHELL, born John Mitchell in London, England, 1946. Drummer with the Jimi Hendrix Experience.

Notes:

Funeral of Brian Jones—leaving the church are, (from left) Canon Hugh Hopkins, Brian's parents, his sister and girlfriend Suki Poitier.

JULY 10

IT'S A WOMAN'S PREROGATIVE! Cher files for divorce from Allman brother keyboardist, Greg Allman . . . ten days after their wedding! She accuses him of moonlighting with an old flame. And so it goes. (1975)

1965 "Satisfaction" becomes **The Rolling Stones'** first #1 U.S. single.

1967 **Kenny Rogers** quits the **New Christie Minstrels** to form **The First Edition.**

1975 **Mick Taylor** (former Stone) and **Carla Bley** both quit the **Jack Bruce Band.**

1979 **Chuck Berry** is sentenced to four months in prison after pleading guilty to charges of income tax evasion. According to the IRS, Berry shortchanged Uncle Sam by more than $200,000 on his 1973 return.

🎵 **RECORD RELEASES** include **Martha and the Vandellas** "Heatwave" (1963). . . **Wilson Pickett** "In The Midnight Hour" and **Sonny & Cher** "I Got You Babe" (1965) . . . and **Three Dog Night** "Liar" (1971).

Birthdays:

ARLO GUTHRIE, New York City, 1947. Son of legendary folk singer, Woody Guthrie, best known for *Alice's Restaurant,* the song and the movie.

RONNIE JAMES DIO, 1949. Vocalist with Black Sabbath, after spending time with Deep Purple and Rainbow.

Notes:

The New Christy Minstrels

REGROUP! Jimi Hendrix's new Band of Gypsies appeared in concert for the first time at the Apollo Theater in Harlem, a benefit for BIAFRA. A somewhat different approach from the Jimi Hendrix Experience, the Band of Gypsies has a more rhythmic sound, with Billy Cox on bass, Buddy Miles on drums, and Jimi's vocals and sizzling guitar. (1969)

1959 **Joan Baez** makes her first recording, a duet with **Bob Gibson** at the Newport Film Festival.

1967 **The First Edition** forms and begins recording their first album the day after group leader and vocalist, **Kenny Rogers,** quits the **New Christie Minstrels.**

1979 **Neil Young's** film *Rust Never Sleeps* opens in L.A. The title song becomes one of Neil's biggest hits.

🎵 RECORD RELEASES include the **Supremes** "Where Did Our Love Go" (1964) . . . **David Bowie's** LP *Space Oddity* (1969) . . . **Mungo Jerry** "In The Summertime," **Edwin Starr** "War," and the **Who** "Summertime Blues" (1970).

Birthdays:

JEFF HANNA, Detroit, Michigan, 1947. Singer, guitarist and percussionist with the Nitty Gritty Dirt Band.

Notes:

Kenny Rogers and the First Edition

PLEASED TO MEET YOU! Mick Jagger and his newly formed The Rolling Stones appear for the first time at the Marquee Club in London. The early line-up includes Keith Richard, Brian Jones (still using the pseudonym Elmo Lewis), Dick Taylor and Mick Avery, all former members of Blues Incorporated. (1962)

1969 An all-acoustic **John Mayall Band** records *The Turning Point* album live-in-concert at the Fillmore East in New York.

1969 Supergroup, **Blind Faith,** makes its U.S. debut at Madison Square Garden in New York.

1969 **Bob Dylan** releases "Lay Lady Lay."

1970 **Janis Joplin** appears in concert for the first time with her new group, **The Full Tilt Boogie,** in Louisville, Kentucky.

1971 The first authorized touring company of Rice-Webber's *Jesus Christ Superstar* begins its cross-country rounds in Pittsburgh. Promoter **Robert Stigwood** put together this cast of 60, only one of whom performed on the original recording . . . **Yvonne Elliman** as Mary Magdalene.

1979 Singer-songwriter, **Minnie Ripperton,** dies of cancer in her husband's arms in Los Angeles. Minnie first grabbed the national limelight with her 1974 hit "Lovin' You."

1979 Chicago disc jockey, **Steve Dahl,** dynamites disco records at Kamisky Park between games of a Cubs double-header. For 98 cents admission, disco haters are invited to gather up the dreaded records, toss them onto a pile, and watch as Dahl blasts the entire stack.

Birthdays:

CHRISTINE McVIE, born Christine Perfect in England, 1943. Singer and keyboardist, she joined Fleetwood Mac, her husband's group, after a limp solo start.

ERIC CARR, 1950. Replacement for drummer, Peter Criss, in Kiss, disguised in Fox make-up.

Notes:

ENOUGH IS ENOUGH! "The Everly Brothers died ten years ago!" explains Don Everly from the stage of the John Wayne Theater in Buena Park, California, just after brother, Phil, smashes his guitar and stalks off, ending the careers of the Everly Brothers. Their latter years were marked by personal misfortune and disagreement. (1973)

1973   The debut LP from **Queen** is released, featuring lead track "Keep Yourself Alive."

🎵 **RECORD RELEASES** include the **Shirelles** "Dedicated To The One I Love" (1959) . . . **Steppenwolf** "Born To Be Wild" and **Vanilla Fudge** "You Keep Me Hangin' On" (1968) . . . **Billy Preston** "Nothing From Nothing" and **Eric Clapton** "I Shot The Sheriff" (1974).

Birthdays:

ROGER McGUINN, born James Joseph McGuinn, Chicago, Illinois, 1942. Singer-guitarist who formed the Byrds in '65.

Notes:

The Shirelles

I'M THE TAX MAN! Former Beatles and Rolling Stones money man, Allen Klein, surrenders to authorities at New York's Metropolitan Corrections Center to begin serving a two-month sentence for filing a false income tax return. (1980)

1969   Gold Record awarded to **The 5th Dimension** for "The Age of Aquarius."

1973   Former **Byrds** guitarist, **Clarence White,** is killed when he's struck by an automobile near Lancaster, California. The twenty-nine-year-old guitarist is thrown seventy-five feet into the air by the impact.

Birthdays:

WOODY GUTHRIE born Woodrow Wilson Guthrie in Okema, Oklahoma, 1912. A legendary folk singer, from his pen emerged numerous American classics including "This Land is Your Land." He died October 3rd, 1967, of Huntington's Chorea and is survived by son Arlo Guthrie, who carries on the musical tradition.

Notes:

_____

_____

_____

_____

_____

Woody Guthrie

YOU HAD ME BUT I NEVER HAD YOU! John Lennon's mother, Julia, is killed in an auto accident in Liverpool. The loss is expressed over and over in much of John's music. (1958)

1977 **Ray Davies** announces that he is quitting the **Kinks.** Brother, **Dave,** as surprised by the disclosure as anyone, assures the press that Ray's split is only temporary. He was right.

1978 **Bob Dylan** performs at Blackbushe Airport in England before a crowd of 200,000, the largest U.K. gathering ever to attend an open-air concert by a single artist.

RECORD RELEASES include the **Bee Gees** "To Love Somebody," **Jay & The Techniques** "Apples, Peaches, Pumpkin Pie," **Van Morrison** "Brown Eyed Girl," and the **Rascals** "A Girl Like You" (1967).

Birthdays:

LINDA RONSTADT, Tucson, Arizona, 1946. Singer first with the Stone Poneys, she hit paydirt as a solo artist with hits like "You're No Good" and "That'll Be The Day." A lead role in *The Pirates of Penzance* on Broadway introduced her to the musical theater in 1980.

Linda Ronstadt

JULY 16

HELLO CREAM! Rock's premiere supergroup, Cream, forms in the U.K. in the summer of '66 when Eric Clapton, fresh from John Mayall's Bluesbreakers, joins with Ginger Baker and Jack Bruce of the Graham Bond Organization. Their second LP, *Disraeli Gears,* proves their commercial viability with the runaway hit single "Sunshine Of Your Love." (1966)

1960 **Hank Ballard** and the **Midnighters** are the first group to ever score three records on Billboard's Hot 100 chart at the same time . . . "Poppin' Time," "Let's Go, Let's Go," and "The Twist." The record wouldn't last long, 'cause the **Beatles** are comin'.

1969 Gold Record awarded to the **Beatles** for "The Ballad of John & Yoko."

1973 **Bob Dylan's** soundtrack album to *Pat Garrett and Billy the Kid* is released, featuring the hit "Knockin' On Heaven's Door."

1976 **Loggins and Messina** split up after six years of recording hits together. **Kenny Loggins** initiated the break, realizing it was about time he made the solo album he'd set out to make in 1970 . . . the one that became **Loggins and Messina's** *Sittin' In.*

1981 **Harry Chapin** is killed in a car crash on New York's Long Island Expressway when his blue 1975 Volkswagen Rabbit is hit from behind by a tractor-trailer. Harry dies of a massive heart attack.

🎵 **RECORD RELEASES** include the **Lovin' Spoonful** "Summer In The City" (1966) . . . and **The Who** "I'm Free" (1969).

Notes:

BLUE MEANIES & YELLOW ZONKERS! The Beatles full-length animation feature, *Yellow Submarine,* premieres at the London Pavillion. Cartoon Beatles take a psychedelic "trip" in their Yellow Submarine, and find a very real pot of gold, as the film becomes the second biggest box-office draw of 1969. Four new songs are recorded specially for the film. (1968)

1959 Blues singer, **Billy Holiday,** dies of heroin overdose. Billy is hailed as perhaps the finest female blues singer ever.

1972 **Sly Stone** is mistakenly arrested by overzealous police in Santa Monica for possession of dangerous drugs. Charges are dropped when the "dangerous drugs" turn out to be cold capsules.

1972 A **Rolling Stones** equipment van is dynamited while the group is touring Montreal. The blast blows out 30 PA speakers and shatters dozens of windows in nearby apartments.

1974 **The Moody Blues** open their own 32-track recording studio in London, the first U.K. studio specifically for quadraphonic recording.

1974 The United States Justice Department orders **John Lennon** to leave the country within 60 days or be deported. John returns the fire by filing a countersuit against Uncle Sam.

RECORD RELEASES include **The Miracles** "Tracks of My Tears" (1965) . . . **The Who** "We won't Get Fooled Again" (1971) . . . and **Heart** "Magic Man" (1976).

Birthdays:

SPENCER DAVIS, Swansea, Wales, 1941. He formed the Spencer Davis Group with Muff and Steve Winwood, and had a major hit with "Gimme Some Lovin'."

GEEZER BUTLER, born Terry Butler in Birmingham, England, 1949. Bassist with Black Sabbath.

PHOEBE SNOW, New York City, 1952. Had a mid-seventies hit with "Poetry Man" and joined with Paul Simon on "Gone At Last."

MICK TUCKER, Middlesex, England, 1948. Drummer with Sweet until the group disbands in early 1980s.

Notes:

NO NUKES ON FILM! The movie of the three-day series of "No Nukes" concerts at Madison Square Garden opens to favorable reviews in New York. Film highlights include segments of Bruce Springsteen, Carly Simon and James Taylor, and Jackson Browne. Money from the movie is added to the cash from the concert and all is donated to the fight against nuclear power. (1980)

1973   Gold Record award to **Chicago** for *Chicago VI.*

1980   **Billy Joel** tops American record charts with the album *Glass Houses* and single "It's Still Rock and Roll To Me."

♫ **RECORD RELEASES** include the **Ventures** "Walk Don't Run" and **Elvis Presley** "It's Now Or Never" (1960) . . . and the **Beatles** "Hard Days Night" (1964).

Birthdays:

DION, born Dion DiMucci in New York City, 1939. Teen idol-vocalist of Dion and the Belmonts, his hits include "In The Still Of The Night" and "Runaround Sue."

MARTHA REEVES, Detroit, Michigan, 1941. She joined Motown Records as a secretary and ended up earning them millions fronting the Vandellas and hits like "Heatwave," "Jimmy Mack," and "Dancing In The Street."

BRIAN AUGER, London, 1939. Vocalist and keyboardist, first with Long John Baldry, then forming Trinity for the hit "This Wheel's On Fire," then the Oblivion Express in 1971.

Notes:

Pheobe Snow

HUSH HUSH, DEEP PURPLE! British metal rockers, Deep Purple, bite the dust after months of rumors hinting at the breakup. The end was signaled in 1975 when guitarist Ritchie Blackmore quit to form his own group, Rainbow. Purple is best known for their 1972 bombshell "Smoke On The Water." (1976)

1976 **Allman Brothers Band** roadie, **Scooter Herring,** is sentenced to 75 years in prison for distributing cocaine and other narcotics to **Greg Allman.** Greg was granted immunity in exchange for his testimony.

♪ **RECORD RELEASES** include the **Rolling Stones** "Honky Tonk Woman" (1969) . . . and **Orleans** "Dance With Me" (1975).

Birthdays:

BERNIE LEADON, Minneapolis, Minnesota, 1947. Guitarist with the Flying Burrito Brothers before joining Linda Ronstadt's backup group which became the Eagles in '71. He quit in '75 to be replaced by Joe Walsh.

BRIAN MAY, Middlesex, England, 1947. Guitarist with Queen.

KEITH GODCHAUX, San Francisco, California, 1948. Keyboard player with the Grateful Dead, he and wife Donna joined the group during Ron "Pigpen" McKernan's illness.

ALAN COLLINS, Jacksonville, Florida, 1952. A founding member of Lynyrd Skynyrd, now guitarist and founder of the Rossington-Collins Band.

Notes:

Brian May

THANKS, BRIAN! "Surf City" by Jan and Dean is leading American singles charts just two weeks after its release. This anthem of "teen Utopia" where there are "two girls for every boy," was given to them by Beach Boy, Brian Wilson, and begins a close association between the two California surf groups. (1963)

1967   Jimi Hendrix records "Burning Of The Midnight Lamp" at Mayfair Recording Studios in New York.

1968   Iron Butterfly's psychedelic classic "Inna Gadda Da Vida" enters Billboard's Hot 100 chart at #117. It goes on to become one of the biggest selling rock records of all time.

1968   Jane Asher tells a BBC-TV reporter that her engagement to Beatle, **Paul McCartney,** is off. Paul was watching the show at a friend's house and heard the news the same time the rest of Britain did.

1973   *Genesis Live* is released in Britain, a recording made during a live U.S. radio broadcast. Their next live album wouldn't be issued until June, 1982, with *Three Sides Live.*

Birthdays:

CARLOS SANTANA, Autlan, Mexico, 1947. The guitarist's own group, Santana, emerged in the San Francisco music explosion of the sixties. Their Woodstock appearance brought them to the forefront of rock in '69.

JOHN LODGE, Birmingham, England, 1943. Bassist with the Moody Blues, he replaced Clint Warwick after their 1965 hit "Go Now."

MICHAEL ANTHONY, 1955. Bassist with Van Halen.

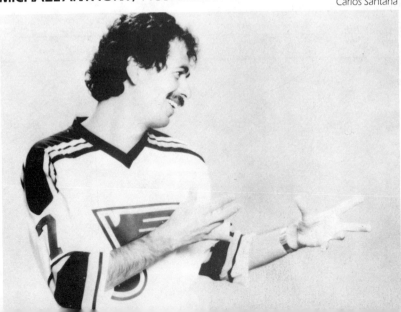

Carlos Santana

ROCK 'N' ROLL GOLD! Two Gold Records are issued on this day in rock history. Carole King takes one of them for her single "It's Too Late" from the multi-million selling *Tapestry* album (1971)... and the other awarded to Michael Murphy for "Wildfire," a horse story. (1975)

1972 **Rod Stewart's** fourth solo effort *Never A Dull Moment* is released on Mercury Records. It features "You Wear It Well," a strong successor to "Maggie May."

♫ **RECORD RELEASES** include **Robert Palmer** "Bad Case Of Lovin' You" and **Little River Band** "Lonesome Loser" (1979).

Birthdays:

CAT STEVENS, born Stephen Demetri Georgiou in London, 1947. A singer-songwriter-guitarist who rose to fame on the strength of hits like "Wild World," "Moon Shadow," and others.

KAY STARR, Dougherty, Oklahoma, 1922. Famous for the "Rock and Roll Waltz."

KIM FOWLEY, Manilla, Phillippines, 1942. He had a 1960 million seller with the novelty song "Alley Oop."

Notes:

_____

_____

_____

_____

_____

_____

_____

IT BEGAN RIGHT HERE! *Introducing The Beatles* is released on Vee Jay Records, the first label contracted to issue John, Paul, George, and Ringo's works in the United States. The album stiffed and Capitol Records subsequently won exclusive rights to press the Beatles' music. (1963)

1969 **Aretha Franklin** is arrested for causing a "disturbance" in a parking lot in Detroit. The feisty soul singer pays the $50 fine, and runs over a road sign on her way out of the police station lot.

1969 Gold Record awarded to **Led Zeppelin** for their album debut.

1977 Stiff Records releases **Elvis Costello's** first LP *My Aim Is True,* featuring the single "Allison."

1979 **Little Richard** quits rock 'n' roll for religion, he announces at a fundamentalist tent revival meeting in North Richmond, California. "I gave up rock 'n' roll for the Rock of Ages."

♪ RECORD RELEASES include the **Monkees** "Pleasant Valley Sunday" (1967) . . . and the **Who** "Join Together" (1972).

Birthdays:

DON HENLEY, Linden, Texas, 1947. Drummer with the Eagles after backup with Linda Ronstadt.

Notes:

Aretha Franklin

JULY 23

IN MEMORY OF KEITH! Grateful Dead piano player, Keith Godchaux, 32, dies of head injuries sustained in an auto accident two days earlier in Marin County, California. Keith and his wife, Donna, both joined the Dead in 1971 at a time when Ron McKernan was seriously ill with a liver disease. (1979)

1969 Gold Records awarded to **Blood, Sweat and Tears** for "Spinning Wheel" . . . and to **Three Dog Night** for "One."

♫ **RECORD RELEASES** include **Napoleon XIV** "They're Coming To Take Me Away, Ha Ha" and the **Hollies** "Bus Stop" (1966). . . **Carly Simon** "Nobody Does It Better" and **Foreigner** "Cold As Ice"(1977).

Birthdays:

DINO DANELLI, Jersey City, New Jersey, 1945. Original drummer with the Young Rascals, later forming Photomaker with ex-Rascal, Gene Cornish.

ANDY McKAY, England, 1946. Sax and oboe player with Roxy Music, plus solo career.

DAVID ESSEX, born David Cook in London, 1947. Singer-songwriter-actor, had a seventies hit with "Rock On."

TONY JOE WHITE, 1947. Famous for "Polk Salad Annie."

BLAIR THORNTON, Canada, 1950. Guitarist who joined Bachman-Turner Overdrive in '75 in place of Tim Bachman.

Notes:

ACCEPT NO IMITATIONS! Robert Stigwood's film *Sgt. Peppers Lonely Hearts Club Band* opens in New York, starring Peter Frampton as Billy Shears and the Bee Gees as The Henderson Brothers. Musical performances by Aerosmith, Alice Cooper and Earth, Wind and Fire give the soundtrack LP some sizzle, but nothing can save the film. It's a major box-office flop. (1978)

1965   **The Animals** enter British rock charts for the first time with "We've Gotta Get Out Of This Place."

1972   Drummer **Bobby Ramirez,** 23, of White Trash is killed in a bar brawl in Chicago. One of his three attackers turns himself over to police and is charged with first-degree murder.

♫ **GOLD RECORDS** awarded to **Elton John** for the *Honky Chateau* LP (1972) . . . and to **Jim Croce** for "Bad, Bad, Leroy Brown" (1973).

♫ **RECORD RELEASES** include the **Beach Boys** "California Girls," **We Five** "You Were On My Mind," and **Bob Dylan** "Like A Rolling Stone" (1965) . . . **Hall & Oates** "She's Gone" and the **Jefferson Starship** "With Your Love" (1976).

Notes:

SWITCHED ON DYLAN! The boos are almost deafening as Bob Dylan makes his "electric debut" at the Newport Folk Festival. The crowd jeers as Bob introduces his new style, namely electrically amplified instruments rather than his usual acoustic ones. The times, they were a changin'. (1965)

1966 **The Rolling Stones** play their last American concert with guitarist **Brian Jones.**

1968 *Big Brother and the Holding Company,* the first album featuring **Janis Joplin,** is released on Mainstream Records and contains "Piece of My Heart." It earns a Gold Record when Columbia Records later re-issues it.

1969 **Neil Young** joins **Crosby, Stills and Nash** for the first time at a concert at New York's Fillmore East. Soon he would become the final gear of the **Crosby, Stills, Nash and Young** hit-making machine.

1971 **The Beach Boys**' critically acclaimed *Surf's Up* album is released on Capitol Records.

1980 **Kiss** unveils their new drummer, **Eric Carr,** at a New York Palladium show. Carr's "fox" replaces **Peter Criss's** "cat."

1980 **The Rolling Stones** top American charts with "Emotional Rescue."

1981 **The Moody Blues,** back recording after a five-year break, hold the #1 spot on U.S. album charts with "Long Distance Voyager," while Canada's **Air Supply** pins down #1 on the singles charts.

🎵 **RECORD RELEASES** include **Chicago** "25 Or 6 To 4" . . . and **Dawn** "Candida" (1970).

Birthdays:

JIM McCARTY, Liverpool, England, 1944. A founding member and drummer of the Yardbirds, before leaving with singer Keith Relf to form Renaissance.

STEVE GOODMAN, Chicago, Illinois, 1948. Discovered by Kris Kristofferson, he penned "City Of New Orleans" made famous by Arlo Guthrie, a classic train song.

Notes:

STAIRWAY TO HEAVEN! Led Zeppelin's U.S. tour is abruptly halted when singer, Robert Plant, gets word from England that his six-year old son, Karac, died. The boy was a victim of complications resulting from a virus. The tour is never resumed. (1977)

1968   **Mick Jagger** is heard playing guitar for the first time with the release of the **Rolling Stones** *Beggars Banquet,* featuring the hit ''Street Fighting Man.''

1974   The first **Beatles** Convention.

Birthdays:

MICK JAGGER, Kent, England, 1943. After starting with Alex Korner's Blues Incorporated, he co-founded the Rolling Stones in '63. The group is second perhaps only to the Beatles for setting the pace of sixties rock and, twenty years later, is going as strong as ever.

ROGER TAYLOR, Norfolk, England, 1949. Drummer with Queen, he also released a first solo LP in 1981.

Notes:

Mick Jagger

GIVE US YOUR TIRED, YOUR BEATLES! John Lennon's struggle to remain in the United States finally ends when his application to become a permanent resident is approved. U.S. Immigration Service lawyers state that the government no longer objects to John's presence and awards him his long-awaited green card . . . #A17-597-321. (1976)

1971   **George Harrison** announces his plans to organize a benefit concert for the starving people of Bangla Desh.

1972   **Tony Banks,** keyboardist of **Genesis,** marries in Farnham, Surrey, England. All Genesis members, former and present, are on hand.

1974   **Neil Young's** *On The Beach* LP is released on Reprise Records.

1976   **Bruce Springsteen** files a massive breach-of-contract suit against his manager **Mike Appel,** demanding $1 million damages plus the return of all monies paid to Appel during their association. In response, Mike Appel sought and won a court order barring Bruce from entering a recording studio while the suit is in litigation.

🎵 **RECORD RELEASES** include **Santo & Johnny** "Sleepwalk" (1959) . . . and **Lynyrd Skynyrd** "Sweet Home Alabama" (1974).

Birthdays:

BOBBY GENTRY, Chickasaw County, Mississippi, 1944. Famous for the "Ode To Billy Joe."

Notes:

BIGGER THAN WOODSTOCK! Six hundred thousand young people gather at Watkins Glenn Racetrack in New York for "Summer Jam," featuring the Grateful Dead, The Band, and The Allman Brothers. Unlike the Woodstock concert, there was no politicking, no births, and but a single death . . . that of a skydiver whose parachute caught fire. (1973)

1970   **Mick Jagger** makes his acting debut in the title role of the film *Ned Kelly,* which premieres in Glenrowan, near Melbourne, Australia, home of the real-life Ned Kelly.

1972   Gold Record awarded to **Cheech and Chong** for their debut LP.

1979   **Ted Nugent, Aerosmith, Journey** and **Thin Lizzy** headline the World Series of Rock at Cleveland Stadium in Ohio. Of the 65,000 people who attended, one 18 year old man is shot to death in the parking lot, thirty people are robbed, and two women raped.

♬ RECORD RELEASES include **Tommy Roe** "Sheila" (1962) . . . **Grand Funk Railroad** "We're An American Band" and **B.W. Stevenson** "My Maria" (1973).

Birthdays:

RICK WRIGHT, London, 1945. Keyboardist with Pink Floyd from the group's beginning.

SIMON KIRKE, Shropshire, England, 1948. Drummer with Free before he and Paul Rogers form Bad Company in '73.

Notes:

JULY 29

WIPEOUT IN WOODSTOCK! Bob Dylan is badly injured when he crashes his Triumph motorcycle on the way to a repair shop near his home in Woodstock, New York. The folk legend goes into semi-retirement, as bizarre rumors circulate about his physical and mental state. (1966)

1962   **Bob Dylan's** first radio appearance is on WRVR-FM in New York, as part of a 21-hour hootenany Saturday Special.

1965   The **Beatles'** second film *Help!* has its world premiere at the London Pavillion, with the Queen among those in attendance. The movie wins first prize at the Rio De Janeiro Film Festival later that year.

1970   **The Rolling Stones** announce that **Allen Klein** and his ABKCO Industries will no longer represent them.

1971   A would-be gate crasher at a **Who** concert in New York makes good on his threat to kill someone if he doesn't get into the sold-out concert, and stabs a 22-year-old security guard.

1973   **Led Zeppelin** is ripped off of more than $180,000 in $100 bills when a thief makes off with the band's safe deposit box at the New York Hilton. That money represented most of the cash receipts from two sold-out concerts at Madison Square Garden.

1974   **Cass Elliot** of the **Mamas and the Papas** dies of a heart attack in the London flat of **Harry Nilsson.** The 32-year-old singer is at first believed to have choked on a ham sandwich.

1978   **Fleetwood Mac** cancels shows in Pittsburgh and Cleveland after guitarist, **Lindsey Buckingham,** collapses before a show in Philadelphia.

🎵 **RECORD RELEASES** include **Peter, Paul & Mary** "Blowin' In The Wind" (1963) . . . **Simon & Garfunkel** "Fakin' It" and the **Temptations** "You're My Everything" (1967) . . . **Arlo Guthrie** "City Of New Orleans" and **Rick Nelson** "Garden Party" (1972). . . **Kenny Loggins** "Whenever I Call You 'Friend'" and the **Little River Band** "Reminiscing" (1978).

Notes:

214

BACK TOGETHER AGAIN! Eric Burden and all the original Animals release their reunion album, appropriately titled *Before We Were So Rudely Interrupted,* containing all new music. The group just doesn't have the magic the second time around. (1977)

1968   The **Beatles**-owned Apple Boutique closes its doors.

Birthdays:

JEFFREY HAMMOND-HAMMOND, England, 1946. He replaced original Jethro Tull bassist, Glen Cornick, and first appeared on Tull's *Aqualung* LP. He departed the group in the late seventies.

PAUL ANKA, Ottawa, Ontario, 1941.

Notes:

_____

_____

_____

_____

_____

_____

_____

_____

Fleetwood Mac

PILL PUSHIN' PAPA! John Phillips of the Mamas and the Papas is arrested at his summer home in Water Mill, Long Island, as a principle in a major pill-pushing ring. John, known to have been a long-time cocaine addict, is later found guilty of the crime. (1980)

1964   A **Rolling Stones** concert in Belfast, Ireland, is stopped by police after just twelve minutes due to rioting fans.

1967   **Mick Jagger** and **Keith Richard** are released from jail after spending a month behind bars for possession of dangerous drugs. Public outcry over their imprisonment succeeds in overturning Keith's conviction completely, while Mick is given a conditional discharge.

1971   **James Taylor** has the #1 record in the U.S. with "You've Got A Friend," a **Carole King** song. Carole herself later records it on her best-selling *Tapestry* LP.

1972   Gold Record awarded to **Chicago** for *Chicago V.*

1981   **Debbie Harry** steps outside **Blondie** and releases a solo album, *Koo Koo.*

🎵 **RECORD RELEASES** include the **Yardbirds** "Heart Full of Soul" (1965). . . **Lee Michaels** "Do You Know What I Mean" (1971) . . . **Blue Oyster Cult** "Don't Fear The Reaper" and **Orleans** "Still The One" (1976).

Birthdays:

BOB WELCH, Los Angeles, California, 1946. A singer-guitarist, he joined Fleetwood Mac in '71 and left to pursue solo ventures in '75. Best known for "Sentimental Lady" and "Ebony Eyes."

HUGH McDOWELL, England, 1953. Celloist with Electric Light Orchestra, he joined in place of Colin Walker in '71.

Notes:

Deborah Harry

AUGUST 1

BANGLA DESH! BANGLA DESH! One of the greatest indoor rock events ever is held at Madison Square Garden in New York . . . George Harrison's landmark Concert For Bangla Desh. Its unparalleled cast includes Eric Clapton, Ringo Starr, Billy Preston, Leon Russell, Bob Dylan and others. The entire show is recorded and later issued as a triple-album set, the proceeds of which are eventually donated to aid the starving children of Bangla Desh. (1971)

1942 American Federation of Musicians Union president, **James Petrillo,** views records as a threat to musicians' jobs, and bans its membership from recording.

1964 Singer **Johnny Burnette** ("You're Sixteen") dies at the height of his career in a boating accident in Clear Lake, near San Francisco, California.

1970 *Performance,* starring **Mick Jagger,** premieres two years after its completion when the distributor insists that a scene in which Mick and co-star **Anita Pallenberg** have sexual intercourse be cut.

🎵 **RECORD RELEASES** include **Chubby Checker** "The Twist" (1960) . . . **Ronny & The Daytonas** "GTO" (1964) . . . and **Dave Mason** "Only You Know and I Know" (1970).

Birthdays:

JERRY GARCIA, San Francisco, California, 1942. Guitarist and founder of the Grateful Dead.

BOZ BURRELL, born Raymond Burrell, Lincolnshire, England, 1946. Bassist, he joined Bad Company after leaving King Crimson.

JOE ELLIOT, Birmingham, England, 1960. Vocalist for Def Leppard.

Notes:

GETTING HIS DUE! Singer John Phillips of the Mamas and the Papas sues ABC/Dunhill Records for $9 million, claiming the label cheated his and other groups out of perhaps as much as $60 million in royalties. The financially troubled record label wouldn't survive the decade. (1973)

1972 **Brian Cole,** 28, one of the original members of the **Association,** dies in his Los Angeles home of a heroin overdose.

🎵 **GOLD RECORDS** are issued to **Rod Stewart** for the LP *Every Picture Tells A Story* (1971) . . . and to **Dr. Hook and the Medicine Show** for their hit single "Sylvia's Mother" (1972).

🎵 **RECORD RELEASES** include **Leon Russell** "Lady Blue" (1975).

Birthdays:

GARTH HUDSON, Ontario, Canada, 1942. Keyboardist with The Band, from their earliest days as The Hawks through their final concert in November 1976.

ANDREW GOLD, Burbank, California, 1951. L.A. session musician who backed Linda Ronstadt before striking out on his own.

Rod Stewart

AUGUST 3

WE'RE SORRY BUT IT'S TIME TO GO! The Beatles make their 294th and last appearance at the Cavern Club in Liverpool, the place where they'd gotten their start. "Please Please Me" had just been released and the future was looking bright. (1963)

1966 **The Rolling Stones** record "Have You Seen Your Mother Baby" at RCA Studios in London.

1966 Counterculture comedian, **Lenny Bruce,** dies of morphine overdose. His style of comedy paved the way for **George Carlin, Richard Pryor** and others.

1968 **The Doors'** "Hello, I Love You" is #1 in America.

1968 The first Newport Pop Festival.

1971 **Paul McCartney** announces the formation of his new band **Wings,** which includes wife **Linda** and **Denny Laine,** an original member of the **Moody Blues.**

1974 Steel guitar player, **Jeff Baxter,** and drummer, **Jim Hodder,** both quit **Steely Dan.** Baxter proceeds to join the **Doobie Brothers.**

1974 Guitarist, **John Grimaldi,** joins **Argent,** replacing **Russ Ballard** who goes it solo after seven years with the group.

🎵 **RECORD RELEASES** include the **Beach Boys** "Surfer Girl," **Martha and the Vandellas** "Heat Wave," and **Allan Sherman** "Hello Mudda, Hello Fadda" (1963) . . . and **Stevie Wonder** "You Haven't Done Nothing" (1974).

Notes:

_____

_____

_____

_____

_____

_____

_____

BIGGER THAN JESUS! Radio stations in six U.S. cities ban the playing of Beatles records after the *London Evening Standard* quotes John Lennon's comment that the Beatles are more popular than Jesus Christ. The blasphemous statement sets off an international uproar, complete with public burnings of Beatles records. (1966)

1970   **Jim Morrison** is arrested and charged with public drunkenness in Los Angeles when he falls stone cold asleep on an old woman's front porch.

1975   **Led Zeppelin's Robert Plant,** his wife, and two children are seriously injured in an auto accident while vacationing in Greece. Plant has to record his vocals for the *Presence* LP from a wheelchair.

1979   Twenty thousand fans, including California Governor **Jerry Brown,** pack the Los Angeles Forum for a tribute to **Lowell George,** the prolific songwriter and leader of **Little Feat** who died earlier that year. Among the performers are **Linda Ronstadt, Jackson Browne** and **Bonnie Raitt.**

1980   **John and Yoko** begin recording the album that will become *Double Fantasy,* their last.

♬ **RECORD RELEASES** include **Elvis Presley** "Hound Dog" (1956) . . . **Paul Simon** "Love Me Like A Rock" (1974) . . . and **Electric Light Orchestra** "Don't Bring Me Down" (1979).

Birthdays:

MAUREEN COX STARKEY, 1946. First wife of Beatles drummer, Ringo Starr, the marriage lasted until July, 1975.

Jim Morrison

WE'RE GOIN' HOPPIN'! Television's original dance party "American Bandstand" makes its debut live from Philadelphia and becomes the longest running network television program ever. It makes a star and a millionaire of host, Dick Clark. (1957)

1967 **Pink Floyd's** first album, *The Piper At The Gates Of Dawn*, is released. Lead guitarist, **Syd Barrett,** penned ten of the eleven songs on it.

1971 Gold Record awarded to *Blood, Sweat & Tears IV.*

1974 **Joan Jett** forms **The Runaways,** an all-girl, jailbait band.

1975 **Stevie Wonder** signs a $13 million deal with Motown Records, the biggest recording contract offered a musician, including former top money-makers **Elton John** and **Paul McCartney.**

1981 *Heavy Metal* premieres, a futuristic cartoon fantasy highlighted by music of **Black Sabbath, Blue Oyster Cult, Cheap Trick, Devo, Sammy Hagar, Journey, Stevie Nicks,** and a hit title song by **Don Felder.**

🎵 **RECORD RELEASES** include **Eric Burden and the Animals** "San Franciscan Nights," **Bobby Gentry** "Ode To Billy Joe" (1967) . . . and the **Moody Blues** "Nights In White Satin" (1972).

Birthdays:

RICK DERRINGER, born Richard Zehringer, Celina, Ohio, 1947. Had an international hit at age 15 with the McCoy's "Hang On Sloopy." Later joined Johnny Winter's backup group, then Edgar Winter's White Trash before becoming a solo artist and recording another big hit "Rock and Roll Hoochiekoo."

RICK HUXLEY, Dartford, England, 1942. Guitarist with the Dave Clark Five.

JIMMY WEBB, Elk City, Oklahoma, 1946. Singer-songwriter, best known for composing "By The Time I Get To Phoenix" and "Up, Up and Away."

Notes:

GETTING BIGGER AND BIGGER! Singer, Stevie Nicks, steps out of Fleetwood Mac for the release of her first solo LP, *Bella Donna*. Among its lead tracks are "Stop Dragging My Heart Around," a duet with Tom Petty, and "Edge Of Seventeen." One of her performances on a brief trip tour to support this album is taped for cable television and simulcast for radio on The Source. (1981)

1966 British record charts put the **Troggs** at #1 with "With A Girl Like You" and the **Beach Boys** just entering with "God Only Knows."

1973 **Stevie Wonder** is hospitalized in a coma from serious head injuries when a car in which he is a passenger collides with a logging truck near Salisbury, North Carolina.

🎵 **RECORD RELEASES** include the **Kinks** "Sunny Afternoon" and **Simon & Garfunkel** "Dangling Conversation" (1966) . . . and the **Little River Band** "Help Is On The Way" (1977).

MORE THAN A PRETTY FACE! Fleetwood Mac welcomes its first female member, Christine McVie, wife of Mac bassist, John McVie. Prior to joining the group she recorded solo under her maiden name of Christine Perfect. "Dragonfly," a 1970 single, marked her record debut with the Mac. (1970)

1971 **The Mothers of Invention** record *Just Another Band From L.A.* live at UCLA, featuring a Zappa Mini-Opera *Billy The Mountain.*

1974 **Peter Wolf** of the **J. Geils Band** marries actress, **Faye Dunaway,** in Beverly Hills after dating for nearly a year.

1979 A crazed **Marshall Tucker Band** fan in California steals a car from the parking lot outside the Long Beach Arena and drives right in, smashing down two banks of metal exit doors and one concrete wall inside.

🎵 **RECORD RELEASES** include the **Turtles** "It Ain't Me, Babe" (1965) . . . and the **Moody Blues** "The Story In Your Eyes" (1971).

Birthdays:

ANDY FRASER, London, England, 1952. Bassist with Free ("Alright Now") after starting with John Mayall's band.

Notes:

_____

_____

_____

_____

_____

_____

_____

_____

BANNED IN . . . BRITAIN! Wendy O. Williams and her outrageous Plasmatics are banned from making their British debut. The Greater London Council objects to the "blowing-up" of cars and cancels the Hammersmith Odeon show three hours before showtime. (1980)

1966 The **Beatles** *Revolver* album is released in America on Capitol Records.

1967 **Patti** and **George Harrison** stroll unrecognized in the Haight Ashbury district of San Francisco, until George blows their cover by borrowing a guitar and playing.

1975 **Julian "Cannonball" Aderly,** alto saxophonist, famous for his 1965 Grammy Award winner "Mercy, Mercy, Mercy," dies of a stroke in Gary, Indiana.

🎵 **RECORD RELEASES** include the **Animals** "House of the Rising Sun" (1964) . . . **Diana Ross** "Ain't No Mountain High Enough" and **Creedence Clearwater Revival** "Looking Out My Back Door" (1970).

Birthdays:

JOE TEX, Baytown, Texas, 1933. Singer-songwriter who rose from church choirs to making hits like "Hold What You've Got." Influenced Mick Jagger's stage manner.

Notes:

_____

_____

_____

_____

_____

_____

_____

_____

HELTER SKELTER! Actress, Sharon Tate, and four others are victims in a bizarre night of murder. Charles Manson, who is charged and found guilty of the crime, claims the Beatles spoke to him through "secret messages" in the lyrics of five songs on the White Album and told him to do it. (1969)

1963   Britian's *Ready Steady Go* rock and roll television program is first broadcast. The show gives early breaks to **Bob Dylan, The Rolling Stones, The Who,** and many others.

1964   **Bob Dylan** and **Joan Baez** sing together for the first time in concert in Forest Hills, New York.

1973   **Lillian Roxon,** author of the *Rock Encyclopedia,* dies of a severe asthma attack at age 41. The Australian-born writer was one of the world's premiere rock journalists, whose columns appeared regularly in *Mademoiselle, Oui,* and *The New York Sunday Times.*

1974   Trumpeter, **Bill Chase,** 39, and three members of his group are killed in a plane crash in Jackson, Minnesota.

1975   **Don Kirshner's** first annual *Rock Music Awards* is televised as an alternative to the Grammys. **Elton John** is the first big "Rocky" winner.

🎵 **GOLD RECORDS** awarded to the **Rolling Stones** for *Aftermath* LP (1966) . . . and to **Looking Glass** for the hit single "Brandy" (1972).

🎵 **RECORD RELEASES** include **Sly and the Family Stone** "Hot Fun In The Summertime" and **Three Dog Night** "Easy To Be Hard" (1969).

_____

_____

_____

_____

_____

_____

_____

_____

WHAT A DAY! American album charts are hot with two classics . . . The Band's record debut *Music From Big Pink* enters, while Cream sits solidly at #1 with *Wheels of Fire*. (1968)

1970 "The State of Florida VS. Jim Morrison" case begins. Jim was literally "caught with his pants down" on stage in Miami seventeen months earlier.

1972   Paul and Linda McCartney are accused of drug possession by authorities in Sweden.

🎵 **RECORD RELEASES** include **Lloyd Price** "I'm Gonna Get Married" (1959) . . . the **Chambers Brothers** "Time Has Come Today" and the **Who** "Magic Bus" (1968).

Birthdays:

IAN ANDERSON, Edinburgh, Scotland, 1947. Vocalist and flutist, he formed Jethro Tull from the ashes of the John Evans Band in '68. A colorful and flamboyant front man.

RONNIE SPECTOR, born Veronica Bennett, New York City, 1947. Singer-songwriter with the Ronettes when producer, Phil Spector, spotted them, made them hit-makers with "Be My Baby," and she married him.

BOBBY HATFIELD, Beaver Dam, Wisconsin, 1940. Member of the Righteous Brothers, considered the leading exponents of "blue-eyed soul."

Notes:

Ronnie Spector

THE BIG APPLE! The Beatles launch their own label, Apple Records, and declare the week of August 11th "National Apple Week." The first discs issued are the Beatles' single "Revolution" and George Harrison's movie soundtrack to *Wonderwall*. (1968)

1972 The mayor of San Antonio declares August 11th, 1972, **Cheech and Chong** Day when he learns that the comics donated a free concert as a prize in a local high school voter registration contest.

1973 Producer, **Bill Aucoin,** first sees **Kiss** playing at a New York hotel, offers to become their manager, and promises them a record contract within two weeks. A handshake seals the deal.

1975 Gold Record awarded to **Aerosmith** for *Toys In The Attic* LP.

1976 Who drummer, **Keith Moon,** is hospitalized after collapsing flat in a Miami Hotel. This was the second time Keith was stricken ill during the Who's U.S. Tour that year.

🎵 **RECORD RELEASES** include **Elvis Presley** "Don't Be Cruel" (1956). . . **The Beach Boys** "Surfin' Safari" (1962) . . . and the **Edgar Winter Group** "Free Ride" (1973).

Birthdays:

ERIC CARMEN, Cleveland, Ohio, 1949. An original member of the Raspberries, he hit as a solo artist in '74 with "All By Myself."

ERIK BRANN, Boston, Massachusetts, 1950. Guitarist with Iron Butterfly, Eric left to form Flintwhistle in '69.

MIKE HUGG, Hampshire, England, 1942. Drummer who formed the Mann Hugg Blues Band with Manfred Mann in '63, and continued with Mann thru '72.

JEFF HANNA, Detroit, Michigan, 1947. Guitarist-vocalist with the Nitty Gritty Dirt Band.

Notes:

MARY HAD A LITTLE LAMB! Thomas Edison invents sound record-ing with his Edisonphone, a tin-foil-wrapped cylinder on which sound from a megaphone was "etched" with a thin metal needle. He records an intense version of "Mary Had A Little Lamb." (1877)

1957 **Buddy Holly** enters U.S. singles charts with "That'll Be The Day," a tune **Linda Ronstadt** would once again take into the Ameri-can charts twenty years later.

1966 The **Beatles** begin their 1966 American Tour.

1967 **Peter Green's Fleetwood Mac** make their stage debut at Great Britian's National Blues and Jazz Festival. Also on the bill is **Cream, Small Faces, Ten Years After, Donovan,** and **Pink Floyd.**

1978 Former Who manager, **Pete Meaden,** commits suicide.

🎵 **RECORD RELEASES** include **Diana Ross** and the **Su-premes** "Reflections," **Jackie Wilson** "Higher and Higher," and **The Box Tops** "The Letter" (1967).

The Clash

BTO BITES THE DUST! Bachman-Turner Overdrive disbands when group founder, Randy Bachman, quits to pursue a solo career. BTO recorded six best-selling albums in their seven-year history to become the #1 Canadian band of the seventies (1977).

1952 Songwriters **Leiber and Stoller's** first record, "Hound Dog," is recorded by **Big Mamma Thornton.**

1965 **The Jefferson Airplane** make their first public appearance at the Matrix Club in San Francisco, a place owned by group co-founder, **Marty Balin.** The original group line-up includes **Balin, Paul Kantner, Signe Anderson, Jorma Kaukonen, Jack Casady** and **Skip Spence.**

1966 **The Lovin' Spoonful's** classic summer song "Summer In The City" is #1 on American charts.

1971 Soul saxophonist, **King Curtis** is stabbed to death following an argument with an associate in front of his New York brownstone apartment.

1976 **The Clash** make their concert debut in London.

1977 **Cherie Currie** quits the **Runaways** to go it solo. She lands a role in "Foxes."

🎵 **RECORD RELEASES** include the **Beatles** "Help!" (1965) . . . **Los Bravos** "Black is Black" and the **Supremes** "You Can't Hurry Love" (1966).

Birthdays:

DAN FOGELBERG, Peoria, Illinois, 1951. Singer-songwriter of such critically acclaimed albums as *Souvenirs, Captured Angel,* and *Netherlands.*

Notes:

_____

_____

_____

_____

_____

_____

_____

_____

WHEN THE HEARTACHES BEGIN! Elvis Presley's mother, Gladys, dies in Memphis Methodist Hospital of a heart attack at age 42. Elvis is furloughed from his Army post in Fort Hood, Texas, to attend the funeral. (1958)

1965 The biggest **Sonny and Cher** hit, "I Got You Babe," is #1 on the U.S. charts.

1965 The **Beatles** begin their 1965 U.S. Tour.

1970 **Steve Stills** is arrested in a motel room in La Jolla, California, for possession of cocaine and barbituates. When police are summoned by the motel manager, Stills is found crawling in the hallways.

1976 "So It Goes" by **Nick Lowe** is released, the first single on Stiff Records. Soon Stiff would introduce America to **Elvis Costello, Ian Dury** and **Lena Lovitch.**

1979 Gold records awarded to the **Beach Boys** for their *Endless Summer* LP (1974) . . . and to the **Knack** for "My Sherona" (1979).

🎵 **RECORD RELEASES** include the **Animals** "We Gotta Get Out Of This Place" and the **McCoys** "Hang On Sloopy" (1965) . . . **Rod Stewart** "Maggie May" (1971) . . . **Chicago** "If You Leave Me Now" and the **Steve Miller Band** "Rock 'n' Me" (1976).

Birthdays:

DAVID CROSBY, Los Angeles, California, 1941. First with the Byrds, he left in '68 to form Crosby, Stills and Nash with Steve and Graham. Several solo recordings.

DASH CROFTS, Cisco, Texas, 1940. Dash met Jim Seals in a music jamboree and played together in several bands before finding fame as Seals and Crofts in 1970.

LARRY GRAHAM, Beaumont, Texas, 1946. A member of Sly and the Family Stone from '66, he formed his own Graham Central Station in the mid-seventies.

TIM BOGERT, Peoria, Illinois, 1944. Bassist with Vanilla Fudge, he later formed a trio with Jeff Beck and Carmine Appice. He and Carmine formed Cactus in the early seventies.

Notes:

_____

_____

_____

_____

THREE DAYS OF FUN AND MUSIC! The historic Woodstock Music and Arts Fair begins, a three-day festival held on Max Yasgur's dairy farm in upstate New York. The roster of groups appearing reads like a Who's Who of sixties rock . . . Janis Joplin, Santana, The Who, Jefferson Airplane, Grateful Dead, Jimi Hendrix, Joe Cocker and many others. Four hundred and fifty thousand fight torrential rainstorms and incredible traffic jams to be part of the music and brotherhood of what would forever be known as the Woodstock Generation. (1969)

1958 **Buddy Holly** marries **Maria Elena Santiago** in his home town of Lubbock, Texas, just two weeks after they'd met.

1965 The **Beatles** play Shea Stadium in New York, their biggest concert to date.

1974 *John, Paul, George, Ringo . . . and Bert,* a **Beatles** musical, opens at the London Lyric Theater to rave reviews.

1976 Violence and arrests plague the concert scene. In Detroit, racial violence prompts the arrest of 47 at an **Average White Band** concert . . . in Los Angeles 188 are arrested, mostly for drug possession, at a **Jethro Tull** concert at the Coliseum . . . and in San Francisco, it took the combined efforts of 17 police departments to quell a bottle-throwing melee involving some 300 angry **Z Z Top** fans who couldn't get tickets.

1980 **George Harrison's** autobiography *I Me Mine* is published.

Birthdays:

TOMMY ALDRICH, Jackson, Mississippi, 1942. Drummer with Ozzy Osbourne. Tommy was an original member of Black Oak Arkansas before joining the Pat Travers Band, and finally the Blizzard of Ozz in 1981.

PETER YORK, Birmingham, England, 1942. Drummer with the Spencer Davis Group.

Notes:

THE KING IS DEAD! Millions mourn the world over when Elvis Presley, the King of Rock 'n' Roll, dies at his Graceland Mansion in Memphis, Tennessee, under confused and sordid circumstances. First reported to be a heart attack, it's later learned that his passing is almost certainly due to drug abuse. Elvis's personal physician is later found guilty of overprescribing medication to Elvis. (1977)

1962   The **Beatles** sack their original drummer, **Pete Best,** in favor of **Ringo Starr.** In 1982 Pete releases an album of his early Decca Records audition with the legendary group.

1975   **Peter Gabriel,** the founder, leader and vocalist of **Genesis,** announces that he is leaving the band in favor of a solo career. Many predict the demise of the group, not anticipating the emergence of drummer, **Phil Collins,** as leader.

1980   **Bill Ward** quits **Black Sabbath, Jools Holland** leaves **Squeeze,** and **Cozy Powell** splits from **Rainbow** . . . all on the same day.

🎵 **RECORD RELEASES** include the **Temptations** "I Can't Get Next To You" and **Harry Nilsson** "Everybody's Talking" (1969).

Elvis Presley

CHANGING OF THE GUARD! Keyboardist, Patrick Moraz, replaces Rick Wakeman in supergroup Yes. The classically trained Moraz made his Yes debut on the *Relayer* LP, while Wakeman adds more steam to his solo career which has already started with the release of his *The Six Wives of Henry VIII* LP. (1974)

1969 **Pete Townshend** pushes **Abbie Hoffman** offstage when the Yippie leader tries to make a political pitch during **The Who's** set on the third day of the Woodstock concerts. Pete said he didn't know it was Hoffman when he gave him the "Heave Ho."

1973 **Paul Williams,** singer and arranger of the original **Temptations,** was found dead slumped over the steering wheel of his car in Detroit. He had a gun in his hand and a bullet in his head. The coroner rules suicide.

1974 **Fleetwood Mac** wins an injunction to prevent another group of musicians from touring as "Fleetwood Mac."

🎵 **RECORD RELEASES** include the **Bee Gees** "Gotta Get A Message To You" and **Deep Purple** "Hush" (1968) . . . and **Bad Company** "Can't Get Enough" (1974).

Birthdays:

SIB HASHIAN, 1949. Drummer with Boston.

Notes:

_____

_____

_____

_____

_____

_____

_____

_____

MILLION DOLLAR TEAM! Two of contemporary music's biggest superstars will combine efforts, as Paul McCartney announces his forthcoming collaboration with Stevie Wonder. Nineteen eighty-two sees the fruits of their efforts, a huge hit record "Ebony and Ivory." (1981)

1969 **Mick Jagger** is accidentally shot on the set of *Ned Kelly* in Australia.

1977 Outside the gates of Graceland Mansion in Memphis, two young girls are killed and another seriously injured, by a runaway car which strikes them as they pay final respects to their idol, **Elvis Presley.**

1978 **The Who's** *Who Are You* is released, the final album with which drummer, **Keith Moon,** appears.

1979 **Nick Lowe** marries singer, **Carlene Carter,** daughter of country music's **June Carter.** The two collaborate on Carlene's third album later that year.

🎵 **RECORD RELEASES** include **Peter, Paul & Mary** "If I Had A Hammer" (1962) . . . and the **Doobie Brothers** "China Grove" (1973).

Birthdays:

DENNIS ELLIOT, London, England, 1950. Drummer and original member of Foreigner.

Notes:

BEATLES OVER AMERICA! John, Paul, George and Ringo began their first U.S. concert tour of North America. Their 26 U.S. concerts included the Beatles' first appearances at the giant outdoor stadiums that would become fixtures of future visits. (1964)

1967 **Ringo Starr** becomes a father at 3:25 in the afternoon, when wife, Maureen, gives birth to a baby boy, Jason.

1973 Singers, **Kris Kristofferson** and **Rita Coolidge,** marry in Los Angeles.

1976 **Kiss** tops U.S. singles charts with a love ballad, "Beth," an uncharacteristic tune for the heavy metal rockers.

1976 Presidential candidate, **Jimmy Carter,** appears at the 5th annual Capricorn Records barbecue. Coincidentally, Capricorn folds at about the same time Carter leaves the White House.

🎵 **RECORD RELEASES** include **Elvis Presley** "Burning Love" (1972).

Birthdays:

JOHN DEACON, Leicester, England, 1951. Bassist with Queen since group formed in the early seventies.

GINGER BAKER, born Peter Baker, London, England, 1939. One of rock's leading drummers of the sixties and seventies, best known for work in Cream and Blind Faith, and a somewhat less successful solo venture Ginger Baker's Airforce.

Notes:

Ginger Baker

235

PRESENTING . . . ROBERT PLANT! One of rock's most amazing vocalists, Robert Plant was born in Worcestershire, England, in 1948. Originally with the Band Of Joy with drummer, John Bonham, Plant joined Jimmy Page's New Yardbirds in '68 which would soon become known as Led Zeppelin. "I never really envisioned myself as being a particularly strong personality outside. I've spent a lot of time keeping myself to myself." Zeppelin disbanded after the death of John Bonham in '80, and Plant released his first solo LP, *Pictures At Eleven* in June, 1982.

1981   Bruce Springsteen plays a special concert to benefit Vietnam War veterans at the Los Angeles Sports Arena, the first in a series.

🎵 **RECORD RELEASES** include the **Temptations** "Beauty Is Only Skin Deep" (1966) . . . and the **Marshall Tucker Band** "Can't You See" (1977).

Birthdays:

JIM PANKOW, Chicago, Illinois, 1947. Original trombonist with Chicago.

ISAAC HAYES, Covington, Tennessee, 1943. Sax and piano player-composer, he's best known for his score to the film *Shaft.*

Robert Plant

ON THE DOTTED LINE, PLEASE! Columbia Records president, Clive Davis, re-signed Bob Dylan to the label, after his original five-year agreement ended the previous April. Lucky break for Columbia, as Bob had already signed a million-dollar deal with MGM Records, but MGM never countersigned the contract. Columbia moved in and won back their artist. MGM Records, incidentally, went out of business. (1967)

1965 **The Rolling Stones**' fourth LP, *Out Of Our Heads,* is leading American album charts, largely on the strength of its hit single "Satisfaction."

1972 Police mace **Grace Slick** and manhandle **Paul Kantner** in an after-concert scuffle in Akron, Ohio, **The Jefferson Airplane's** equipment manager, **Chick Casady,** started the mess when he called the police "pigs."

1973 Gold Albums awarded to two sets of brothers, the **Allmans** for *Brothers and Sisters* and the **Doobies** for *Toulouse Street.*

1980 **Linda Ronstadt** opens on Broadway in Gilbert and Sullivan's "The Pirates of Penzance," a starring role which would later be played by **Maureen McGovern** and **Karla DeVito.**

♫ **RECORD RELEASES** include the **Lovin' Spoonful** "Do You Believe In Magic" and **Barry McGuire** "Eve Of Destruction" (1965) . . . and **Linda Ronstadt** "That'll Be The Day" (1976).

Birthdays:

JACKIE DE SHANNON, Hazel, Kentucky, 1944. Singer-songwriter who's appeared with James Brown and the Beatles, she's best known for writing hits for others, including "Put A Little Love In Your Heart" and "Bette Davis Eyes."

KENNY ROGERS, Houston, Texas, 1938. Early successes in the New Christy Minstrels and the First Edition led to a superstar country music career.

Notes:

LED ZEP'S FINAL VINYL! No one realizes that the release of *In Through The Out Door* would mark the final recording of Led Zeppelin to be issued before the group's demise. (The group disbands in 1980 after the death of drummer, John Bonham.) *Out Door* contains lead tracks "All My Love" and "In The Evening." (1979)

1970 **Neil Young's** *After The Gold Rush* released, his third solo LP, with guitarist, **Nils Lofgren,** and **Crazy Horse** backing.

🎵 **GOLD RECORDS** awarded to the **Stories** for "Brother Louie" (1973) . . . the **Hollies** for "The Air That I Breathe" (1974) . . . and the **Jefferson Starship** for their LP *Red Octopus* (1975).

🎵 **RECORD RELEASES** include **Martha and the Vandellas** "Dancing In The Streets" and the **Shangri-Las** "Remember (Walkin' In The Sand)" (1964).

Birthdays:

DONNA GODCHAUX, San Francisco, Caifornia, 1947. Vocalist of the Grateful Dead with husband, Keith.

IAN MITCHELL, Downpatrick, Ireland, 1958. Bassist with the Bay City Rollers.

Notes:

YOU ONLY LIVE TWICE! Guitarist, Paul Kossoff, best known for his work in the group, Free, suffers a major heart attack and is rushed to a hospital where he is pronounced clinically dead. Miraculously doctors are able to revive him 35 minutes later. He wouldn't survive a second heart attack on March 19, 1976. (1975)

1962 **John Lennon** marries art student, **Cynthia Powell,** at Mount Pleasant Registry Office in Liverpool, with **Paul McCartney** as best man.

1966 The **Beatles** movie, *Help,* makes its U.S. premiere.

1974 **John Lennon** reports seeing a UFO from the rooftop of his New York City apartment at 9 PM.

1974 Gold Record awarded to **Bachman-Turner Overdrive** for the *Not Fragile* LP.

1980 "Ashes To Ashes" is **David Bowie's** first British #1 since the reissuing of "Space Oddity" in '75.

🎵 **RECORD RELEASES** include **Orpheus** "Can't Find The Time" (1969) . . . the **Four Seasons** "Who Loves You" and the **Jefferson Starship** "Miracles" (1975).

Birthdays:

KEITH MOON, London, England, 1947. Drummer with the Who, whose sheer energy more than made up for any lack of technical proficiency. Keith died of a drug overdose in September, 1978.

Notes:

Keith Moon

YOU CAN GET ANYTHING YOU WANT! The movie version of Arlo Guthrie's Thanksgiving ballad, *Alice's Restaurant,* premieres in New York and Los Angeles. Arlo plays himself in this celluloid adaptation directed by Arthur Penn. (1969)

1964 **Marianne Faithful** has her first British hit with the release of "As Tears Go By," a **Mick Jagger-Keith Richards** tune.

1965 **The Rolling Stones** first meet **Allen Klein,** who would soon become their financial manager.

1979 **BB King** celebrates his 30th anniversary in music at the Roxy in Los Angeles.

1979 **The Cars** play New York's Central Park and set a record for drawing the largest crowd there ever, nearly a half-million. That mark is broken a year later by **Elton John.**

1981 **Mark David Chapman** is sentenced after his conviction in the shooting death of **John Lennon** the previous December.

♫ **RECORD RELEASES** include **Iron Butterfly** "In-A-Gadda-Da-Vida" and **Jeanie C. Riley** "Harper Valley P.T.A." (1968) . . . and **America** "Tin Man" (1974).

Birthdays:

JIM CAPALDI, Worcester, England, 1944. Drummer with Traffic, he also appeared on the first Steve Winwood solo LP.

DAVID FREIBERG, Boston, Massachusetts. Bassist, he joined the Jefferson Airplane in '72 after leaving Quicksilver Messenger Service, and continued with the Jefferson Starship.

JOHN CIPOLLINA, Berkely, California, 1943. Guitarist with Quicksilver Messenger Service until their break up in '72.

MALCOLM DUNCAN, Montrose, Scotland, 1945. Sax player with the Average White Band.

Notes:

DO THE LOCOMOTION! Baby-sitting turned out to be a lucrative job for Eva Boyd, who had the #1 song in America with "Locomotion," thanks to her employers, Carole King, and husband, Gerry Goffin. King and Goffin co-wrote, produced and recorded the song with "Little Eva" singing, and the three of them scored a major hit record. (1962)

1967   **Brian Wilson** makes a rare live appearance with **The Beach Boys** on stage in Hawaii, which is recorded and issued as *Lei'd In Hawaii*.

1973   **Allman Brothers Band,** drummer, Butch Trucks, breaks his leg in an auto accident in Macon, Georgia, mere yards from the spot where **Duane Allman** died in a motorcycle accident two years before.

1973   **Henry McCullough** quits **Wings,** leaving **Paul McCartney** minus a guitar player.

1977   **Kiss** plays three sold-out concerts at the Los Angeles Forum. Recordings made that night are released as *Kiss Alive II.*

🎵 **RECORD RELEASES** include the **Four Seasons** "Sherry" (1962). . . and the **Allman Brothers Band** "Ramblin' Man" (1973).

Birthdays:

GENE SIMMONS, Haifa, Israel, 1949. Fire-breathing bassist with Kiss.

Notes:

_____
_____
_____
_____
_____
_____
_____
_____

HAVE YOU EVER BEEN TO ELECTRIC LADYLAND?! Jimi Hendrix opens the doors to his own Electric Ladyland Recording Studios in New York City, one of the first anywhere to offer 36 track recording capability. Many top bands are lured there, including Led Zeppelin and The Rolling Stones. (1970)

1967 The Beatles, **Mick Jagger** and his girlfriend **Marianne Faithful** go to meet the **Maharishi** in Bangor, North Wales.

1967 **Jimi Hendrix's** first album *Are You Experienced?* enters the charts, while **Bobby Gentry's** "Ode To Billy Jo" is the #1 song in America.

1970 **Jimi Hendrix** gives his last performance ever at the Isle of Wight Pop Festival.

1980 Bassist, **Tom Peterson,** quits **Cheap Trick,** a decision "mutually agreed upon" by both he and the group. Italian born, **Pete Comita** fills the void in the band.

♪ **GOLD RECORDS** awarded to the **Rolling Stones** for "Honky Tonk Woman" (1969) . . . and to the **Bee Gees** for "How Can You Mend A Broken Heart" (1971).

♪ **RECORD RELEASES** include the **Association** "Never My Love" and **Jimi Hendrix** "Purple Haze" (1967) . . . and the **Who** "Who Are You" (1978).

Jimi Hendrix

ALL THINGS MUST PASS! Beatles manager, Brian Epstein, is found dead at his home in London from an accidental overdose of Carbitol, a sleeping pill. Stunned by the news, the four Beatles rushed back from their visit with the Maharishi Mahesh Yogi in Bangor. (1967)

1965 **Elvis Presley** plays host to **John, Paul, George,** and **Ringo** at his home in Bel Air while the **Beatles** are touring America. John Lennon remembered the visit as one of the most exciting times of his life.

1965 **The Rolling Stones** announce their new business agreement which put **Andrew Oldham** in as personal manager, Allen Klein as business manager.

1970 **Elton John** makes his American concert debut at the Troubador in Los Angeles. **Mike Maitland,** President of MCA Records, is in the audience and signs Elton soon after.

🎵 **GOLD RECORDS** awarded to **Peter, Paul & Mary** for their *Moving* LP (1963) . . . and to **Freda Payne** for "Bring The Boys Home" (1971).

🎵 **RECORD RELEASES** include **Bob Dylan's** *Highway 61 Revisited* LP (1965) . . . and the **Association** "Cherish" (1966).

Birthdays:

SIMON KIRKE, 1949. Drummer first with Free. When the group broke up, he helped form Bad Company with fellow Free man, Paul Rodgers.

PHIL SHULMAN, Glasgow, Scotland, 1937. Founding member of Gentle Giant, with brothers Ray and Derek.

GLEN MATLOCK, England, 1956. Original bassist with the Sex Pistols, he was replaced by Sid Vicious in '77. Formed Spectors in the early '80s.

Notes:

AUGUST 28

IT TAKES ALL KINDS! Two records that could hardly be more different, both are awarded Gold Records on the same day, each for sales of a half-million copies ... Deep Purple's heavy metal anthem "Smoke On The Water" and the lighthearted novelty tune "The Monster Mash" by Bobby Pickett & The Crypt Kickers. (1973)

1965 **Bob Dylan** is booed off stage in Forest Hills, New York for playing electric guitar rather than his usual acoustic one. The scene repeats itself often over the next year.

1966 The **Beatles** play Dodger Stadium in Los Angeles, the next-to-last stop on their final concert tour.

1969 **Paul and Linda McCartney** become the proud parents of a new baby girl, Mary, born in London.

Birthdays:

DAVE HLUBER, Jacksonville, Florida, 1951. Guitarist and founding member of Molly Hatchet.

DAN SERAPHINE, Chicago, Illinois, 1948. Drummer with Chicago.

Notes:

_____

_____

_____

_____

_____

_____

_____

AUGUST 29

GEORGE JOINS JOHN & PAUL! Guitarist George Harrison joins the Quarrymen, whose members include John Lennon and Paul McCartney, at the opening of the Casbah Club in Liverpool, a new night spot run by drummer Pete Best's mother. (1958)

1966 The **Beatles** play their final concert ever at Candlestick Park in San Francisco.

1976 The original members of **Spirit** reunite for a concert in Santa Monica, California . . . their first performance together since the group broke up in 1971.

🎵 **RECORD RELEASES** include **Roy Orbison,** "Oh, Pretty Woman" (1964) . . . and the **Kinks** "Lola" (1970)

Birthdays:

CHRIS COPPING, England, 1945. Bass and keyboardist with Procal Harum from '69 to their breakup in the late seventies.

MICHAEL JACKSON, Gary, Indiana, 1958. Youngest of the Jackson Five, he rises to superstardom in the late seventies as a solo act.

Notes:

Michael Jackson

ONE ON ONE! John and Yoko Lennon stage one of the most successful benefit concerts ever . . . "One On One," an all-star night of music at New York's Madison Square Garden, staged to benefit retarded children. Stevie Wonder, Roberta Flack, and Sha Na Na are among those who perform free that night. Their efforts raise a quarter-million dollars. (1968)

1968 "Hey Jude," the **Beatles** song with the never-ending fade out, is released in the United States.

1973 **Denny Seiwell** quits **Wings,** the second member of **Paul McCartney's** band to leave that week . . . **Henry McCullough** split just five days before.

Birthdays:

JOHN PHILLIPS, Paris Island, South Carolina, 1935. Singer and songwriter with the Mamas and the Papas, a group he reformed in 1982 after a break of more than a decade.

Notes:

_____

_____

_____

_____

_____

_____

_____

_____

PHIL SPECTOR'S FIRST! Legendary composer/arranger/producer, Phil Spector has his first #1 hit record with the Ronettes "Be My Baby." This and three other Spector songs would sell a million before the years' end. (1963)

1968 *Super Session,* the highly acclaimed collaboration of **Al Kooper, Steve Stills,** and **Mike Bloomfield,** enters American rock charts.

1970 **Peter Yarrow** of **Peter, Paul and Mary** is arrested for taking "immoral liberties" with a fourteen-year-old girl.

1973 Gold Record awarded to **Paul McCartney** for "Live and Let Die," the movie theme.

1976 The judge rules that **George Harrison** is guilty of subconsciously plagerizing the tune from the **Chiffon's** "He's So Fine" in composing his hit single "My Sweet Lord."

🎵 **RECORD RELEASES** include **Carole King** "Jazz Man" (1974).

Birthdays:

VAN MORRISON, Belfast, Ireland, 1945. Singer, songwriter and multi-instrumentalist, Morrison had an early hit in the group Them with "Gloria," and several as a solo artist, including "Moon Dance."

JERRY ALLISON, Hillsboro, Texas, 1931. Friend of Buddy Holly and member of The Crickets.

Notes:

_____

_____

_____

_____

_____

_____

_____

_____

CAN'T YOU HEAR US KNOCKIN'! The Rolling Stones sue manager, Allen Klein, for falsely representing the group with intent to deceive and defraud them. Lawyers for The Stones say Klein's deception is worth $7.5 million. (1971)

1973 **Bob Dylan's** "Knockin' On Heaven's Door" is released, from the film soundtrack *Pat Garrett and Billy The Kid.*

1976 Ode Records president, **Lou Adler,** is kidnapped at gunpoint from his Malibu home and held by two men and a woman demanding $25,000 ransom. Adler pays and is released eight hours later.

1977 **Blondie** signs a deal with Chrysalis Records, an occasion noted as one of the few days lawyers put in time on Labor Day.

1980 **Ken Hensley** quits **Uriah Heep,** twelve years after founding the group.

Birthdays:

BARRY GIBB, Isle of Man, 1946. Singer and guitarist with The Bee Gees, married on his birthday in 1970 to Scottish beauty queen, Linda Gray.

GREG ERRICO, San Francisco, California, 1946. Drummer with Sly and The Family Stone.

DRESSES FOR THE TOP! Rod Stewart reaches the fame he's been working toward when his single "You Wear It Well" tops the British charts. (1972)

🎵 **RECORD RELEASES** include **The Soul Survivors** "Expressway To Your Heart" (1967) . . . and **The Doobie Brothes** "Listen To The Music" (1969).

Birthdays:

ROSALIND ASHFORD, Detroit, Michigan, 1943. Singer with Martha and The Vandellas.

MIK KAMINSKI, England, 1951. Cellist with Electric Light Orchestra as replacement for Michael Edwards in 1973.

Notes:

A VERY COSMIC HIGH! Donovan firmly holds the #1 position on the U.S. singles charts with "Sunshine Superman," a euphoric anthem of the mid-sixties. At the same time, the British Invasion strengthens with The Hollies making their first appearance on the charts with "Bus Stop." (1966)

1970   Al Wilson is found dead in the back yard of the home of fellow **Canned Heat** member, **Bob "The Bear" Hite.** Wilson, the band's guitarist, singer and harmonica player, is recognized as one of the world's foremost authorities on the blues.

RECORD RELEASES include **The Four Seasons** "I've Got You Under My Skin," **The Four Tops** "Reach Out, I'll Be There," and **? and The Mysterians** "96 Tears" (1969) . . . and **The Rolling Stones** "Angie" (1973).

Birthdays:

AL JARDINE, Lima, Ohio, 1942. Guitarist with The Beach Boys.

GEORGE BIONDO, Brooklyn, New York, 1945. Bassist with Steppenwolf as replacement for Nick St. Nicholas.

DON BREWER, Flint, Michigan, 1948. Drummer with Terry Knight and The Pack, then Grand Funk Railroad.

GETTING IT ON THE RECORD! The Beatles begin their first recording session at EMI Studios in St. John's Wood, London, with George Martin producing. (1962)

1965 **The Who** are vandalized while **Pete Townshend** and **Roger Daltry** are shopping for a guard dog to protect their equipment van. The van and $10,000 worth of equipment is ripped off while the two Who members are inside the Battersea Dogs' Home in London. The van is recovered, but not the equipment.

1976 **Aerosmith** is awarded a Platinum Record for the LP *Rocks*.

1976 **Dave Edmunds** is signed to a deal with Swan Song Records, one of the few artists to record for **Led Zeppelin** backed label.

1980 **Yes** performs their final concert at Madison Square Garden with new members, **Geoff Downes** and **Trevor Horn,** formerly of **The Buggles.** The concert is broadcast live on The Source.

🎵 **RECORD RELEASES** include **The Marvelettes** "Please Mr. Postman" (1961) . . . and **Kiss** "Beth" (1976).

Birthdays:

GARY DUNCAN, San Diego, California, 1946. Singer and guitarist with Quicksilver Messenger Service.

GREG ELMORE, California, 1946. Drummer with Quicksilver Messenger Service.

Notes:

_____

_____

_____

_____

_____

_____

_____

_____

SUPREME SACRIFICE! An ironic combination of hits at the top of the charts at the same time, as The Animals "House Of The Rising Sun" replaces "Where Did Our Love Go" by The Supremes at #1 in the U.S. (1964)

1965 **The Rolling Stones** record "Get Off My Cloud" during a session in Los Angeles.

1971 Five films by **John and Yoko** are screened at the London Art Spectrum at Alexandria Palace . . . *Cold Turkey, The Ballad of John and Yoko, Give Peace A Chance, Instant Karma* and *Up You Leg.*

1976 **Gary Rossington** is injured in a serious car accident in Jacksonville, Florida. The former **Lynyrd Skynyrd** guitarist loses most of his teeth and breaks a knee cap when his car hits a telephone pole, a tree and then a house.

🎵 **GOLD RECORDS** awarded to **Emerson, Lake & Palmer** for *Trilogy* (1972) . . . and to **Wings** for the single "Listen To What The Man Said" (1975). **RECORD RELEASES** include **Manfred Mann** "Do Wah Diddy Diddy" (1964) and **R. Dean Taylor** "Indiana Wants Me."

Birthdays:

BUDDY MILES, Omaha, Nebraska, 1946. Drummer with a number of artists in the early sixties before forming Electric Flag and later joining Jimi Hendrix's Band of Gypsies. Then group leader of The Buddy Miles Express.

DAVID "CLEM" CLEMSON, England, 1949. Guitarist with Humble Pie as replacement for Peter Frampton, then the Jack Bruce Band.

LOUDON WAINWRIGHT III, Chapel Hill, North Carolina, 1946. Singer and songwriter noted for his humerous folk songs of the late sixties and seventies.

Notes:

WHERE DID OUR LOVE GO
HE MEANS THE WORLD TO ME

THE SUPREMES

79¢

The Supremes

MOTOWN 1060

SEPTEMBER 6

GOODBYE TO THE MAN WITH THE TOUCH! Tom Wilson, influential record producer of the sixties, dies of a heart attack at his Los Angeles home at age 47. Wilson is best known for producing three early Bob Dylan LPs and the single "Like A Rolling Stone," Simon and Garfunekl's "Wednesday Morning, 3AM" and the *Freak Out* LP for Frank Zappa and The Mothers Of Invention." (1978)

1961   Bob Dylan debuts at the Gaslight Cafe in New York's Greenwich Village, which becomes one of his regular venues in the early sixties.

1969   Thunderclap Newman's "Something In The Air" is released.

1980   Ginger Baker quits the recently reformed Atomic Rooster to join Hawkwind, which crumbles soon after.

Birthdays:

ROGER WATERS, Cambridge, England, 1947. Bassist and founding member of Pink Floyd, major creative participant in the 1982 film, *Pink Floyd The Wall.*

BANNER THOMAS, 1954. Bassist with Molly Hatchett.

Bob Dylan

TOO MUCH, MUCH TOO SOON! Keith Moon dies of a drug overdose in the bedroom of his London flat after attending the film premiere of *The Buddy Holly Story.* The legendary drummer with The Who was plagued by progressively failing health during the last years of his life, due to his quick-paced, overindulgent lifestyle. (1978)

1963 **Bob Dylan** charts for the first time with his *Freewheelin' Bob Dylan* LP, featuring the classic "Blowin' In The Wind."

1974 **Elton John** is awarded a Gold Record for "Don't Let The Sun Go Down On Me."

1975 **Steve Anderson,** a 22-year-old from Los Angeles, sets a new record for "guitar picking" when he strums and picks for 114 hours, 7 minutes nonstop, beating the old record by more than four hours.

1975 **The Guess Who** perform their final concert in Montreal to wrap up a North American tour.

1976 **Paul McCartney** declares "Buddy Holly Week" in honor of Holly's birthday. McCartney, incidentally, owns publishing rights to nearly all of Holly's material.

🎵 **RECORD RELEASES** include **The Crazy World of Arthur Brown** "Fire" (1968).

Birthdays:

BUDDY HOLLY, born Charles Hardin Holley, Lubbock, Texas, 1936. Legendary fifties rock star who, in two years, created singles history with "That'll Be The Day," "Peggy Sue" and other hits.

LITTLE MILTON, born Milton Campbell, Mississippi, 1934. Blues guitarist and singer who recorded with Ike Turner and Howlin' Wolf.

Notes:

YOUNG, THE YOUNGER! Zeke Snodgrass Young is born to singer, Neil Young, and actress, Carrie Snodgrass, at Neil's ranch near Santa Cruz, California. (1972)

1977 **Jimmy McCullough** quits **Wings** to join the recently re-united Small Faces, but the group disbands a few months later.

Birthdays:

RONALD "PIGPEN" McKERNAN, San Bruno, California, 1945. Multi-instrumentalist and original member of The Grateful Dead until his death in 1973.

FREDDIE MERCURY, born Frederick Bulsara, Zanzibar, 1946. Lead singer with Queen.

KELLY GROUCUTT, 1945. Bassist with Electric Light Orchestra.

Freddie Mercury

THE WORLD IS WATCHING! Elvis Presley makes his first appearance on The Ed Sullivan Show, boosting Sullivan's rating to an unheard of 82.6% of the total TV viewing audience. Elvis is only shown from the waist up to avoid showing the mostly-family audience Presley's famous hip gyrations. Elvis performs "Don't Be Cruel" and "Ready Teddy." (1955)

1979 **Cat Stevens,** now known as Yusef Island, marries **Fouzia Ali** at Kensington Mosque, England.

1979 Promoter, **Sid Berstein,** takes a full page ad in *The New York Times* suggesting a Beatles reunion to benefit the Boat People. Bernstein asks for three concerts, one each in Cairo, Jerusalem and New York, but receives no response from the **Beatles.**

🎵 **RECORD RELEASES** include **Lulu** "To Sir With Love," **The Rascals** "How Can I Be Sure," **Sam and Dave** "Soul Man" (1967) . . . **Smith** "Baby, It's You" (1969) . . . **John Lennon** "Imagine" (1971) . . . **The Eagles** "Witchy Woman," **Seals and Crofts** "Summer Breeze" (1972) . . . and **The Rolling Stones** "Beast Of Burden" (1978).

Birthdays:

OTIS REDDING, Macon, Georgia, 1941. Singer and songwriter famous for his soul wrenching R&B hits, "Try A Little Tenderness" and "Sittin' On The Dock Of The Bay."

BILLY PRESTON, Houston, Texas, 1946. Keyboardist and singer with Little Richard in 1963, then featured soloist with various artists including The Beatles on "Get Back." Various solo recordings.

Notes:

_____

_____

_____

_____

_____

_____

_____

A HOT LITTLE COMBINATION! Rod Stewart records his first single "Good Morning Little Schoolgirl" with John Paul Jones of future Led Zeppelin fame on bass. (1964)

1969 Two films by **John and Yoko** are presentd at The Institute of Contemporary Arts . . . the British premiere of *Rape* and the world premiere of *Self Portrait*.

1974 The **New York Dolls** disband.

1975 *Kiss Alive,* the million-seller double LP recorded mostly in Detroit, is released by Casablanca Records and yields the hit single "Rock 'n' Roll All Night," the **Kiss** anthem.

1975 **Bob Dylan** tapes a segment for National Educational Television, a tribute to Columbia Records executive, **John Hammond,** who signed Dylan and **Bruce Springsteen** among others.

1975 **Elton John** is awarded a Gold Record for "Someone Saved My Life Tonight."

1980 **Tom Peterson** quits **Cheap Trick** by "mutual agreement" and is replaced by **Peter Comita.**

1981 **Rick Derringer** loses his instruments and sound equipment when a van parked outside his New York home is ripped off.

RECORD RELEASES include **Count Five** "Psychotic Reaction," **The Left Banke** "Walk Away Renee," and **The Monkees** "Last Train To Clarksville" (1966) . . . and **Linda Ronstadt** "Blue Bayou" (1977)

Birthdays:

JOE PERRY, Boston, Massachusetts, 1950. Founding member and guitarist with Aerosmith, then The Joe Perry Project.

JOSE FELICIANO, Lorenz, Puerto Rico, 1945. Singer and songwriter, blind from birth, a Grammy winner for his version of "Light My Fire."

BARRIEMORE BARLOW, England, 1949. Drummer with Jethro Tull as replacement for Clive Bunker.

CYNTHIA LENNON Blackpool, England, 1939. First wife of John Lennon and mother of Julian.

Notes:

IF YOU DON'T GET IT RIGHT THE FIRST TIME! Ringo joins The Beatles in a recording session for the first time, replacing Pete Best. The band does seventeen takes on "Love Me Do" before they're satisfied. (1962)

1964   **The Kinks** "You Really Got Me" is #1 in England.

1965   **The Rolling Stones** score #1 in England with "Satisfaction," arguably the finest Jagger-Richards contribution to date.

1969   *The Great White Wonder* bootleg LP of Dylan material first surfaces in Los Angeles and will soon become the biggest selling pirated album of all time.

1976   **Bernie Taupin,** lyricist with **Elton John,** makes his acting debut as leader of a touring musical group in *The Hardy Boys and Nancy Drew Meet Dracula.*

🎵 **GOLD RECORDS** awarded to **The Hollies** for "Long, Cool Woman In A Black Dress" (1972) . . . and to **Aerosmith** for the debut LP *Aerosmith* (1975).

Birthdays:
PHIL MAY, England, 1944. Original singer with Pretty Things until 1976, then pursued a solo career.

Notes:

_____

_____

_____

_____

_____

_____

_____

WHAT A DIFFERENCE A PLACE MAKES! Elvis Presley moves with the rest of his family from Tupelo, Mississippi to Memphis, Tennessee. Thirteen years old and at the beginning of his formative years, Elvis would use Memphis as a springboard to his explosive career by availing himself to the local music scene. (1948)

1966   Mickey Dolenz, Peter Tork, Mike Nesmith and **Davy Jones** make their TV debut as **The Monkees** and become a home-grown phenomena as the first ever made-for-TV rock group.

1970   The Woody Guthrie Memorial Concert is held at the Hollywood Bowl, featuring performances from **Bob Dylan, Joan Baez** and **Arlo Guthrie.**

1977   James Lewis McCartney is born to **Paul and Linda.**

1980   The investigation into the death of **Elvis Presley** is re-opened, spurred by an ABC-TV "20/20" segment alleging wrong-doing by Presley's doctor.

RECORD RELEASES include **Jay and The Americans** "Come A Little Bit Closer" (1964) . . . and **James Taylor** "Fire and Rain" (1970).

Birthdays:

GARY BECKLEY, Texas, 1952. Founding member and singer with America.

MARIA MULDAUR, born Maria Grazia Rosa Domenica D'Amato, New York City, 1943. Singer with The Even Dozen Jug Band and John Sebastian before venturing out as a solo artist. Best known for her hit single "Midnight At The Oasis."

Notes:

_____

_____

_____

_____

_____

_____

_____

_____

NO MORE PAY FOR PLAY! The Federal Communications Act is amended to outlaw the payment of cash or gifts in exchange for airplay and makes radio stations responsible for policing the policy. No more "payola." (1960)

1965   Zak Starkey is born to Ringo and Maureen in Queen Charlotte's Hospital, Hamersmith, London.

1969   The Plastic Ono Band makes its concert debut at The Toronto Peace Festival, a rock revival show at Varsity Stadium organized by **John Lennon** and **Yoko Ono.** Plastic Ono features John in his first stage performance in four years, accompanied by **Eric Clapton, Klaus Voorman** and **Alan White.** The concert recording is later relesed as *Live Peace In Tornto.*

1969   Santana's debut LP enters the U.S. charts and gains immediate public acclaim.

1971   James Taylor is awarded a Gold Record for "You've Got A Friend," a **Carole King** composition.

1974   Stevie Wonder begins his first major concert tour since his near-fatal auto accident, with a performance at Nassau Caoliseum on Long Island.

1975 Atlanta vice squad officers bust members of **Dr. Hook** after finding an ounce of pot in one of their hotel rooms.

1980   Jackson Browne's *Hold Out* LP tops the U.S. charts.

♪ **RECORD RELEASES** include **Elvis Presley** "Suspicious Minds" (1969) . . . and **The Eagles** "Lyin' Eyes" (1975).

Birthdays:

DAVID CLAYTON THOMAS, Surrey, England, 1941. Co-founder and lead singer of Blood, Sweat and Tears.

PETER CETERA, Chicago, Illinois, 1944. Founding member and bassist with Chicago.

TIM HARDIN, Eugene, Oregon, 1940. Singer and songwriter best known for "If I Were A Carpenter" and "Reason To Believe."

Notes:

SEPTEMBER 14

ROCK 'N' ROLL PREACHERMAN! Richard Penniman, known as Little Richard, records the classic "Tutti Frutti" during one of his first recording sessions in New Orleans. (1955)

1976 **Bob Dylan's** *Hard Rain* television special airs, featuring film footage of the Colorado concert during which 25,000 fans were drenched by rain.

Birthdays:

JON "BAUSER" BAUMAN, New York City, 1947. Founding member of the singing group Sha Na Na.

PETE AGNEW, Scotland. Bassist and singer with The Shadettes, evolving into Nazareth in 1969.

PAUL KOSSOFF, Hampstead, England, 1950. Guitarist and founding member of Free until he departed to form Backstreet Crawler.

SEPTEMBER 15

HOT GUITAR LICKS! Uriah Heep bassist, Gary Thain, is nearly electrocuted on stage while playing a concert in Dallas. He pulls through but accuses the group of being insensitive to his injuries and quits soon after. (1974)

1962 **The Four Seasons** are #1 in the U.S. with "Sherry."

1975 **Pink Floyd** follows up the hugely successful *Dark Side Of The Moon* with the LP *Wish You Were Here,* a release that is greeted less than enthusiastically by fans and critics.

1977 Fifteen top record industry executives meet with President Carter at The White House, the first time the music business has been officially recognized by a President.

1978 **Bob Dylan's** longest concert tour begins, a series of one-night stands covering 62 cities in the U.S. and Canada.

1979 **Bob Dylan's** "Slow Train Comin'" is released.

1980 **David Bowie** makes his debut on Broadway in *The Elephant Man.*

Birthdays:

LEE DORMAN, St. Louis, Missouri, 1945. Bass and guitar player with Iron Butterfly.

WHOLE LOTTA SHAKIN'! "Shindig" premiers on TV featuring hit songs by current rock groups in a "dance party" atmosphere, complete with mini-skirted go-go girls. (1964)

1963   "She Loves You," the fifth single by the **Beatles,** is released in the U.S. on **Swan Records.**

1967   **The Vanilla Fudge** enters the charts for the first time with a debut LP that includes the seven-minute version of "You Keep Me Hangin' On," the Fudge's only hit.

1974   **Bob Dylan** begins recording *Blood On The Tracks.*

1977   **The Rolling Stones** release *Love You Live,* the double LP recored on the road.

1977   **Marc Bolan,** the lead singer and founding member of **T. Rex,** is killed when a car in which he's riding crashes into Barnes Bridge, London.

1978   **The Grateful Dead** play the pyramids and become the first western rock band ever to headline a concert in Cairo.

Birthdays:

B.B. King, Itta Bena, Mississippi, 1925. Blues singer and guitarist noted as a driving force

Notes:

_____

_____

_____

_____

_____

_____

_____

_____

SEPTEMBER 17

NOW FOR SOMETHING COMPLETELY DIFFERENT! RCA gives birth to the LP, the long playing record, with the introduction of the world's first 33¹/₃ record playing system. It takes some time to catch on, but consumers soon realize the LP can offer more music than the popular 78 RPM disc.

1966   **Johnny Rivers'** "Poor Side Of Town" is released.

1975   **Pink Floyd** is awarded a Gold Record for "Wish You Were Here."

1977   **Fleetwood Mac's** *Rumors* LP begins its 19th week as the #1 album in the U.S., joining only four other albums as all-time chart toppers.

1979   **Keith Richards'** trial on heroin trafficking charges ends in Toronto.

Birthdays:

LOL CREME, Manchester, England, 1947. Guitarist and singer with Kevin Godley in Hot Legs, evolving into 10cc in 1973. Both exited the band in 1977 to perform as a duo.

BILL BLACK, Memphis, Tennessee, 1926. Originally the bassist for Elvis Presley, then formed The Bill Black Combo.

Notes:

THE GUITAR IS SILENCED! Jimi Hendrix dies of asphyxiation when he chokes on his own vomit after taking an overdose of sleeping pills in the apartment of girlfriend, Monika Danneman. Eric Burdon, with whom Jimi was visiting at the time, claims Hendrix left a suicide note, although it was never seen. (1970)

1969   **Tiny Tim** announces his engagement to **Miss Vicki Budinger** at the New Jersey State Fair. The Wedding is to be telecast nationwide on The Tonight Show with Jonny Carson.

1978   The **Kiss** albums are released simultaneously on **Casablanca Records,** four separate solo works from each of the four members of the band.

1979   **The Who** perform the first of five sold-out concerts at Madison Square Garden.

1980   **Jimi Hendrix** fans commemorate the tenth anniversary of his death with a two-day tribute at The Paradise Club in Amsterdam.

🎵 RECORD RELEASES include **The Bee Gees** "Love So Right" . . . and **Boston** "More Than A Feeling" (1976).

Birthdays:

FRANKIE AVALON, born Francis Avallone, Philadelphia, Pennsylvania, 1940. Teen idol of the fifties with various "beach party" film credits, best known for the hit single "Venus."

KERRY LIVGREN, 1949. Keyboards and guitarist with Kansas, an original mamber of the group.

DEE DEE RAMONE, New York City, 1952. Bassist with The Ramones.

Notes:

_____

_____

_____

_____

_____

_____

_____

SEPTEMBER 19

ON A HORSE OF EVERY COLOR! Gram Parsons of the Flying Burrito Brothers dies of multiple drug use while rehearsing in the desert outside of Los Angeles. His coffin is stolen from the grave a week later and his body cremated at Joshua Tree National Monument, according to Parsons' wish as expressed to friend and road manager, Phil Kaufman. (1973)

1974 Gold Records awarded to **Bad Company** for their debut LP . . . **Eric Clapton** for the single "I Shot The Sheriff" . . . and to **Emerson, Lake & Palmer** for the three record set *Welcome Back My Friends To The Show That Never Ends—Lakes and Gentlemen.*

1975 **Dave Mason's** "Split Coconut" is released.

1976 Promoter, Sid Bernstein, offers $230 million for the **Beatles** to reunite.

1979 The MUSE concerts begin at Madison Square Garden, organized by Musicians Units for Safe Energy, starring **Bruce Springsteen, John Hall, Crosby, Stills & Nash** and others. The four days of music produces a double-live LP and the film *No Nukes,* as well as $750,000 for the fight against the use of nuclear energy.

1981 **Simon and Garfunkel** reunite for the first time in eleven years to perform a special concert in New York's Central Park. Five hundred thousand gather to hear the performance and millions of others recapture the experience later on cable. TV.

Birthdays:

BRIAN EPSTEIN, Liverpool, England, 1934. Manager of The Silver Beatles, then The Beatles, Gerry and The Pacemakers, The Cyrkle and Billy J. Kramer and The Dakotas.

"MAMA" CASS ELLIOT, born Naomi Cohen, Baltimore, Maryland, 1943. Singer with the Mugwumps in 1964, then an original member of The Mamas and The Papas, with a successful solo career beginning in 1968.

BILL MEDLEY, Santa Ana, California, 1940. Co-founder of The Righteous Brothers with Bobby Hatfield.

Notes:

264

LET'S SPLIT THE DIFFERENCE! Bubblegum and magic lead the U.S. charts. The Archies' "Sugar, Sugar" is #1 on the singles charts and the supergroup, Blind Faith, starring Eric Clapton, Steve Winwood, Ginger Baker and Rick Grech, is #1 on the album charts. (1969)

1966 **George Harrison** is in India for his first visit with the Maharishi.

1970 **Jim Morrison** is found "not guilty" of lewd and lascivious behavior for the pants-dropping scene during a concert in Miami. He is "guilty" of indecent exposure and profanity in a decision handed by a Miami judge.

1972 **Paul McCartney** is busted for growing pot on his farm in Scotland, the first of his three famous pot busts.

1973 **The Roxy Theater** opens in Hollywood with **Neil Young** performing for the first four sold-out nights. The audience is buzzing with stars . . . **Elton John, Carole King, Jackson Browne** and others.

1973 **Jim Croce** dies with six others in a chartered plane that crashes on take-off at Natchitoches, Louisiana.

1974 **Lynyrd Skynyrd** is awarded a Gold Record for the LP *Second Helping.*

1975 **Linda Ronstadt** "Heat Wave" and **Bruce Springsteen** "Born To Run" released.

1975 **David Bowie's** "Fame" is #1 in the U.S.

1980 **Kathy Collins,** wife of **Rossington-Collins** founder, **Al Collins,** dies of a heart attack after an extremely difficult pregnancy. The band's tour is postponed.

Notes:

_____

_____

_____

_____

_____

_____

_____

SEPTEMBER 21

A DOOBIE ON THE SIDE, PLEASE! Jeff "Skunk" Baxter joins The Doobie Brothers following a memorable career as slide guitarist with Steely Dan. Some critic view Baxter's choice as a backwards move, but he rides The Doobies' wave of success for five years. (1974)

1971 **Paul McCartney** is awarded a Gold Record for "Another Day" and "Uncle Albert/Admiral Halsey."

1974 **Ariel Bender** quits **Mott The Hoople** after recording with the band for two albums.

1979 **"BEATLES ARE BACK"** is the headline banner on *The New York Post*. It's a premature and innaccurate report that the Fab Four will reunite for a benefit concert for the Boat People.

1979 **Crosby, Stills & Nash** reunite for the MUSE concerts at Madison Square Garden.

🎵 **RECORD RELEASES** include **Jimi Hendrix** "All Along The Watchtower . . . **The Turtles** "Elenore," and **Gary Puckett and The Union Gap** "Over You" (1968) . . . and **Bachman-Turner Overdrive** "You Ain't Seen Nothin' Yet" and **Lou Reed** "Sally Can't Dance" (1974).

Birthdays:

DON FELDER, Topanga, California, 1947. Original member and guitarist with The Eagles and various solo performances.

LEONARD COHEN, Montreal, Canada, 1935. Poet and singer best known for "Suzanne.

Notes:

SEPTEMBER 22

WHEN FOLK SINGING WAS A HOOT! Bob Dylan performs at Carnegie Hall for the first time as one of the cast in all-star Hootenanny. He plays five original songs, including "The Talking John Birch Society Blues." (1962)

1980 **John Lennon** signs with **Geffen Records,** a new lable formed by **David Geffen. Lennon** and **Elton John** are the label's first new artists.

Birthdays:

JOAN JETT, Landsdowne, Pennsylvania, 1958. Singer and guitarist with The Runaways before success as a solo artist with "I Love Rock and Roll."

GEORGE E. CHAMBERS, Flora, Mississippi, 1931. The eldest of the brothers in The Chambers Brothers.

LONG LIVE BILLY SHEARS! "Paul Is Dead" rumors sweep the country when an Illinois University newspaper runs the headline "Clues Hint At Beatles Death." Some of the "clues" include playing segments of Beatles' songs backwards, a barefooted Paul on the *Abbey Road* LP cover and lyrical hints like "the walrus is Paul." Some suspect Capitol Records is behind the scam to bolster sagging record sales. (1969)

1967 **The Box Tops** are #1 with "The Letter."

1974 **Average White Band** drummer, **Robbie McIntosh,** dies from a heroin overdose at a party in North Hollywood, apparently mistaking the heroin for cocaine.

♫ **RECORD RELEASES** include **Elvis Presley** "Good Rockin' Tonight" (1954) . . . **The Doors** "People Are Strange" (1967) . . . **Mott The Hoople** "All The Young Dudes" (1972) . . . **John Lennon** "Whatever Gets You Through The Night" (1974) . . . and **Foreigner** "Double Vision" (1978).

Birthdays:

BRUCE SPRINGSTEEN, Freehold, New Jersey, 1949. Singer and songwriter most commonly revered as "The Boss" for his commanding style and charisma. A relative unknown until the mid-seventies press campaign that brought him to the covers of Newsweek and Time and hailed Springsteen as "the next Bob Dylan."

RAY CHARLES, Albany, Georgia, 1930. Singer and pianist blinded in early childhood, respected as one of the most influential black musicians in the last three decades. Best known for "Georgia On My Mind" and "What'd I Say."

Notes:

WHEN YOU'RE A STAR . . . ! The first Elvis Convention is organized in Cincinnati, Ohio, and nearly 2,500 fans join in to buy any and all Elvis memorabilia available . . . hats, t-shirts, buttons, belt buckles, pictures and original Presley 45RPM singles that sell for as much as $300 each. (1977)

 **RECORD RELEASES** include **The Bee Gees** "How Deep Is Your Love" . . . and **Styx** "Come Sail Away." (1977)

Birthdays:

LINDA McCARTNEY, born Linda Eastman, Scarsdale, New York, 1941. A freelance photographer, married to Paul McCartney in 1969 and has recorded and performed in concert with him since.

GERRY MARSDEN, London, England, 1942. Lead singer with Gerry and The Pacemakers, the Brian Epstein-managed English Invasion band of the mid-sixties best known for "Ferry Crossed The Mersey."

Notes:

WHAT'D I SAY
RAY CHARLES
ATLANTIC 8028

AND IT GOES LIKE THIS! "The Twist" by Chubby Checker is #1 in the U.S. and "Twist Fever" has touched nearly every fabric of society, from *Life Magazine* to the nightly TV news. Chubby will attempt to revive the craze 22 years later with "T-82" from his return-to-rock LP *The Change Has Come.* (1960)

1965   Barry McGuire's "Eve Of Destruction" is #1 in the U.S.

1979   Elton John's manager is charged with assault and battery for hitting a doorman with a cane at San Francisco's Fairmont Hotel as he and Elton leave for the airport. **John Reid** is sentenced to work in a crime diversion program.

1979   *Evita* premieres on Broadway, the third rock opera musical from **Tim Rice** and **Andrew Lloyd Webber.**

1980   The Grateful Dead begin recording live at The Warfield Theater in San Francisco, then move to New York's Radio City Music Hall to complete *The Dead Set,* a double LP.

1980   John Bonham of **Led Zeppelin** dies at the home of guitarist, **Jimmy Page,** after a long night of heavy drinking. The coroner's report reveals Bonham has ingested 40 measures of vodka. His death means the end of the historic supergroup.

1981   The Rolling Stones open their U.S. tour with a performance at JFK Stadium in Philadelphia.

🎵 **RECORD RELEASES** include **Cat Stevens** "Peace Train" and **Yes** "Your Move" (1971). . . and **The Eagles** LP *The Long Run* (1979).

Birthdays:

JOHN LOCKE, Los Angeles, California, 1943. Keyboardist with Spirit, then with Nazareth.

RONNIE McINTYRE, Lennox Town, Scotland, 1945. Guitarist with Average White Band.

Notes:

_____

_____

_____

_____

_____

_____

A LITTLE BEFORE HIS TIME! Emile Berliner, a German immigrant living in Washington, D.C., receives a patent for his new machine, which he calls the Gramophone. Things have come a long way, Emile! (1887)

1937 Jazz and blues singer, **Bessie Smith,** dies in a car accident.

1968 **Brian Jones** is fined $150 plus court costs after a judge finds the **Rolling Stones** guitarist guilty of possession of marijuana.

1968 **Eric Burdon's** "San Franciscan Nights" is #1 in the U.S.

1974 **John Lennon's** *Walls and Bridges* is released, featuring "Whatever Gets You Through The Night" and "No. 9 Dream."

♪ **RECORD RELEASES** include **The Kinks "You Really Got Me" (1964) . . . and The Who** "See Me, Feel Me" (1970).

Birthdays:

OVIVIA NEWTON-JOHN, Cambridge, England, 1948. Singer and songwriter who began at age 14 in the Sol Four, then a successful solo career and film roles in *Grease* and *Xanadu.*

CRAIG CHAQUICO, 1954. Guitarist with The Jefferson Starship.

BRIAN FERRY, Duram, England, 1945. Keyboardist and singer with Roxy Music and various LP's.

JOSEPH BAUER, Memphis, Tennessee, 1941. Drummer with The Youngbloods, an original member with Jesse Colin Young.

Notes:

_____

_____

_____

_____

_____

_____

_____

A SIGN OF THE TIMES! Bob Dylan's career gets a big boost when *The New York Times* writes a favorable review of him titled "Bob Dylan: A Distinctive Folksong Stylist." (1962)

1962   **Martha and The Vandellas** release their first Motown single "I'll Have To Let Him Go."

1971   **Black Sabbath** is awarded a Gold Record for the LP *Masters of Reality.*

1972   **Rory Storme** dies from an overdose of sleeping pills and his mother commits suicide on the same day. Storme was Storme was leader of **Rory Storme** and **The Hurricanes,** which featured Ringo Starr on drums.

1976   **Jackson Browne** puts the finishing touches on his LP *The Pretender*

1979   **Jimmy McCullough** is found dead in his flat in Maida Vale, England. Before joining and leaving **Paul McCartney's** band, **Wings,** McCullough played with **Thunderclap Newman** and **Stone The Crows.**

Birthdays:

MEAT LOAF, born Marvin Lee Aday, Dallas, Texas. Singer who started with The Amboy Dukes before landing a role in *The Rocky Horror Picture Show,* where he met lyricist Jim Steinman. The pair were successful on Meatloaf's debut LP *Bat Out Of Hell.*

DON NIX, Memphis, Tennessee, 1941. Singer and original member of The Bar-Keys and producer on LPs by John Mayall, Jeff Beck, Delanie and Bonnie and others.

Notes:

_____

_____

_____

_____

_____

_____

_____

THE LONG SIDE OF SINGLE LIFE! "Hey Jude" is #1 on the U.S. singles charts and despite the length of the song, nearly seven minutes, it finds nearly continual airplay on radio stations everywhere. "Hey Jude" appears only on the Beatles compilation of previously unreleased singles, which some call the *Hey Jude* album. (1968)

1968 **Mary Hopkin** is #1 in Britain with "Those Were The Days," produced by **Paul McCartney.**

1973 **The Rolling Stones** appear on American TV for the first time since *The Ed Sullivan Show* when **Don Kirshner's** *Rock Concert* presents a twenty-minute promotional film of the Stones performing "Angie," "Silver Train" and "Dancin' With Mr. D." from the *Goats Head Soup* LP.

1974 **King Crimson** disbands after five years together, but only **Robert Fripp** remains as the original member.

1974 **Mick Ronson** joins **Mott The Hoople** as replacement for **Ariel Bender.**

1976 A&M Records sues **George Harrison** for missing the deadline to deliver his LP *33 1/3*. Harrison is ill with hepatitis at the time.

Birthdays:

NICK ST. NICHOLAS, Germany, 1943. Bassist with Steppenwolf, an original member of the group.

BEN E. KING, born Benjamin Nelson, Henderson, North Carolina, 1938. Discovering singing at his father's diner in 1956, King first joined The Five Crowns, which evolved into The Drifters.

Notes:

JUST BLOWIN' IN THE WIND! Bob Dylan's first recording is on Caroline Hester's debut LP for Columbia Records. Dylan plays harmonica and catches the attention of Columbia executive, John Hammond, who signs Dylan based on his performance that day. (1961)

1963 **The Rolling Stones** begin their first tour of Britain at London's New Victoria Theater, accompanied by **The Everly Brothers** and **Bo Diddley.**

1969 **Jackie De Shannon** is awarded a Gold Record for "Put A Little Love In Your Heart."

1975 **Jackie Wilson's** career ends when he's struck with a massive heart attack while performing in Philadelphia. Neither the orchestra nor audience realizes what is happening when the singer slumps to his knees during the concert.

Birthdays:

JERRY LEE LEWIS, Ferriday, Louisiana, 1935. Singer and pianist known to millions as "The Killer," Lewis began recording in 1957 with a string of hits to follow, including "Great Balls Of Fire" and "Whole Lotta Shakin' Going' On." Lewis suffered a serious illness in 1981, but recovered and continues vigorous performances.

MARK FARNER, Flint, Michigan, 1948. Guitarist and lead singer with Grand Funk Railroad.

MIKE PINERA, Tampa, Florida, 1948. Guitarist with The Blues Image, then as replacement for Erik Brann in Iron Butterfly.

Notes:

TO GO SO FAST AND LIVE SO HIGH! James Dean dies in a car crash on a winding, narrow road in central California. His short film career in *East Of Eden, Rebel Without A Cause* and *Giant* allowed Dean to carve an image of the misunderstood teenager. It has never faded. (1955)

1977 **Ian Dury's** debut LP is released on Stiff Records.

🎵 **RECORD RELEASES** include **Strawberry Alarm Clock** "Incense and Peppermint" (1967) . . . and **Al Stewart** "Time Passages" (1978).

Birthdays:

DEWEY MARTIN, Chesterville, Ontario, 1942. Folksinger with The Dillars before forming Buffalo Springfield as the group's drummer.

MIKE HARRISON, Cumberland, England, 1945. Keyboardist and original member of Spooky Tooth.

FRANKIE LYMON, New York City, 1942. Lead singer with The Teenagers on "Why Do Fools Fall In Love."

FREDDIE KING, Longview, Texas, 1934. Blues guitarist on sessions with Muddy Waters and others before Leon Russell signed him to a solo contract with Shelter Records.

JOHNNY MATHIS, San Francisco, California, 1935. Distinctive pop singer of "Chances Are" and "Twelfth Of Never" and scores of other songs, his "best of" LP is one of the biggest selling albums of all time.

GUD DUDGEON, 1942. Producer best known for his work with Elton John, but also for work with David Bowie, Kiki Dee and Joan Armatrading.

Notes:

Ian Dury

END OF THE LONG AND WINDING ROAD! The Beatles' *Abbey Road* is released in the U.S., the last album the group will ever make as a foursome. The "B" side of the LP is largely a medley of unfinished and previously unrecorded songs that flow together, rather amazingly, as a complete song. (1969)

1970 Two thousand fans unable to get tickets to a **Rolling Stones** concert at the Sports Palace in Milano, Italy, go on a rampage. Riot police end the trouble with 63 arrests.

1971 **John Lennon** and **The Plastic Ono Band** are awarded a Gold Record for the LP *Imagine.*

1975 **Al Jackson** of **Booker T. and The MGs** is shot to death in his East Memphis home by burglars. The drummer is 39.

1979 **Elton John** begins an eight-night concert series in New York City.

Birthdays:

SCOTT McKENZIE, Arlington, Virginia, 1944. Singer and songwriter with The Journeymen, then as a soloist with the international hit "San Francisco (Wear Some Flowers In Your Hair)."

Notes:

Abbey Road LP

NOT A VERY GRATEFUL EVENT! The Grateful Dead band members, Bob Weir and Ron "Pigpen" McKernan, are busted on a variety of drug charges when San Francisco police raid the group's Haight-Ashbury home armed with warrants, guns . . . and reporters. (1968)

1965   The McCoys "Hang On Sloopy" is #1 on the U.S. singles charts at the same time **Bob Dylan** enters the LP charts with his second "electric" album, *Highway 61 Revisited.*

1973   Cheech and Chong are awarded a Gold Record for their debut comedy LP *Los Cochinos.*

1980   The Bee Gees sue manager, **Robert Stigwood,** for $200 million, accusing him of misrepresentation and fraud in his handling of their business affairs.

🎵 **RECORD RELEASES** include **Bob Dylan** "Positively 4th Street" (1965) . . . and **Rod Stewart** "Tonight's The Night" (1976).

Birthdays:

MIKE RUTHERFORD, England, 1950. Bassist with Genesis, the band he formed with former Yes keyboardist, Tony Banks.

DON McLEAN, New Rochelle, New York, 1945. Singer and guitarist who received national acclaim in 1971 with the hit single "American Pie."

Notes:

THIS LAND WAS HIS LAND! Woody Guthrie dies of Huntington's Chorea, a rare hereditary disease, after nearly fifteen years of paralysis. The legendary folksinger wrote scores of great American standards including "This Land Is Your Land" and influenced the styles of many folksingers who followed his career . . . Pete Seeger, Bob Dylan and Woody's son, Arlo. (1967)

1901 The Victor Talking Machine Company is formed. The pioneer of the phonograph industry will become RCA/Victor after a merger.

1964 **The Supremes** "Baby Love" is released.

1977 "Sentimental Lady" is released as a single from composer **Bob Welch's** first solo LP, a song that originally appeared on **Fleetwood Mac's** *Bare Trees* LP.

1977 The "Bunch of Stiffs" tour begins in England, sponsored by the new wave label, Stiff Records. The entourage includes **Elvis Costello, Ian Dury, Nick Lowe** and others.

1980 **Bruce Springsteen** begins his 1980 tour in Ann Arbor, Michigan. His opening night "butterflies" show when he forgets the words to the first song "Born To Run."

1980 **Rockpile's** debut LP is released five years after the group is formed and it marks the band as one of the most promising groups of the eighties. Unfortunately, personality clashes will force the group to disband six months later.

Birthdays:

CHUBBY CHECKER, born Ernest Evans, Philadelphia, Pennsylvania, 1941. Singer noted for the international hit "The Twist."

EDDIE COCHRAN, Albert Lea, Minnesota, 1938. Singer and guitarist in the fifties rock scene, best known for "Summertime Blues."

LINDSAY BUCKINGHAM, California, 1947. Guitarist and singer with Fleetwood Mac after a duo career with Stevie Nicks. His solo career blossomed in the early eighties.

Notes:

A PIECE OF OUR HEARTS FADES! Janis Joplin dies of a heroin overdose in a Hollywood hotel room. Her talents were brought to international attention following her performance with Big Brother and The Holding Company at The Monterey Pop Festival. Her most successful LP *Pearl* is released posthumously. (1970)

1980 **Carly Simon** collapses on stage at The Stanley Theater in Pittsburgh of nervous exhaustion.

1980 Original **Deep Purple** singer, **Rod Evans,** fronts a "bogus" Deep Purple tour of Central and North America, but is prevented from performing when other members of the group file a court injunction.

1980 Stiff Records is fined 50 pounds Sterling for making an "indecent exhibition" with their official T-shirt, which bears the slogan "If It Ain't Stiff It Ain't Worth A Fuck."

 RECORD RELEASES include **Crosby, Stills & Nash** "Suite: Judy Blue Eyes" (1969) . . . and **The Bee Gees** "Nights On Broadway" (1975).

Birthdays:
NONA HENDRIX, Trenton, New Jersey, 1944. Singer with The Del Capris before joining Patti LaBelle in 1962.

JAMES FIELDER, Denton, Texas, 1947. Bassist with Blood, Sweat and Tears after playing briefly with The Buffalo Springfield.

Notes:

OCTOBER 5

THEY GET THERE FROM HERE! The Beatles first single, "Love Me Do," is released. Two versions are recorded, one with Ringo on drums and the other with a session player drumming and Ringo on tambourine. The latter becomes the single. (1962)

1970 **Papa John Creach** joins **The Jefferson Airplane.** The elderly fiddler is first recruited into **Hot Tuna,** a group formed from within the Airplane by **Jack Cassady** and **Jorma Kaukonen.**

1970 *Led Zeppelin III* is released.

🎵 **RECORD RELEASES** include **Cream** "White Room" and **Steppenwolf** "Magic Carpet Ride" (1968) . . . and **Harry Chapin** "Cat's In The Cradle" (1975).

🎵 **GOLD RECORDS** awarded to **Led Zeppelin** for *III* (1970) . . . and to **Santana** for their third release, **Santana** (1971).

Birthdays:

STEVE MILLER, Dallas, Texas, 1943. Singer, songwriter and guitarist with a college band, The Marksmen Combo, before forming The Steve Miller Blues Band in 1966, followed by a successful solo career.

BRIAN CONNOLY, Middlesex, England, 1948. Singer and founder of Sweet in 1968.

Notes:

CAN'T ALWAYS GET WHAT YOU WANT! Mick Jagger apologizes to the Reverend Jesse Jackson for the lyrics in "Some Girls," but refuses to grant Jackson's request that the song be changed to exclude the line "black girls just love to get fucked all night long." Jackson has denounced the song for being "racially insulting" and "degrading to blacks and women." (1978)

1966 LSD is made illegal in California.

1967 "Death Of A Hippie" funeral service is held by **The Diggers** in Haight-Ashbury in San Francisco, as participants ceremoniously fill a coffin with stereotyped hippie artifacts and set it aflame to symbolize the end of the "media-hyped movement."

1975 *Who By Numbers* is released, featuring the hit single "Slip Kid."

1980 **Johnny Lydon,** a former member of **The Sex Pistols,** is given a three-month jail sentence for assaulting a customer in a Dublin bar.

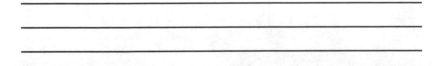 **RECORD RELEASES** include **Ringo Starr** "Photograph" and **Todd Rundgren** "Hello, It's Me" (1973) . . . **The Eagles** "Heartache Tonight" and **Fleetwood Mac** "Tusk" (1979).

Birthdays:

MILLIE SMALL, Jamaica, 1948. Singer noted for a #2 single in the sixties on both sides of the Atlantic, "My Boy Lollipop."

Notes:

_____

_____

_____

_____

_____

Eagles Live

THE BEGINNING OF STARTING OVER! John Lennon's immigration battle ends when the U.S. Court of Appeals overturns the order to deport him. The court rules that the British law under which John is convicted of "possession of cannabis resin" in 1968 is unjust by U.S. standards, and that he therefore has been denied due process. (1975)

1969 **The Youngbloods** are awarded a Gold Record for "Get Together."

1977 **Steve Hackett** quits **Genesis** to devote more time to his solo career, after seven years with the band. "It was a relief in a way. You could tell there just wasn't the energy there anymore."—Genesis drummer **Phil Collins.**

🎵**RECORD RELEASES** include **David Bowie's** LP *Heroes* (1977) . . . and the **Toto** single "Hold The Line" (1978).

Birthdays:

DINO VALENTI, New York City, 1943. Guitarist and singer with Quicksilver Messenger Service.

KEVIN GODLEY, Manchester, England, 1945. Drummer with 10cc until 1977 when he left to form a duo with guitarist, Lol Creme.

Notes:

David Bowie

LOOSE LIPS SINK SHIPS! The Sex Pistols sign a 40,000 pound deal with Britain's EMI label and release their debut single, "Anarchy in the U.K." The contract ends three months later after the group is involved in a series of embarrassing incidents, including the use of profanity during a live interview, and much bad press. (1976)

1979 **Fleetwood Mac's** *Tusk* LP is rush-released by Warner Brothers Records weeks ahead of schedule when songs from the album mysteriously appear on FM radio stations.

1980 **Bob Marley** is hospitalized in New York City after collapsing in Central Park. Rumors that Marley has cancer are denied.

🎵 **RECORD RELEASES** include **Peter & Gordon** "Lady Godiva," **Mitch Rider and The Detroit Wheels** "Devil With A Blue Dress/Good Golly, Miss Molly," and **The Rolling Stones** "Have You Seen Your Mother, Baby (Standing In The Shadows)" (1966) . . . and **Linda Ronstadt** "It's So Easy" (1977).

Birthdays:

RAY ROWYER, England, 1945. Guitarist with Procol Harum on the first hit "Whiter Shade of Pale," replaced by Robin Trower.

HAMISH STUART, Glasgow, Scotland, 1949. Guitarist with Average White Band as replacement for Michael Rosen.

JOHNNY RAMONE, New York City, 1951. Guitarist with The Ramones.

Notes:

Ramones

OCTOBER 9

THE PRICE OF CRUMBLING SUCCESS! Elvis and Priscilla Presley are divorced in Santa Monica, California. Priscilla is awarded a generous settlement of nearly $1.5 million cash, $4,200 a month alimony for one year, half the sale price of the couple's $750,000 home and a 5% interest in two of Elvis' publishing companies. (1973)

1965   The **Beatles'** "Yesterday" is #1 in the U.S.

1973   Gold Records awarded to **Grand Funk Railroad** for "We're An American Band" . . . and to **Paul Simon** for "Loves Me Like A Rock."

1975   **Sean Ono Lennon** is born to **John and Yoko** on his father's birthday.

1978   **Jaques Brel** dies of lung cancer. The Belgian-born songwriter's impact on French popular music is often compared to that of **Bob Dylan** on American folk music.

1980   **Yoko** hires a skywriter to wish **John** a Happy 40th Birthday.

♫ **RECORD RELEASES** include **The Four Seasons** "Let's Hang On" (1965) . . . **Van Morrison** "Wild Night" (1971) . . . and **Styx** "Babe" (1979).

Birthdays:

JOHN WINSTON LENNON, Liverpool, England, 1940. Singer, songwriter, guitarist and producer who formed the legendary Beatles in 1962, a group that created some of the most definitive music of the sixties. Lennon continued to record after the group disbanded in 1970, but stopped in 1975 when he was granted permanent resident status in the U.S. after a grueling court battle. A revitalized career in music was ended in 1980 when Lennon was shot to death in front of his apartment building in Manhattan shortly after the release of the LP *Double Fantasy.*

JOHN ALEX ENTWISTLE, London, England, 1944.   Bassist and original member of the supergroup, The Who, with occasional solo projects.

JACKSON BROWNE, Heidelberg, Germany, 1948. Singer, guitarist and songwriter with The Nitty Gritty Dirt Band then a successful solo artist.

Notes:

_____

_____

_____

IT JUST TAKES THE RIGHT ONE! Pink Floyd's *Atom Heart Mother* LP is released as the group's fifth album and eventually reaches #1 in England, launching Pink Floyd to stardom. (1970)

1962 "Monster Mash," the novelty single by Bobby "Boris" Pickett and The Crypt Kickers, is #1 in the U.S.

1978 **Steve Tyler** and **Joe Perry** of **Aerosmith** are injured when a fan tosses a cherry bomb on stage during a concert in Philadelphia, an incident that leads to a crackdown on concert violence in the City of Brotherly Love.

1979 "Fleetwood Mac Day" in Los Angeles, when the group gets its own star on Hollywood Boulevard's Walk Of Fame.

RECORD RELEASES include **The Shangri-Las** "Leader Of The Pack" (1964) . . . **Frank Zappa** *Hot Rats* LP (1969) . . . and **Smokey Robinson and The Miracles** "Tears Of A Clown" (1970).

Birthdays:

DAVID LEE ROTH, 1955. Lead singer with Van Halen.

JOHN PRINE, Maywood, Illinois, 1946. Singer, songwriter and guitarist discovered by Paul Anka and Kris Kristofferson in 1969. Prine's songs have been widely recorded by such artists as Al Kooper and Bonnie Raitt and he has a number of solo LPs.

John Lennon

VERY READY FOR PRIME TIME! *Saturday Night Live* premieres on NBC-TV, starring Chevy Chase, John Belushi, Dan Ackroyd, Gilda Radner, Larraine Newman, Jane Curtin and Garrett Morris. Buck Henry is the first host and the show is to become the highest rated late-night TV program ever. (1975)

1969   Blues great, **Muddy Waters,** is injured in an auto accident in Illinois that kills three others.

1975   **Elton John's** "Island Girl" is released.

1978   **Nancy Spungen** is found murdered in the bathroom of the Greenwich Village apartment she shared with boyfriend **Sid Vicious** of **The Sex Pistols.** Vicious is arrested a day later and charged with the stabbing death.

1980   **Queen** is #1 in the U.S. with the single "Another One Bites The Dust" and the LP *The Game.*

Birthdays:
DARYL HALL, Philadelphia, Pennsylvania, 1948. Singer and keyboardist, founding member of Hall & Oates.

Notes:

OCTOBER 12

ABOUT TO BE EXPERIENCED! The Jimi Hendrix Experience is formed in London, featuring bassist Noel Redding, a good-looking British player, and Mitch Mitchell, a cocky and very confident drummer who channeled his personal contempt for Hendrix into his playing. They record three authorized LPs together. (1966)

1968 **The Moody Blues** "Ride My Seesaw" is released.

1968 **Big Brother and The Holding Company,** featuring **Janis Joplin,** is #1 on the U.S. LP charts with *Cheap Thrills.*

1970 An **Ian Anderson** flute, a mutilated **Pete Townshend** guitar and a 1966 black Cadillac limo once used to transport the **Beatles, Janis Joplin, Bob Dylan** and others are a few of the items offered at the Rock Memorabilia Auction held at Bill Graham's Fillmore East in New York City.

1971 *Jesus Christ Superstar,* opens in New York.

1974 **David Bowie's** *David Live* is released as a double LP, recorded at The Tower Theater in Philadelphia.

1978 **Sid Vicious** is arrested and charged with the murder of **Nancy Spungen.**

1979 **Jethro Tull** is forced to cancel two concerts when **Ian Anderson** is struck in the face by a rose tossed to the stage at Madison Square Garden by a fan, a rose thorn piercing his eye.

1980 Seven people are stabbed at a **Blood, Sweat and Tears** concert in Los Angeles.

GOLD RECORDS awarded to **The Rolling Stones** for "Out Of Our Heads" (1965) . . . and to **Elton John** for the double LP *Goodbye Yellow Brick Road* (1973).

Birthdays:
SAMUEL MOORE, Miami, Florida, 1935. Half of sixties singing team Sam & Dave.

RICK PARFITT, London, England, 1948. Guitarist with Status Quo.

Notes:

MORE PEACEFUL THAN LIFE! Janis Joplin's ashes are scattered at sea off the coast of California. It is, symbolically, a more peaceful end than the gutsy singer had enjoyed when alive, often the object of self abuse from drugs and alcohol. (1970)

1963   The **Beatles** appear on "Sunday Night At The London Palladium" on ABC-TV, their first major TV show.

1975   **Neil Young** undergoes successful surgery in Los Angeles to remove a growth from his vocal chords.

1979   **Supertramp's** "Take The Long Way Home" is released.

Birthdays:

PAUL SIMON, Newark, New Jersey, 1941. Singer, songwriter and multi-instrumentalist who teamed with Art Garfunkel to form Tom and Jerry, evolving into Simon and Garfunkel. He is noted for both his duo and solo work, particularly "Sounds Of Silence" and "Mother And Child Reunion."

ROBERT LAMM, Brooklyn, New York, 1944. Keyboardist with Chicago.

MARIE OSMOND, 1959. The only female singer in the Osmond Family, she joined with brother Donnie to co-host a successful TV variety show in the late seventies.

LENNY BRUCE, New York City, 1925. Counter-culture comedian whose style paved the way for comics George Carlin, Richard Pryor and others.

Notes:

_____

_____

_____

_____

_____

_____

_____

_____

THE GREAT WHITE TURNING POINT! The Beatles complete the 18-week recording session and put the finishing touches to the *White* album, a faceless LP jacket that contains a disc with a truly brilliant collection of Beatles tunes. Many critics will cite the *White* album as the last great cooperative effort of the foursome. (1968)

1964 **Charlie Watts,** drummer with **The Rolling Stones,** marries **Shirley Ann Shepherd** in Bradford, England.

1967 **Clive Davis** is named president of Columbia Records.

1971 **John and Yoko** appear on *The Dick Cavett Show* and, in the course of the interview, manage to plug John's new LP, Yoko's new single, Yoko's new book, a film by John, two films by Yoko and her first art show.

1972 **Joe Cocker** and six members of his band and road crew are busted for drug possession after a concert in Adelaide, Australia.

🎵 **RECORD RELEASES** include **Elvis Presley** "Jailhouse Rock" (1957). . . **Spanky and Our Gang** "Lazy Day" and **The Who** "I Can See For Miles" (1967) . . . **The Temptations** "Papa Was A Rolling Stone" (1972). . . **Kiss** "Rock and Roll All Night" (1975) . . . and **Ace Frehley** "New York Groove" (1978).

Birthdays:
JUSTIN HAYWARD, Wiltshire, England, 1946. Guitarist and often lead singer with The Moody Blues, as replacement for Denny Laine.

CLIFF RICHARD, born Harry Rodger Webb, Lucknow, India, 1940. Singer, guitarist and actor best known in the U.S. for "Devil Woman" and "Don't Turn Out The Light."

Notes:
_____
_____
_____
_____
_____
_____
_____
_____

OCTOBER 15

TASTE OF THINGS TO COME! Led Zeppelin performs on stage for the first time in a small London pub after just three rehearsals. (1969)

1960   The Miracles "Shop Around" becomes Motown's first million seller.

1966   Pink Floyd's first major concert is at the London Roadhouse before a crowd of 2,000 for a party to launch the *International Times,* Europe's first underground newspaper.

1968   Big Brother and The Holding Company, featuring **Janis Joplin,** awarded a Gold Record for *Cheap Thrills.*

1970   Derek and The Dominos begin a U.S. concert tour in Trenton, New Jersey.

1973   Keith Richards and **Anita Pallenberg** are busted for drug possession in Nice, France.

1976   Fleetwood Mac's *Rumors* LP is released.

1976 RKO owned radio stations ban **Rod Stewart's** "Tonight's The Night" single because of "suggestive lyrical content."

1977   Lynyrd Skynyrd's *Street Survivors* LP is released featuring an album cover showing group members enveloped in flames. The cover is changed when three members of the band are killed in a plane crash five days later.

🎵 **RECORD RELEASES** include **The Lovin' Spoonful** "Rain On The Roof" (1966)... **Paul Simon** "Slip Slidin' Away" and **Bob Welch** "Sentimental Lady" (1977).

Birthdays:

BARRY McGUIRE, Oklahoma, 1935. Singer and songwriter with The New Christy Minstrels, best known for his solo single "Eve Of Destruction."

RICHARD CARPENTER, New Haven, Connecticut, 1946. Half of the brother-sister act The Carpenters.

Notes:

WHEN NOTHING IS SOMETHING! Billy Preston reaches the height of his career in the mid-seventies when he's awarded a Gold Record for the hit "Nothing From Nothing." Preston has turned his key-boards prowess into a successful career of featured solo perform-ances with the Beatles and others, as well as on his own. He will fade from popularity from this point on. (1974)

1969 **Leonard Chess** dies at age 52. The founder of Chess Records assured success for the label, when he and his brothers signed **Chuck Berry.**

🎵 **RECORD RELEASES** include **Isaac Hayes** "Theme From Shaft" . . . and **Santana** "Everybody's Everything" (1971).

Birthdays:
BOB WEIR, San Francisco, California, 1947. Guitarist and singer with The Grateful Dead, as well as founder of his own band Bobby and The Midnights. Born with a rare brain disorder, Weir cannot read, al-though he aspires to be a writer.

Notes:

_____

_____

_____

_____

_____

_____

_____

Santana

PUBES IN PUBLIC! *Hair* opens at New York's Public Theater, a Joseph Papp production. The tribal rock musical soon moves uptown to Broadway and gives theater-goers a taste of something they aren't used to—nudity on stage. A huge success! (1967)

1964   **Manfred Mann's** "Do Wah Ditty Ditty" is #1 on the U.S. singles charts.

1972   **Billy Williams** dies, best known for his hit "Write Myself A Letter."

1975   **Maurice Gibb** of **The Bee Gees** marries former restaurant manager, **Yvonne Spencely,** a woman he met shortly after being separated from his first wife, British pop singer, **Lulu.**

1975   **David Bowie** is awarded a Gold Record for "Fame."

🎵 **RECORD RELEASES** include **The Zombies** "She's Not There" (1964) . . . and **Eric Clapton** "After Midnight" (1970).

Birthdays:

GARY PUCKETT, Hibbing, Minnesota, 1942. Lead singer and founder of Gary Puckett and The Union Gap.

JAMES SEALS, Sydney, Texas, 1941. Singing partner with Dash Crofts in the seventies hit band, Seals & Crofts.

Chuck Berry

WRONG PLACE, WRONG TIME, FOR A LONG TIME! John and Yoko are busted at Ringo's basement apartment in London's Montague Square for possession of cannabis resin. John pleads guilty so police won't press charges against Yoko, though he swears the hashish has been planted in the flat by police. The arrest becomes the backbone of the U.S. Immigration Department case to keep Lennon from becoming a U.S. citizen. (1968)

1967   **John Lennon's** first solo film appearance comes at the premiere of *How I Won The War* at the London Pavillion.

1969   Britian's New Music Express reports that **Rod Stewart** has joined **Small Faces** as replacement for **Steve Marriott,** who has left to form **Humble Pie.**

1969   **Paul Kantner** is busted in Honolulu and charged with possession of marijuana after police catch the **Jefferson Airplane** guitarist crawling through bushes outside his home with a joint clenched between his teeth. Kantner denies the police report and claims he was setup.

1974   Soul singer, **Al Green,** is scalded when his girlfriend, **Mary Woodson,** throws boiling grits at him, before shooting herself. Green suffers severe burns on his back. Mary dies instantly.

1975   **Simon and Garfunkel** reunite on *Saturday Night Live* for their first post-split up collaboration when they perform "My Little Town."

🎵 **RECORD RELEASES** include **Blood, Sweat and Tears** "And When I Die," **Steam** "Na Na Hey Hey Kiss Him Goodbye," and **Stevie Wonder** "Yester-Me, Yester-You, Yesterday" (1969).

Birthdays:

CHUCK BERRY, San Jose, California, 1926. Legendary singer and guitarist noted as the inspiration for many contemporary guitarists. Berry rose to fame in the mid-fifties with "Johnny B. Goode" and "Maybelline" and many of his classics have been covered by newer rock groups, including "Roll Over Beethoven" by the Beatles and Electric Light Orchestra.

Notes:

OCTOBER 19

A WHOLE LOTTA FAME! Led Zeppelin's second LP, *Led Zeppelin II,* is released to hordes of anxious fans who are quick to discover a heavy metal anthem on the disc, "Whole Lotta Love." (1969)

1974 **The Who's** *Odds and Sods* LP is released, featuring material previously recorded for other albums but never released.

1974 Bassist, **Mike D'Albuquerque,** quits **Electric Light Orchestra** and is replaced by **Kelly Groucutt.**

♫ RECORD RELEASES include **Diana Ross and The Supremes** "Love Child" (1968) . . . and **Neil Sedaka** "Laughter In The Rain" (1974).

Birthdays:

PETER TOSH, born Peter McIntosh, Jamaica, 1944. Singer and guitarist, original member of Bob Marley's Wailers. Solo career after 1975 with support from Mick Jagger and his Rolling Stones Records.

KEITH REID, London, England, 1944. Lyricist with Procol Harum.

Peter Tosh

THE TRAGIC FALL OF RISING STARS! Three members of Lynyrd Skynyrd are killed when their tour plane crashes in Mississippi. Dead are lead singer, Ronnie Van Zandt, guitarist, Steve Gaines and singer, Cassie Gaines. The other band members who survive do not reform the group, even though it is on the verge of stardom, but choose to cast the survivors as The Rossington-Collins Band. (1977)

1964   One hundred fifty excited, rowdy fans are arrested as **The Rolling Stones** perform their first Paris concert at the Olympia.

1969   **John and Yoko's** *Wedding* album is released, with a photo of the newlyweds dressed in virginal white on the cover.

1972   **Pink Floyd** cancels three recording dates so the band can perform "War On Want," a charity concert at Wembley Park in England.

1974   **Mirage** is a daughter born to **Eric** and **Rose Burdon.**

1979   **Bob Dylan** is the musical guest on *Saturday Night Live* performing "You Gotta Serve Somebody."

1979   **The Eagles** "Long Run" enters the U.S. charts at #2.

🎵 **RECORD RELEASES** include **Elvis Presley** "Love Me Tender" (1956) . . . **The Four Seasons** "Big Girls Don't Cry" (1962) . . . and **The Steve Miller Band** "The Joker" (1973).

Birthdays:

AL GREENWOOD, New York City, 1951. Keyboardist with Foreigner, an original member of the band until his departure in 1980 to pursue a solo career.

TOM PETTY, Florida, 1953. Guitarist, singer and founder of Tom Petty and The Heartbreakers.

RIC LEE, Staffordshire, England, 1945. Drummer with Ten Years After.

Notes:

NEW THINGS FOR THE LAST TIME! Buddy Holly performs his last studio recordings at Pythian Temple Studios in New York City using orchestral strings as backing for the first time on any of his recordings. Among the tunes recorded during the session is "It Doesn't Matter Anymore." (1958)

1965 **Bill Black,** the original bassist with **Elvis Presley** and later of his own Bill Black Combo, dies in Memphis, Tennessee.

1969 **Jack Kerouac,** author of the Beat Generation classic *On The Road,* dies of a hernia.

1971 **Jade** is a daughter born to **Mick** and **Bianca Jagger** at the Belvedere Nursing Home, Paris.

1972 **America's** "Ventura Highway" is released.

1975 **Elton John** is awarded a Gold Record for "Rock Of The Westies" and later is awarded his own star on Hollywood Boulevard's Walk Of The Stars. For the first time, police are forced to close down neighboring streets to keep the crowd of fans away.

1976 *The Song Remains The Same* premieres in New York City. The mix of fantasy sequences with **Led Zeppelin** concert footage from the 1973 Madison Square Garden date is the group's first attempt at cinema. Both the movie and soundtrack LP are commercial successes.

Birthdays:

MANFRED MANN, born Michael Leibowitz, Johannesburg, South Africa, 1940. Keyboardist and founding member of the Mann-Hugg Band in 1963, evolving into Manfred Mann.

ELVIN BISHOP, Tulsa, Oklahoma, 1942. Guitarist with The Butterfield Blues Band in the mid-sixties, then a solo career marked by the hit "Fooled Around And Fell In Love."

STEVE CROPPER, Willow Spring, Missouri, 1941. Guitarist and original member of Booker T. and The MGs, followed by a solo career and featured performances, including The Blues Brothers Band.

ERIC FAULKNER, Edinburgh, Scotland, 1954. Guitarist with The Bay City Rollers, then The Rollers.

Notes:

WHO WOULD KNOW BETTER! The Who fail to impress the British record giant EMI with a test recording and are turned down by the label, a situation similar to the Beatles flunking their first audition at a major label. (1964)

1966   The Beach Boys release the classic "Good Vibrations," the most expensive single ever produced up to this point.

1974   *Hotter Than Hell* by **Kiss** is released. The cover art features cat-like drummer, **Peter Criss,** without his red whiskers and chin fur as part of a new make-up look.

🎵 GOLD RECORDS awarded to **Joan Baez** for "The Night They Drove Old Dixie Down," and to **John Lennon** for his LP *Walls And Bridges.*

Birthdays:

LESLIE WEST, Queens, New York, 1945. Guitarist and singer with The Vagrants, then Mountain with Felix Pappalardi. Later he formed West, Bruce & Laing.

EDDIE BRIGATI, New York City, 1946. Singer with The Young Rascals, then The Rascals.

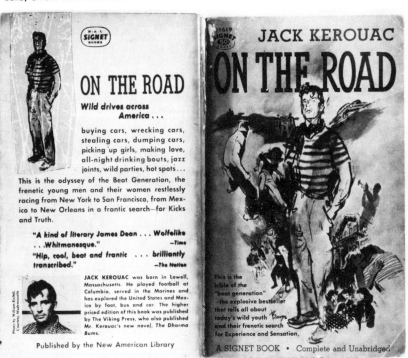

THOSE WERE THE DAYS! Elton John packs Dodger Stadium to end his 1975 concert tour of the West Coast, becoming the first rock star to appear at the stadium since the Beatles in 1966. (1975)

1960 **The Drifters** "Save The Last Dance For Me" is #1 in the U.S.

1962 **Stevie Wonder** makes his first Motown recording, "Thank You For Loving Me All The Way," when he's twelve years old.

1978 **Billy Joel** is awarded a Platinum Record for the LP *52nd Street,* his second platinum award of the year.

1978 CBS Records leads other labels in hiking the suggested retail price of some LPs to $8.98, a one dollar increase.

🎵 **RECORD RELEASES** include **The Byrds** "Turn, Turn, Turn" (1965)... **Bread** "Baby, I'm A Want You" (1971)... **Electric Light Orchestra** "Livin' Thing" and **Leo Sayer** "You Make Me Feel Like Dancing" (1976).

Birthdays:

GREG RIDLEY, Cumberland, England, 1947. Bassist with Spooky Tooth, then formed Humble Pie with Steve Marriott.

Notes:

GETTING OFF EASY! Keith Richards is found guilty of heroin possession by a Toronto judge, but is given a suspended sentence and one year probation. The verdict comes one year and a half after Canadian Mounties found 22 grams of heroin in Keith's hotel room. The court's leniency is severely criticized. (1978)

1964   The Ronettes "Walking In The Rain" is released.

1967   Pink Floyd arrive in the U.S. for their first American tour, to begin at The Fillmore West in San Francisco.

1975   John Lennon's *Shaved Fish* an oddly titled greatest hits LP, is released.

1976   Carlos Santana, James Taylor and **Pete Seeger** perform at the United Nations Day Concert for the First Planetary Celebration, a benefit to encourage dual citizenship . . . to planet earth as well as to one's country.

1977   Cameras begin to roll on the set of *The Buddy Holly Story,* with **Gary Busey** in the title role.

Birthdays:

BILL WYMAN, born William Perks, Kent, England, 1941. Bassist and original member of The Rolling Stones, joining the group shortly after Mick Jagger and Keith Richard left Blues Incorporated to form The Stones. Wyman occasionally records solo, producing three LPs of his own by the early eighties.

JERRY EDMONTON, Canada, 1946. Drummer with Steppenwolf, an original member of the band.

DALE "BUFFIN" GRIFFIN, Ross-On-Wye, England, 1948. Drummer and founding member of Mott The Hoople.

THE BIG BOPPER, born J.P. Richardson, Sabina, Texas, 1930. Singer and songwriter best known for "Chantilly Lace" in the mid-fifties, before he died in a plane crash with Buddy Holly and Richie Valens.

Notes:

FIRST CASTING OF THE STONES! The Rolling Stones make their first appearance on *The Ed Sullivan Show*. Hundreds of concerned parents write letters of complaint to CBS causing Sullivan to promise he will never let the band make a second appearance. But they do, less than a year later. (1964)

1969 **The Guess Who** is awarded a Gold Record for "Laughing."

1969 **Pink Floyd's** *Ummagumma* is released, a double LP featuring one disc of live recordings and a second disc of experimentation by each of the four members of the group.

1973 **John Lennon** sues Uncle Sam, charging the U.S. Immigration Department has engaged in wiretaps against him and his lawyer. The suit is part of Lennon's fight to gain U.S. citizenship.

1974 **The Incredible String Band** disbands after nearly ten years together.

1976 **Phillip Reed** dies in a fall from a Salt Lake City hotel room. Before joining **Flo and Eddie** as guitarist, Reed is known as one of the best session players in Los Angeles.

♫ **RECORD RELEASES** include **Peter, Paul & Mary** "Leaving On A Jet Plane" and **Three Dog Night** "Eli's Coming" (1969).

Birthdays:

JON ANDERSON, Lancashire, England, 1944. Singer and founding member of Yes until the demise of the supergroup in 1981. Then a solo career and collaborations with Vangelis.

GLEN TIPTON, Birmingham, England, 1948. Guitarist with Judas Priest, a founding member of the group.

HELEN REDDY, Melbourne, Australia, 1941. Singer best known for her 1971 single "I Am Woman."

Notes:

_____

_____

_____

_____

_____

_____

_____

_____

FABULOUS AWARDS FOR FOUR! The Beatles are presented with the MBE medals (Member of The British Empire) by Her Majesty The Queen at an investiture at Buckingham Palace. (1965)

1955 New York City's famed underground newspaper, *The Village Voice,* is first published. Author **Norman Mailer** is among the financial backers.

1961 **Bob Dylan** signs with Columbia Records, his first recording contract guaranteeing him 4% royalties from the sales of his records.

1963 **Bob Dylan** performs at Carnegie Hall in New York City.

1974 **The Rolling Stones** *It's Only Rock And Roll,* the final LP with guitarist Mick Taylor, is released.

1980 **Paul Kantner** of **The Jefferson Starship** suffers a brain hemorrhage during a recording session for the group's *Modern Times* LP and spends fifteen days recuperating at Cedars-Sinai Medical Center in Los Angeles.

1981 **The David Bowie-Queen** collaboration "Under Pressure" is released.

🎵 RECORD RELEASES include **The Classics IV** "Stormy," **Johnny Taylor** "Who's Making Love" (1968) . . . and **John Lennon** "Mind Games" (1973).

Notes:

THE BOSS IS COVERED! Bruce Springsteen is on the covers of both *Time* and *Newsweek,* which appear at newstands the same day. The magazines spotlight Springsteen as a typical example of how publicists and the media can create a rock star, regardless of his talent. It becomes apparent that the two weekly giants have simply added to the hype they fervently criticize. The publicity accelerates Bruce's career. (1975)

1970 *Jesus Christ Superstar* is unveiled at St. Peter's Lutheran Church in New York City. Composers, **Tim Rice** and **Andrew Lloyd Webber,** interpret the music as the record plays. The LP features **Deep Purple** vocalist Ian Gillan, as Jesus and, **Yvonne Elliman,** as Mary Magdalene.

Bruce Springsteen

IN SEARCH OF THE BEATLES! Brian Epstein's curiosity is aroused when a patron at his record store asks for "My Bonnie" by the Beatles. Epstein discovers the record is available only in Germany and sets out to find the Liverpool musicians who recorded it. (1961)

1962 "Bob Dylan is not the author of 'Blowin' In The Wind' " is the claim of a high school teacher in Milburn, New Jersey, who says he wrote the classic protest tune and sold it to Dylan for $1,000. The truth is revealed twelve years later in a *New York Times Magazine* article in which the teacher admits that after several unsuccessful attempts to write a protest song himself, he simply presented Dylan's as his own and started the rumor to save face.

1968 **Cynthia Lennon** sues **John** for divorce on grounds of adultery, a charge John doesn't defend because **Yoko** is pregnant with his child at the time.

1969 **Elvis Presley** is awarded a Gold Record for "Suspicious Minds."

1972 **The Who's** "Join Together" is chosen as the official theme of the United States Council for World Affairs.

Birthdays:

CHARLIE DANIELS, Wilmington, North Carolina, 1936. Singer, guitarist, fiddler and songwriter who began as a session player for Bob Dylan, Peter Seeger, Ringo Starr and others before recording his own material in the early seventies. Best known for his 1980 hit "In America."

RICKI LEE REYNOLDS, Manilla, Arkansas. 1948. Guitarist with Black Oak Arkansas.

WAYNE FONTANA, born Glyn Ellis, Manchester, England, 1945. Singer who auditioned for a record deal with Fontana Records, prompting his name change. Best known for the sixties hit "A Groovy Kind Of Love."

Notes:

LOSS OF A BROTHER! Duane Allman dies in a motorcycle crash on a winding road near Macon, Georgia. The leader and guitarist with The Allman Brothers Band is just 24 years old. (1971)

1965   The Rolling Stones score a first when "Get Off Of My Cloud" becomes #1 in the U.S. and England on the same day.

1966   ? and The Mysterians "96 Tears" is #1 in the U.S.

🎵 **RECORD RELEASES** include **The New Vaudeville Band** "Winchester Cathedral" and **The Supremes** "You Keep Me Hanging On" (1966) . . . and **Rod Stewart** "You're In My Heart" (1977).

🎵 **GOLD RECORDS** awarded to the **Beatles** for "Something" and "Come Together" (1969) . . . and to **The Who** for the double LP *Quadrophenia.* (1973)

Birthdays:

PETER GREEN, London, England, 1946. Guitarist with John Mayall's Bluesbreakers before forming Fleetwood Mac in 1967, then a solo career in 1970.

DENNY LAINE, born Brian Arthur Hines, on a boat off the coast of New Jersey, 1944. Guitarist with The Diplomats in the early sixties, then with The Moody Blues in 1964 and with Wings in 1971, pursuing a solo career in 1981.

Notes:

"ARE WE ROLLING, BOB!" Bob Dylan's Rolling Thunder Review begins its American tour in Plymouth, Massachusetts, featuring Joan Baez and Ramblin' Jack Elliot. Much of the tour is filmed and is included in Dylan's film *Renaldo and Clara.* (1975)

1978 *Kiss Meets The Phantom Of The Park,* a TV movie starring the comic-book rock band as they battle the forces of evil in an amusement park, airs on network TV.

🎵 **RECORD RELEASES** include **The Supremes** "I Hear A Symphony" and **The Yardbirds** "I'm A Man" (1965) . . . and **Melanie** "Brand New Key" (1971).

Birthdays:

GRACE SLICK, Chicago, Illinois, 1939. Lead singer with The Great Society before replacing Signe Anderson in The Jefferson Airplane in 1966. She has engaged in various solo projects during her on-again, off-again relationship with The Jefferson Airplane-Starship.

TIMOTHY B. SCHMIDT, Oakland, California, 1947. Bassist and singer with Poco in 1969, then with The Eagles as replacement for Randy Meisner in 1977 and various solo and session projects following the disbanding of The Eagles in 1982.

EDDIE HOLLAND, Detroit, Michigan, 1939. Singer and songwriter responsible for many of the sixties Motown hits with writing team of Holland-Dozier-Holland.

Notes:

A MAJESTIC REIGN BEGINS! Queen's "Bohemian Rhapsody" is released in England and begins the climb to #1, a position it remains at for eight consecutive weeks, unequaled in twenty years on the British charts. (1975)

1938 *War Of The Worlds,* the **Orson Welles** radio presentation of the classic H.G. Wells sci-fi tale, scares America into believing that a martian invasion of Earth is actually taking place.

1956 **Mary Patricia McCartney,** mother of Paul, dies in Liverpool.

1964 **Bob Dylan** performs his Halloween concert at Philharmonic Hall in New York City, with **Joan Baez** as special guest.

1966 **Pink Floyd** forms **Blackhill Enterprises** with **Peter Jenner** and **Andrew King** as a six-way partnership to manage the band's affairs.

1966 **The Monkees** are awarded a Gold Record for "The Last Train To Clarksville."

1967 **Brian Jones** of **The Rolling Stones** is sentenced to nine months in jail on drug charges and is released on bail.

1970 **Michelle Phillips,** formerly with The Mamas and The Papas, marries actor, **Dennis Hopper,** star of *Easy Rider.*

1976 **Pink Floyd** completes the quadrophonic mix of the *Wish You Were Here* LP.

Birthdays:

TOM PAXTON, Chicago, Illinois, 1937. Folksinger and guitarist best known for "The Last Thing On My Mind."

RUSS BALLARD, Waltham Cross, England, 1947. Guitarist and singer with The Roulettes in the early sixties, then with Unit 4 + 2 before co-founding Argent with Rod Argent in 1968. A solo career followed in 1974.

KINKY FRIEDMAN, Rio Duckworth, Texas, 1944. Singer and guitarist with his own band, Kinky Friedman and The Texas Jewboys, known for his irreverent lyrics.

Notes:

_____

_____

_____

_____

CAPTURED LIVE! The Beatles open at The Star Club for a two-week stint. Another musician performing there tapes the band one night and, years later, releases the recordings as *The Beatles Live! At The Star Club, Hamburg, Germany.* (1962)

1963 **The Rolling Stones** release "I Wanna Be Your Man," a song given to them by **Paul McCartney** and **John Lennon.**

1968 **George Harrison's** *Wonderwall,* a film soundtrack, is released as the first solo LP from any of the four **Beatles** and is the first record on the Apple label.

1969 **Elvis Presley's** "Suspicious Minds" is #1 in the U.S.

1969 **The Faces,** featuring **Rod Stewart,** sign with Warner Brothers Records.

1969 *Abbey Road,* the final group effort by the **Beatles** is #1 on the U.S. album charts.

1973 **The Rolling Stones** are awarded a Gold Record for "Angie."

1974 **Bob Dylan's** "Blood On The Tracks" is released.

1977 *Never Mind The Bullocks, Here Are The Sex Pistols,* the punk band's first and only LP, is released.

1979 **Bob Dylan** tells the world he's a Christian at his first all-gospel concert at The Warfield Theater in San Francisco.

1980 **Graham Bonnet** quits **Rainbow** two weeks after the departure of drummer **Cozy Powell.** Replacements, **Joe Lynn Turner** and **Bob Rondinelli,** become the 15th and 16th musicians to play in the **Ritchie Blackmore** group in its five-year history.

1981 RCA leads other labels in raising the price of 45 RPM singles from $1.69 to $1.99.

♪ **RECORD RELEASES** include **The Band** "Up On Cripple Creek," **Creedence Clearwater Revival** "Fortunate Son," and **B.J. Thomas** "Raindrops Keep Falling On My Head" (1969) . . . and **Diana Ross** "Theme From *Mahogany*" (1975).

Birthdays:

RICK GRECH, Bordeaux, England, 1945. Bassist with Family and co-founder of Blind Faith in 1969.

ON THE ROAD ALONE! George Harrison is the first former Beatle to embark on a U.S. tour with a concert at The Forum in Los Angeles. Surprisingly, the opening night audience barely fills half the house. (1974)

1963   *With The Beatles* is released on Parlophone Records in England. This original British debut LP is issued in the U.S. as *Meet The Beatles.*

1967   **The Monkees** are awarded a Gold Record for "Pisces, Aquarius, Capricorn & Jones Ltd."

1968   **Jimi Hendrix's** *Electric Ladyland* LP enters the U.S. charts at #1!

1969   Two rock films premiere in San Francisco on the same day. *Popcorn,* a documentary featuring footage of **The Rolling Stones, Otis Redding, Jimi Hendrix** and **The Bee Gees** . . . and *Sympathy For The Devil,* documenting the **Stones** in rehearsal.

1973   **John Lennon's** "Mind Games" is released.

1979   **Little Feat's** *Down On The Farm* is released, the group's last LP recorded shortly before the death of **Lowell George.**

1979   **The Who's** *Quadrophenia* movie opens at theaters across the U.S. starring **Sting** of **The Police.** For the soundtrack, **The Who** re-record and re-mix the entire original album.

🎵 **RECORD RELEASES** include **The Beach Boys** "Be True To Your School" (1963) . . . and **Stevie Wonder** "For Once In My Life" (1968).

Birthdays:

KEITH EMERSON, England, 1944. Keyboardist with The Nice before co-founding Emerson, Lake & Palmer in 1970.

DAVE PEGG, England, 1947. Bassist with Fairport Convention as replacement for Ashley Hutchings in 1969, then with Jethro Tull.

DAVID "JAY" BLACK, New York City, 1938. Lead singer and founder of Jay and The Americans.

Notes:

GOODNESS GRACIOUS, IT'S JERRY LEE! Jerry Lee Lewis' classic "Great Balls Of Fire" is released and sets the stage for a lengthy career of piano stomping hits from "The Killer." Within a month his first single is firmly lodged in the Top Ten. (1957)

1962 **The Crystals'** "He's A Rebel" is #1 in the U.S., one of a string of **Phil Spector** productions which flooded the record charts in the early sixties.

1967 **Peter Green's Fleetwood Mac** has its first single released in England, "I Believe My Time Ain't Long," with vocals by **Jeremy Spencer.**

1972 **James Taylor** and **Carly Simon** are married in her Manhattan apartment at 6:30 PM. With the exception of **Liz** and **Dick,** the couple are said to be the highest paid married couple in the world and on the eve of the marriage, Carly takes a bow with James at his concert at Radio City Music Hall.

Birthdays:

NICHOLAS SIMPER Middlesex, England, 1946. Bassist various sixties bands before joining Deep Purple in 1968, replaced a year later by Roger Glover.

Jerry Lee Lewis

A NIGHT FIT FOR A QUEEN! The Beatles play a Royal Command Performance at Prince of Wales Theater in London, as part of an evening of variety entertainment for Queen Elizabeth. (1963)

1962 **Bob Dylan** performs at Carnegie Hall in New York City, his first major concert outside of Greenwich Village. Attendance is poor.

1967 **The Doors'** *Strange Days* enters the U.S. album charts.

1970 **Jethro Tull** performs in a sold-out benefit to aid Phoenix House, the country's largest drug rehabilitation facility. Most of Tull's 80-minute set at Carnegie Hall is music from the *Benefit* LP.

1971 The Rainbow Theater opens and is London's first permanent rock 'n' roll theater.

1973 A **Pink Floyd** benefit concert raises 10,000 pounds to aid **Robert Wyatt,** the former **Soft Machine** drummer suffering a broken back.

1978 **Roger Corman** begins filming *Rock & Roll High School* starring **The Ramones.**

1978 **Greg Reeves** sues **Crosby, Stills, Nash & Young** for $1 million, alleging the group failed to pay royalties due him for work on the *Deja Vu* LP.

1979 *The Last Waltz,* director **Martin Scorcese's** film of the final concert by **The Band,** opens in New York and is hailed as one of the finest concert films ever made.

♪ **RECORD RELEASES** include **Smokey Robinson and The Miracles** "I Second That Emotion" (1967) . . . **Jethro Tull** "Living In The Past" (1972) . . . **Billy Joel** "My Life" and **Talking Heads** "Take Me To The River" (1978).

Notes:
_____
_____
_____
_____
_____
_____
_____
_____

OUT AGAIN, IN AGAIN! Ozzy Osbourne quits Black Sabbath and is replaced by Dave Walker. Ozzy's departure lasts only a few weeks before he asks for and gets his old job back. He is soon to quit again and will front his own band. (1977)

1960   Johnny Horton dies in a car crash near Milano, Texas, as his career is in full stride from the 1959 hit "Battle Of New Orleans."

1966   The Beach Boys' "Good Vibrations" enters the British charts on its climb to the top.

1966   Simon and Garfunkel's "A Hazy Shade Of Winter" is released.

1977   Guy Lombardo dies of a heart attack in Houston, Texas, where his band was performing, forever ending a standard tradition of **Guy Lombardo and The Royal Canadians** bringing in the New Year.

Birthdays:

IKE TURNER, Clarksdale, Mississippi, 1931. Singer, songwriter and multi-instrumentalist who formed The Kings Of Rhythm and scored with the song "Rocket 88," before his long association with wife Tina (Annie Mae Bullock.)

PETER NOONE, Manchester, England, 1947. Singer and guitarist, leader of Herman's Hermits in the sixties and then The Tremblers in 1980.

ART GARFUNKEL, New York City, 1941. Singer who joined with Paul Simon to form Tom and Jerry, evolving into Simon and Garfunkel. The combination brought international success in the seventies when the two split, Garfunkel turning his interests to a film career. They reunited in New York's Central Park in 1981 for a concert and album.

GRAM PARSONS, Winterhaven, Florida, 1946. Singer and guitarist with The Byrds as replacement for David Crosby in 1968, then with The Flying Burrito Brothers until his death in 1972.

Notes:

STARTING AT THE BOTTOM, CHEAPLY! Rock promoter Bill Graham produces his first concert, a benefit to aid the San Francisco Mime Troupe, with The Grateful Dead, Jefferson Airplane and three other bands. Graham rents The Fillmore Auditorium for a fee of $60. (1965)

1972 **New York Dolls** drummer, **Billy Muncia,** dies of accidental suffocation when a girl pours coffee down his throat after he nods off in her apartment following a night at the London Speakeasy Club. Muncia is 21.

1972 Gold Records awarded to **Deep Purple** for the *Machine Head* LP and to **The Raspberries** for the single "Go All The Way."

1973 **Gram Parsons**' body is stolen from its grave and cremated at Joshua Tree National Monument in the California desert, an act of "loyalty" by long-time friend and manager, **Phil Kaufman.**

1975 **The Sex Pistols** play their first show at St. Martin's School of Art, London. The concert is arranged by former **New York Dolls** manager, **Malcolm McLaren,** who gave the Sex Pistols their name.

🎵 **RECORD RELEASES** include **The Animals** "It's My Life" (1965) . . . **The Bee Gees** "Lonely Days, Lonely Nights" (1970) . . . **Sly and The Family Stones** "Family Affair" and **The Who** "Behind Blue Eyes" (1971).

Birthdays:

GLENN FREY, Detroit, Michigan, 1948. Guitarist, keyboardist and singer with The Eagles, before going solo in '82 with debut LP *No Fun Aloud.*

CHRIS GLEN, 1950. Bassist with The Sensational Alex Harvey Band.

Notes:

PLEASE STAND FOR A RIOT! A quizzical Jim Morrison demands that the crowd at a Doors concert rise to its feet, prompting Phoenix, Arizona, police to consider the standing fans as a "riot." The Doors are warned never to return. (1968)

1979 *The Rose* has its world premiere in Los Angeles. **Bette Midler** stars as the overindulgent rock superstar who eventually becomes the victim of her own success, a story loosely based on the life of **Janis Joplin.**

🎵 **RECORD RELEASES** include **The Beach Boys** "Dance, Dance, Dance" (1964) . . . **Chicago** "Does Anybody Really Know What Time It Is?" (1970).

Birthdays:

JONI MITCHELL, born Roberta Joan Anderson, Alberta, Canada, 1943. Singer and songwriter who began in coffeehouses around Canada before recording her first LP in 1964. Her songs have been recorded by Judy Collins, Tom Rush and CS&N among others. "Big Yellow Taxi" and "Help Me" established Mitchell as a major recording artist in her own right.

MARY TRAVERS, Louisville, Kentucky, 1937. Singer and founding member of Peter, Paul & Mary.

JOHNNY RIVERS, New York City, 1942. Singer with several major hits in the sixties and early seventies, including "Memphis," "Poor Side Of Town" and "Secret Agent Man."

Notes:

Bette Midler

NOVEMBER 8

JOHN ON HIS OWN! *How I Won The War* starring John Lennon, premieres in the U.S. It is the first time a member of the Beatles appears in a film without the other three. (1967)

1968 **John** and **Cynthia Lennon's** divorce is final. **Yoko** is already pregnant with John's child.

1971 *Zoso,* or **Led Zeppelin** *IV* is released and features the famous classic "Stairway To Heaven." The LP never reaches #1, but does appear somewhere on the charts for a record 158 weeks.

1975 **Fleetwood Mac's** "Over My Head" is released.

1980 **Bruce Springsteen's** *The River,* a double LP, is #1 in the U.S.

🎵 **GOLD RECORDS** awarded to **Ringo Starr** for *Ringo* (1973) . . . **Jethro Tull** for *War Child* and **Elton John** for his *Greatest Hits* (1974).

Birthdays:

ROY WOOD, Birmingham, England, 1946. Singer, songwriter and multi-instrumentalist, co-founder of The Move, which evolved into Electric Light Orchestra in 1972. Later he formed Wizard and in 1980, Helicopter.

BONNIE RAITT, Los Angeles, California, 1949. Guitarist and singer with a country-blues background in the sixties, then rock-pop solo work into the eighties.

BONNIE BRAMLETT, born Bonnie Lynn, Granite City, Illinois, 1944. Singer and songwriter, backing vocals for Ike and Tina Turner before joining with husband, Delaney Bramlett, in 1967 and recording with Eric Clapton, Dave Mason and others.

Bonnie Raitt

TO HAVE YOUR LUNCH AND EAT IT, TOO! Brian Epstein first sees the Beatles perform at a lunchtime concert at The Cavern Club in Liverpool. Epstein is the only person at the club wearing a suit. Not long after his first look, Epstein becomes the band's manager. (1961)

1965 The "lost jam" with **Bob Dylan, Robbie Robertson** and **Brian Jones** takes place in Brian's hotel room in New York City, the night of the big power blackout. No electricity, no recordings.

1966 **John Lennon** meets **Yoko Ono** for the first time at the preview of Yoko's art exhibition, "Unfinished Paintings and Objects," at the Indica Gallery in London.

1967 *Rolling Stone Magazine* is first published by Editor, **Jan Wenner.** The premiere issue includes his note that "Rolling Stone is not just about music, but also the things and attitudes that the music embraces."

1971 **Chicago** is awarded a Gold Record for *Chicago Live At Carnegie Hall,* a four record set.

1973 **Billy Joel's** *Piano Man* LP is released, the title track becoming his first hit record.

1973 **Cat Stevens** makes his U.S. television debut in a specially filmed segment of ABC's "In Concert," showing Stevens performing live at The Hollywood Bowl.

1980 **Bob Dylan** begins his first U.S. tour that features predominately "born again" material.

🎵 **RECORD RELEASES** include **The Kingsmen** "Louie, Louie" (1963) . . . and **Judy Collins** "Both Sides Now" (1968).

Birthdays:

TOM FOGERTY, Berkeley, California, 1941. Guitarist and founding member with brother John of Creedence Clearwater Revival.

Notes:

TAKE THIS GUITAR, SON! Greg Allman's gift on his 13th birthday is an electric guitar, a present from his parents. His brother, Duane, would receive his first electric guitar two weeks later. The rest is Allman Brothers history! (1960)

♪ **GOLD RECORDS** awarded to **Led Zeppelin** for *Led Zeppelin II* (1969) . . . and to **Anne Murray,** who receives hers on **The Merv Griffin Show** for "Snowbird" (1970).

♪ **RECORD RELEASES** include **David Essex** "Rock On" and **Stevie Wonder** "Livin' For The City" (1973).

Birthdays:

GREG LAKE, Bournemouth, England, 1948. Guitarist and singer, one of the founding members of King Crimson, then Emerson, Lake & Palmer, with a solo career in 1981.

BRAM TCHAICOVSKY, 1949. Singer and guitarist, originally a member of The Motors in the late seventies, with a solo career in 1980.

TIM RICE, Amersham, England, 1944. Lyricist and collaborator with Andrew Lloyd Webber on *Jesus Christ Superstar, Evita* and other rock "operas."

Notes:

Greg Allman

TWO BROTHERS DOWN! Barry Oakley, bassist with The Allman Brothers Band, dies when his motorcycle slams into a bus in Macon, Georgia, just three blocks from the site where Duane Allman lost his life in a similar mishap a year before. Oakley is 24. (1972)

1968 **John and Yoko's** *Two Virgins* LP is released, a collection of pants, grunts, and other assorted "just-barely-musical" love sounds, plus the infamous controversial nude cover.

1969 **The Stone Poney's** "Different Drum," featuring **Linda Ronstadt** on vocals, enters the U.S. singles charts.

1969 **Doors'** singer, **Jim Morrison,** is arrested for "interfering with the flight of an intercontinental aircraft and public drunkenness."

1970 **Bob Dylan's** first book is published. *Tarantula* is a collection of his prose and poetry.

1972 The first "official" pinball tournament is held in a restaurant parking lot in Winnsboro, South Carolina. One thousand onlookers see **Jerry Marsh** walk away with the honors as "Pinball Champion."

1973 A bogus **Mott The Hoople** concert is aired on 30 radio stations in the U.S. What is billed as a "live" concert recording is actually a disappointing assemblage of album tracks with concert crowd sound effects dubbed in.

♫ **RECORD RELEASES** include **Buddy Holly** "Peggy Sue" (1957) . . . **Diana Ross and The Supremes** "In And Out Of Love" and **Small Faces** "Itchycoo Park" (1967) . . . **Loggins & Messina** "Thinking Of You" and **Joni Mitchell** "You Turn Me On I'm A Radio" (1972).

Birthdays:

JESSE COLIN YOUNG, New York City, 1944. Singer, songwriter and guitarist with two folk style LPs before he formed The Youngbloods in 1965, with a solo career following the band's breakup in 1972. Best known for "Get Together."

CHRIS DREJA, Surrey, England, 1945. Guitarist and founding member of The Yardbirds.

VINCE MARTELL, Bronx, New York, 1945. Guitarist with Vanilla Fudge.

Notes:

STORY OF HIS LIFE! Marty Balin's rock opera *Rock Justice* opens a four-day run at San Francisco's Old Waldorf Nightclub, the story of a rock star who dreams he's on trial for not having a hit record. The premiere is two weeks after the release of *Freedom At Point Zero,* the first Jefferson Starship LP on which Balin does not appear. (1979)

1966   Simon and Garfunkel's *Parsley, Sage, Rosemary & Thyme* is the #1 LP in the U.S.

1979   **Snowy White** joins **Thin Lizzy** and **John Sloman** joins **Uriah Heep.**

1980   **John Lennon's** last single, "Starting Over," is released on Geffen Records, the black-and-white sleeve photo shows **John and Yoko** kissing.

🎵 **RECORD RELEASES** include **Donovan** "Mellow Yellow" and **The Music Machine** "Talk Talk" (1966) . . . and **Billy Joel** "Just The Way You Are" (1978).

Birthdays:

NEIL YOUNG, Toronto, Canada, 1945. Guitarist, singer and song-writer in the Canadian folk scene until he formed The Buffalo Springfield with Steve Stills in 1966, followed by a solo LP, his partnership with Crosby, Stills, Nash & Young, then solo again.

BOOKER T. JONES, Memphis, Tennessee, 1944. Singer and multi-instrumentalist best known for his mid-sixties hit "Green Onions."

BRIAN HYLAND, New York City, 1943. Singer best known for the 1960 hit "Itsy Bitsy Teenie Weenie Yellow Polka Dot Bikini."

BOB CREWE, Newark, New Jersey, 1931. Leader of The Bob Crewe Generation and best known for the sixties hit "Music To Watch Girls By."

Notes:

THE MAGIC OF MEANIES! The Beatles' *Yellow Submarine* premieres in the U.S. The film not only gives the Beatles a new outlet for their music, but also heightens the career of pop artist, Peter Max, and becomes a cult classic among fans and animators alike (1968).

1964 *Our Own Story* by **The Rolling Stones** is published, a group history edited and compiled by **Pete Goodman.** The book makes it into the British top ten paperbacks list within five weeks.

1971 **Pink Floyd's** *Meddle* is released to lukewarm reviews, but contains one of the group's favorite concert pieces, "Echos," an entire album-side composition.

1973 **Peter, Paul & Mary** are awarded a Gold Record for the LP *In The Wind.*

🎵 **RECORD RELEASES** include **The Tokens** "The Lion Sleeps Tonight" (1961). . . **The McCoys** "Fever" and **The Statler Brothers** "Flowers On The Wall" (1965) . . . **Three Dog Night** "Old Fashioned Love Song" and **Jonathan Edwards** "Sunshine" (1971).

Birthdays:

TERRY REID, Paxton Park, England, 1949. Outstanding British session musician with a number of solo LPs, including *Bang Bang You're Terry Reid* in 1969, and a tour with Cream.

Notes:

_____

_____

_____

_____

_____

_____

_____

_____

JOHN & YOKO & THE ARTS! Two films by John and Yoko are screened in Chicago. *Number 5* is a 52 minute close-up of John's face and *Two Virgins* is similarly artistic, but with little substance. (1968)

1942   *New Music Express,* The British music newspaper, first begins publishing record charts based on sales figures.

🎵**RECORD RELEASES** include **The Supremes** "Come See About Me" (1964) . . . **Todd Rundgren** "We Gotta Get You A Woman," **Van Morrison** "Domino," and **Santana** "Black Magic Woman" (1970).

Birthdays:

FREDDIE GARRITY, Manchester, England, 1940. Leader of sixties British pop group, Freddie and The Dreamers.

Van Morrison

ELVIS, ONE STEP BEYOND! Elvis Presley's first film, *Love Me Tender,* a rock and roll western, premieres. It is the first of dozens of films Presley will make before he dies. (1956)

1969 **Janis Joplin** is busted for using "vulgar and indecent" language on stage in Tampa, Florida, and for allegedly threatening to kick a policeman in the face.

1971 **Grand Funk Railroad's** *E Pluribus Funk* LP is released with its eye-catching, round silver-foiled jacket designed to look like an American coin.

1974 *Here's Johnny: Magic Memories From The Tonight Show* is released and is the most expensive two-record package ever in the history of the record business.

1974 The last single from **The Faces** is released, the title nearly as long as the song . . . "You Can Make Me Dance, Sing, or Anything (Even Take The Dog For A Walk, Mend A Fuse, Fold Away The Ironing Board, Or Any Other Domestic Shortcomings.)"

1975 **The Hunter-Ronson Band** disbands, the two former **Mott The Hoople** members opting for solo careers.

1980 A new season of "Saturday Night Live" premieres on NBC-TV with an all-new cast and new producer. Dismal reviews and slipping ratings finds the producer out of a job after twelve weeks.

1980 *Double Fantasy,* **John and Yoko's** final LP, is released.

🎵 **RECORD RELEASES** include **Tommy Roe** "Jam Up Jelly Tight" (1969) . . . and **The Electric Light Orchestra** "Evil Woman" (1975).

Birthdays:

CLYDE McPHATTER, Durham, North Carolina, 1933. Lead singer with The Drifters until a solo career after military service, best known for his hit "Lover Please."

ANNIFRID "FRIDA" ANDERSON, Stockholm, Sweden, 1945. Singer with Abba following a successful TV show, "Hyland's Corner."

PETULA CLARK, Rugby, England, 1932. Singer best known for her sixties hit "Downtown."

Notes:

THE BRIGHT SIDE OF ROCK! Bill Ham first demonstrates his "Light Show," which becomes a stock item at most concerts during the "psychedelic era," allowing bands to perform against a backdrop of melting colors and flashing lights. (1965)

1971   **Led Zeppelin** is awarded a Gold Record for *Led Zeppelin IV.*

1974   *Red,* **King Crimson's** "final" LP, is released after the group disbands. As it turns out, Crimson reforms in 1980 and has issued two more LPs since.

1979   Infinity Records is shut down by parent company, MCA, after producing only three hit singles and one Gold Album in two years of operation.

♪ **RECORD RELEASES** include **The Temptations** "Cloud Nine" and **B.J. Thomas** "Hooked On A Feeling" (1968) . . . and **Stevie Wonder** "Boogie On Reggae Woman" (1974).

Birthdays:

PATTIE SANTOS, 1949. Singer with It's A Beautiful Day, the group best known for the song "White Bird."

Notes:

NOVEMBER 17

ELTON, DEE, NIGEL AND ALL OF NEW YORK CITY! Elton John's *11/17/70* LP is recorded as it is broadcast live over WABC-FM from A&R Recording Studios in New York City. This marks one of the first times that a rock concert, broadcast live, has been recorded for release intact. The British version of the album is titled *17/11/70/.* (1970)

1971 **The Faces'** LP *A Nod Is As Good As A Wink To A Blind Horse* is released, featuring **Rod Stewart** on vocals.

1979 **John Glascock,** bassist with **Jethro Tull,** dies at age 27 in London following open heart surgery.

Birthdays:

GORDON LIGHTFOOT, Orilla, Ontario, Canada, 1939. Singer and songwriter best known for "If You Could Read My Mind."

EUGENE CLARK, Tipton, Missouri, 1941. Guitarist with The Byrds after an early career with The New Christy Minstrels.

BOB GAUDIO, 1942. Singer with The Four Seasons.

Notes:

BIG BAND AND THE ROCKERS! *Procol Harum Live In Concert With The Edmonton Symphony Orchestra* is recorded in Ontario, Canada. The single "Conquistador" emerges as a hit from this unique blend of rock and symphony. (1971)

1967 **Pink Floyd's** "Apples And Oranges," the group's second single, is released in England.

1970 **Traffic** records their "live" LP.

1971 **Junior Parker** dies during an eye operation, leaving behind a history of famous recordings, including "Bad Women, Bad Whiskey."

1972 **Danny Whitten,** singer and songwriter with **Crazy Horse,** dies of an accidental drug overdose at the home of a friend.

1975 **Chicago** is awarded a Gold Record for *Chicago's Greatest Hits.*

🎵 **RECORD RELEASES** include **The Monkees** "Daydream Believer," **Johnny Rivers** "Summer Rain," and **Gary Puckett and The Union Gap** "Woman Woman" (1967) . . . **Steely Dan** "Do It Again" and **Stevie Wonder** "Superstition" (1972) . . . and **The Bee Gees** "Too Much Heaven" (1978).

Birthdays:

HANK BALLARD, Detroit, Michigan, 1936. Singer and songwriter, leader of The Midnighters, a fifties R&B group that recorded "The Twist" before Chubby Checker made it famous.

Notes:

_____

_____

_____

_____

_____

_____

_____

_____

_____

TIME TO DUCKWALK AGAIN! Chuck Berry is released from the Lompoc Prison Farm in California after serving two and a half months in jail for income tax evasion. Berry had shortchanged the government to the tune of $200,000 on his 1973 return and would soon be back on stage doing his famous "duckwalk" and playing his hits. (1980)

1969 **Fleetwood Mac's** "Oh Well" is released and reaches #2 on the British pop charts.

1974 **Pink Floyd's** concert at Trentham Gardens, Stoke, England, is recorded and bootlegged to 150,000 fans, who mistake the concert recording as an official Pink Floyd release.

1975 A "battle of the bands" hits the airwaves in Cincinnati when **Rick Wakeman** and **Gary Brooker** of **Procol Harum** bad-mouth each other on WEBN radio, The dispute began earlier in the evening when Wakeman, headlining the concert, refused to let Procol Harum play with borrowed instruments because the band's equipment van failed to arrive on time.

1977 **Joey Ramone** is burned by an exploding teapot backstage before a concert in New Jersey.

🎵 **RECORD RELEASES** include **The Temptations** "(I Know) I'm Losing You" (1966) . . . and **Steely Dan** "Peg" (1977).

Birthdays:

RAY COLLINS, 1937. Singer with The Mothers Of Invention.

FRED LIPSIUS, New York City, 1944. Sax player with Blood, Sweat & Tears, a founding member of the band.

Joey Ramone

NOVEMBER 20

WHO, TO THE BEAT OF A DIFFERENT DRUMMER! Nineteen-year-old Scott Halpin is the star of the night at The Who concert at The Cow Palace in San Francisco when he replaces an ailing Keith Moon on drums for the last three songs of the concert. Halpin gets the gig when he responds to Roger Daltry's plea "Is there a drummer in the house?" Young Halpin's set clincher draws cheers from the 14,000 in the audience. (1973)

1961 **Bob Dylan's** first recording session begins for his LP *Bob Dylan*.

1971 **Isaac Hayes** is #1 in the U.S. with his first hit single, theme from "Shaft."

1973 Comedian, **Allan Sherman,** dies of respiratory failure. The Jewish comedian established his popularity in the sixties with the novelty hit, "Hello Mudda, Hello Fadda."

🎵 **RECORD RELEASES** include **Simon and Garfunkel's** "Sounds Of Silence" (1965) . . . and **Manfred Mann's Earth Band** "Blinded By The Light" (1976).

Birthdays:

DUANE ALLMAN, Nashville, Tennessee, 1946. Guitarist and co-founder of The Allman Brothers Band after a highly acclaimed background with Eric Clapton in Derek and The Dominos, Wilson Pickett and Aretha Franklin.

JOE WALSH, Cleveland, Ohio, 1947. Guitarist and singer, founding member of The James Gang in 1965, then formed Barnstorm before joining The Eagles in 1976, with solid contributions to their Grammy winning LP *Hotel California.* Walsh continues to record and perform solo.

Notes:

_____

_____

_____

_____

_____

_____

_____

_____

_____

NOVEMBER 21

WELL, MAYBE ONE MORE TIME! Marty Balin makes a surprise appearance with The Jefferson Starship during a concert in San Francisco. Balin had left the band years before, vowing never to return and his comeback was as much a surprise to the group as to the audience. (1974)

1968   The tragic coincidence of miscarriages for **Yoko** (John recorded the heartbeat of the baby earlier in the day) and, within 24 hours, for **Marianne Faithful,** pregnant with **Mick Jagger's** child.

1968   The **Beatles** are awarded a Gold Record for the *White Album,* an instant million seller.

1974   **Wilson Pickett** is arrested by police in Andes, New York, for possession of a dangerous weapon.

1975   The "Kiss Army" is first organized for a gathering in Terre Haute, Indiana. Mayor William Brighton declares it "Kiss Day" in his city.

1980   **Eagles** drummer, **Don Henley,** is arrested at his home in Los Angeles when a 16-year-old girl is found nude and over-dosed on the premises. Henley is charged with possession of various drugs and contributing to the delinquency of a minor.

RECORD RELEASES include **The Shirelles** "Will You Still Love Me Tomorrow" (1960). . . and **Led Zeppelin** "Immigant Song" (1970).

Birthdays:

LIVINGSTON TAYLOR, 1950. Singer and songwriter, brother of James Taylor, with some success as a solo artist.

DR. JOHN, born Malcolm John Rebennack, New Orleans, Louisiana, 1941. Guitarist, pianist and singer, studio musician with Phil Spector, Sam Cooke, Sonny & Cher and others before forming Dr. John and The Night Trippers in 1978. Mick Jagger and Eric Clapton pay tribute to his talents by appearing on his 1971 LP, *Sun, Moon and Herbs.*

Notes:

THE SIGNING OF A LIFETIME! Elvis Presley signs a contract with RCA Victor after being released from his contract with Sun Records. It proves to be a gold mine for RCA as Presley stays with the company for the remainder of his career. (1955)

1963 **Phil Spector's** *Christmas Album* is withheld from release when the nation's attention is monopolized by news of President Kennedy's assassination.

1965 **Bob Dylan** and **Sara Lowndes** are married. He describes her as "the sad-eyed lady of the lowlands."

1967 **Sam and Dave** are awarded a Gold Record for "Soul Man."

1968 "Alice's Restaurant," **Arlo Guthrie's** 22-minute Thanksgiving classic, is released on **Reprise Records.** The story is later made into a film.

1969 **Joe Cocker** debuts in the U.S. charts for the first time with the LP *With A Little Help From My Friends,* featuring support from **Jimmy Page, Steve Winwood** and **Albert Lee.**

🎵 **RECORD RELEASES** include **Led Zeppelin** "Whole Lotta Love" (1969) . . . and **Nazareth** "Love Hurts" (1975).

Birthdays:

STEVE VAN ZANDT, 1949. Guitarist and singer with Bruce Springsteen's E Street Band, known as "Miami" Steve.

Notes:

_____

_____

_____

_____

_____

_____

_____

_____

FISH OUT OF WATER! Country Joe McDonald quits The Fish, leaving the band without a lead singer, arranger and composer, although the group attempts to survive as The Incredible Fish. McDonald pursues a solo career. (1968)

1899   The first jukebox is installed at the Palais Royal Hotel in San Francisco by the Pacific Phonograph Company.

1964   **The Rolling Stones** are banned by the BBC after they arrive late for a radio program.

1974   **Gary Wright** quits **Spooky Tooth** to pursue a solo career and eight months later releases his *Dream Weaver* LP, featuring a title song that becomes #1.

1974   **Frankie Valli's** "My Eyes Adore You" is released.

1979   **Marianne Faithful** is arrested at Oslo Airport and charged with possession of marijuana. She signs a full confession and is set free to resume her concert tour.

Notes:

VIDEO ROCKS WITH THE RECORD STARS! *In Concert* premieres on ABC-TV, a program created by Don Kirshner to allow rock acts to work in a concert before a live audience with the same high quality sound they would get in a recording studio. The debut program features Alice Cooper, The Allman Brothers Band, Chuck Berry, Blood, Sweat and Tears, Seals and Crofts, Poco and others. (1972)

1958 **Record Releases** include **Richie Valens** "Donna" . . . and **Jackie Wilson** "Lonely Teardrops."

1962 "James Bond Theme" by **Norman Mingo** enters the British charts and will be followed, in years to come, by other Bond themes that will be hits including, "Goldfinger" by **Shirley Bassey** and, "Thunderball," by **Tom Jones.**

1972 **Rick Nelson** is awarded a Gold Record for his single "Garden Party"

Birthdays:

BEV BEVAN, Birmingham, England, 1946. Drummer and original member of The Move, evolving with Jeff Lynne and Roy Wood to ELO.

LEE MICHAELS, Los Angeles, California, 1945. Singer and multi-instrumentalist with his own Lee Michaels Band, best known for the hit single "Do You Know What I Mean?" in 1971.

ROBIN WILLIAMSON, Glasgow, Scotland, 1943. Co-founder of The Incredible String Band.

SCOTT JOPLIN, Father of Dixieland Rag music, his style revived in the mid-seventies on the hit "The Sting," from the film.

Notes:

_____

_____

_____

_____

_____

_____

_____

_____

SAVING THE LAST DANCE! "The Last Waltz," the final concert by The Band, occurs at San Francisco's Winterland theater, the venue where The Band debuted seven years before. Bob Dylan, Neil Young, Joni Mitchell, Van Morrison, Eric Clapton, Steve Stills and Ringo Starr are among the galaxy of stars participating, with director Martin Scorcese filming the event for the film *The Last Waltz.* (1976)

1955 **Bill Haley** and **The Comets**' "Rock Around The Clock" is #1 in Britain.

1968 The **Beatles** *White Album* is released in the U.S., a double album individually numbered with color photos of each of the Beatles, as well as a fold-out poster.

1969 **John Lennon** returns his MBE medal as a protest against British involvment in Biafra and British support of American involvement in Vietnam. Lennon's latest LP *Cold Turkey* is also slipping down the charts.

1972 A disappointing crowd of only 32,000 turn out for the "Woodstock Of The West" concert sponsored by a Los Angeles radio station, starring **Sly and The Family Stone, Stevie Wonder, Mott The Hoople, The Eagles, The Bee Gees** and others.

1976 **Rick Wakeman** rejoins **Yes** as keyboardist, after quitting the group three years earlier to pursue a solo career.

Notes:

_____

_____

_____

_____

_____

_____

_____

_____

NO MORE FRESH CREAM! Cream perform their farewell concert at Royal Albert Hall in London before a capacity crowd of 5,000, the performance filmed by the BBC for release as *The Cream.* (1968)

1966 **The Monkees** are awarded a Gold Record for "I'm A Believer."

1973 **The New York Dolls** make their concert debut in a London restaurant.

1973 **John Rostill** of **The Shadows** is electrocuted. The Shadows had more than twenty hits in Britain before disbanding in 1968.

1976 **Lol Creme** and **Kevin Godley** quit **10cc** to develop their new instrument, "the Gizmo," an electric guitar synthesizer.

1980 *Wings Over America* has its film premiere in New York, capturing the first American tour of **Paul McCartney and Wings.**

Birthdays:

TINA TURNER, born Annie Mae Bullock, Brownsville, Tennessee, 1938. Singer and songwriter with husband Ike Turner, best known for the hit "River Deep, Mountain High." Her film credits include the "Acid Queen" in *Tommy.*

JOHN McVIE, England, 1945. Bassist and original member of John Mayall's Bluesbreakers before forming Fleetwood Mac with Peter Green in 1967.

Jimi Hendrix

FROM THE COLLECTION OF NEAL PETERS

RECORD BREAKING FEVER! *Saturday Night Fever* breaks box office records and makes a star of John Travolta, and The Bee Gees for a second time. The soundtrack LP from the film becomes one of the biggest albums of all time. (1977)

1960 **The Shirelles** are #1 in the U.S. with **Carole King's** "Will You Still Love Me Tomorrow."

1964 **Mick Jagger** fined 16 pounds sterling for reckless driving in Staffordshire, England.

1964 *Beatles For Sale* is released in England, featuring the single "I Feel Fine."

1967 The **Beatles** *Magical Mystery Tour* LP is released in the U.S.

🎵 **RECORD RELEASES** include **The Lovin' Spoonful** "You Didn't Have To Be So Nice" (1965) . . . **Break** "Lost Without Your Love" and **Queen** "Somebody To Love" (1976).

Birthdays:

JIMI HENDRIX, born Johnny Allen Hendrix (then changed to James Marshall Hendrix by his father when he returned from World War II) Seattle, Washington, 1942. Guitarist and singer. Perhaps the most innovative guitarist of rock as a completely free-form experimenter with his instrument. Beginning as a session player with James Brown, The Isley Brothers and Little Richard, he formed The Jimi Hendrix Experience in 1966 in London with a boost into stardom at The Monterey Pop Festival and Woodstock. His unique guitar style remains unmatched.

AL JACKSON, 1935. Drummer with Booker T. and The MGs.

Notes:

333

JOHN AND JOHN, STANDING THERE! John Lennon joins Elton John on stage at Madison Square Garden in New York, the occasion marking Lennon's last concert appearance. The two join voices for "Whatever Gets You Through The Night" and "I Saw Her Standing There." (1974)

1964   **The Shangri-Las** "Leader Of The Pack" is #1 in the U.S.

1968   **John Lennon** pleads guilty to possession of cannabis resin for which he was arrested the previous month.

🎵 **RECORD RELEASES** include **George Harrison** "My Sweet Lord" and **Elton John** "Your Song" (1970).

Birthdays:

RANDY NEWMAN, Los Angeles, California, 1943. Singer, song-writer and pianist best known for his biting lyrics on songs like the hit "Short People." Scored the soundtrack for the 1981 film "Ragtime," which won him an Academy Award nomination.

BERRY GORDY, JR. Detroit, Michigan, 1929. Songwriter and record company executive who wrote the million seller "Lonely Teardrops" for Jackie Wilson and "You Got What It Takes" for Marv Johnson. Formed Tamla Records with $700 loan, which evolved into Motown Records, the hugely successful label for The Supremes, Stevie Wonder, Smokey Robinson and scores of others.

Randy Newman

ON A CRISP NIGHT, OOH LA LA! Supertramp is recorded live during a concert in Paris, a performance to be released as the double LP *Paris*. Outstanding performances and superb production quality makes it one of the most outstanding live sets on disc. (1979)

1965 Colorado governor, **John Love,** declares "Rolling Stones Day" in Denver, the day after the band sells out a concert date.

1968 *The Who Sell Out,* the first concert record from **The Who,** is released. The LP features radio jingles and commercials in between the songs, along with the hit "I Can See For Miles."

1975 "Squeeze Box" by **The Who** is released.

1978 **Paul Simon** sues CBS Records claiming the label is bent on destroying his reputation and career. Simon has already signed with Warner Brothers Records.

Birthdays:

JOHN MAYALL, Cheshire, England, 1933. Singer and multi-instrumentalist, recognized as the "grandfather" of the British rock movement with his Bluesbreakers band, which allowed many of the top rock musicians a place to begin.

DENNY DOHERTY, Halifax, Novia Scotia, 1941. Singer and original member of The Mamas and The Papas and a member of the group when it reformed in 1982.

FELIX CAVALIERE, Pelham, New York, 1944. Keyboardist with Joey Dee and The Starlighters before forming The Young Rascals.

Notes:

S & G and A T & T! Simon and Garfunkel's first TV special airs without the support of the original sponsor, AT&T, which bailed out when the company learned the program features left wing philosophy, illustrated by footage of Bobby Kennedy's funeral march and clips of fighting in Vietnam. (1969)

1973 Jazz drummer, **Buddy Rich,** is busted for possession of marijuana while touring Australia, the second bust of the 56-year-old percussionist. Rich pleads "not guilty" and charges are dropped.

1977 **David Bowie** joins **Bing Crosby** on Crosby's 42nd Annual Christmas Special. The pair sing a duet of "Little Drummer Boy."

♫**RECORD RELEASES** include **Sly and The Family Stone** "Everyday People" (1968) . . . and **The Eagles** "Best Of My Love" (1974).

Birthdays:

ROGER GLOVER, Brecon, South Wales, 1945. Bassist and producer with Deep Purple replacing Nick Simper, then with Ritchie Blackmore's Rainbow.

(NOEL) PAUL STOOKEY, Baltimore, Maryland, 1937. Singer and founding member of Peter, Paul & Mary.

DICK CLARK, New York City, 1929. Disc jockey, concert promoter, TV host and producer. Although not a musician himself, Clark helped the careers of many musicians and singers by inviting them to perform on his "American Bandstand" TV show, one of the longest running TV programs to date.

Notes:

!!#?%?ß#&&! The Sex Pistols shock Britain when group leader, Johnny Rotten, swears on live TV. The network later determines that host, Bill Grundy, provoked the obscenities, but the group's fate is sealed. For days, British newspapers play up the event with headlines like "The Punks . . . Rotten and Proud Of It," and many concert dates are cancelled on their first British tour. (1976)

1966 **The Mamas and Papas** are awarded a Gold Record for the debut LP *Mamas & Papas*.

1969 **Magic Sam** dies at age 32. He's a blues guitarist and singer best known for the 1964 hit "High Heeled Sneakers."

1971 **John Lennon's** "Happy Christmas" is released, furthering his and Yoko's message to the world that "War Is Over, If You Want It. Happy Christmas, John & Yoko."

1975 **Bette Midler** undergoes an emergency appendectomy.

Birthdays:

JOHN DENSMORE, Los Angeles, California, 1945. Drummer with The Doors, an original member of the group until two years after the death of Jim Morrison, then with Robbie Kreiger in the Butts Band and later a career in dance.

BETTE MIDLER, Paterson, New Jersey, 1945. Singer and songwriter who began as an actress and quickly moved to a bawdy cabaret style stage show following the release of her first LP in 1972. Her film credits include the lead role in *The Rose*.

LOU RAWLS, Chicago, Illinois, 1936. Singer and songwriter with a gospel background and credits with Sam Cooke; a successful solo career followed.

Notes:

_____

_____

_____

_____

_____

_____

_____

_____

GOOD TIMES GONE BAD! Kris Kristofferson and Rita Coolidge divorce after six years of marriage, a time during which each has built a successful career. The two appeared together in the film *Pat Garrett and Billy The Kid.* (1979)

1971   Taj Mahal performs a Death Row concert for the inmates at Washington State Penitentiary.

1974   Sitarist, Ravi Shankar, is hospitalized in Chicago while touring with George Harrison. He's released two weeks later and rejoins the tour in Boston.

1980   Joni Mitchell makes her cable TV debut on "Shadows and Light," a Showtime special of an eighty-minute concert taped at the Santa Barbara County Bowl in California.

♫ RECORD RELEASES include **The American Breed** "Bend Me, Shape Me" (1967) . . . **Dr. Hook** "Cover Of The Rolling Stone," **Hurricane Smith** "Oh Babe, What Would You Say?" and **Carly Simon** "You're So Vain" (1972).

Birthdays:

TOM McGUINESS, London, England, 1941. Bassist with Manfred Mann until 1969 when he formed the McGuiness-Flint group.

RICK SAVAGE, Birmingham, England, 1960. Guitarist with Def Leppard, an original member of the band.

Joni Mitchell

DECEMBER 3

TRAGEDY AT THE RIVERFRONT! Eleven concert goers die and dozens are injured during the rush to get good seats at a Who concert in Cincinnati. Festival seating and too few open doors is blamed for the tragedy and, as a result, festival seating is banned in Cincinnati and other cities. (1979)

1938 **Alfred Lennon** marries **Julia Stanley**. They have one child, a son, **John.**

1971 **Frank Zappa and The Mothers of Invention** concert in Montreux, Switzerland, is halted when a fire breaks out. $50,000 worth of equipment is lost as the Montreux Casino burns to the ground.

1976 **The Sex Pistols** first single, "Anarchy In The U.K.," is released.

1976 A tired and punchy **Jackson Browne** drops his pants on stage at the Oakland Paramount Theater in California when a fan shouts to him, "get loose!"

1977 **Fleetwood Mac's** *Rumors* LP slips to #2 in the U.S. after a record 29 weeks at the top. It's replaced by the soundtrack to *Saturday Night Fever.*

🎵 **RECORD RELEASES** include **The Mamas and The Papas** "Words Of Love," **Otis Redding** "Try A Little Tenderness," **Paul Revere and The Raiders** "Good Thing," and **The Seekers** "Georgy Girl" (1966).

Birthdays:

OZZY OSBOURNE, born John Robert Osbourne, Birmingham, England, 1948. Singer and songwriter with Earth, which evolved into Black Sabbath. Ozzy left in 1980 to pursue a successful solo career.

MICKEY THOMAS, 1949. Singer with the Elvin Bishop band until joining The Jefferson Starship during the recording of the LP *Freedom At Point Zero.*

Notes:

THE ZEPPELIN IS GROUNDED! The official announcement comes in a written statement signed by Robert Plant, John Paul Jones and Jimmy Page two months after the death of Led Zeppelin drummer, John Bonham. "We wish it to be known that the loss of our dear friend and the deep respect we have for his family, together with the sense of undivided harmony felt by ourselves and our manager, have led us to decide that we could not continue as we were." (1980)

1965 **Keith Richards** is nearly electrocuted when he attempts to move an ungrounded microphone with the neck of his guitar and is knocked cold for seven minutes.

1971 **Sly and The Family Stone's** "Family Affair" is #1 in the U.S.

1976 **Bob Marley** is shot at his home in Kingston, Jamaica, two days before he was to headline a reggae concert organized by supporters of Prime Minister, **Michael Manley.** Despite an arm wound, Marley performs the concert and leaves himself open for another possible attack.

1976 Guitarist, **Tommy Bolin,** dies of a heroin overdose in a Miami hotel.

🎵 **GOLD RECORDS** awarded to **Fleetwood Mac** for *Fleetwood Mac* LP (1974) . . . and to **Kiss** for *Kiss Alive* (1975).

🎵 **RECORD RELEASES** include **Paul Revere and The Raiders** "Just Like Me" and the **Kinks** "Well Respected Man' (1965) . . . and **Badfinger** "Day After Day" (1971).

Birthdays:

CHRIS HILLMAN, Los Angeles, California, 1942. Bassist and singer, original member of The Byrds and then The Flying Burrito Brothers, later joining with former Byrd's Clarke and McGuinn in a trio.

DENNIS WILSON, Hawthorne, California, 1944. Drummer and original member of The Beach Boys.

GARY ROSSINGTON, Jacksonville, Florida, 1952. Guitarist and original member of Lynyrd Skynyrd, then founding member of The Rossington-Collins Band, formed from survivors of the plane crash that ended Lynyrd Skynyrd.

Notes:

MY WAY . . . OR THE HIGHWAY! Graham Nash quits The Hollies when he learns of plans for the group to record an album of Bob Dylan songs against his advice. Nash goes on to form Crosby, Stills and Nash. (1968)

1964   **The Zombies** and **The Kinks** enter the U.S. singles charts on the same day with two classics, "She's Not There" and "You Really Got Me."

1968   **The Rolling Stones** hold a real "Beggars Banquet" at the Elizabethan Rooms in London to celebrate the release of the album of the same name.

1973   **Pink Floyd** releases *A Nice Pair,* a double LP repackaging of the band's first two albums, *The Piper At The Gates Of Dawn* and *A Saucerful Of Secrets.*

1975   **Seals and Crofts** awarded a Gold Record for the *Greatest Hits* LP.

1976   **Billy Joel's** performance at Palmer Auditorium at the University of Connecticut at New London is recorded and later issued as *Souvenir,* a DJ promotional disc not available to the public but widely played on radio.

🎵 **RECORD RELEASES** include **The Bee Gees** "Lonely Days" (1970).

Birthdays:

JIM MESSINA, Maywood, California, 1947. Singer and guitarist with The Buffalo Springfield, then founding member of Poco in 1968 and later, partner with Kenny Loggins in Loggins & Messina.

LIITTLE RICHARD, born Richard Penniman, Macon, Georgia, 1935. Singer, songwriter and pianist, one of the early innovators of rock 'n' roll with a string of hits, including "Long Tall Sally," "Good Golly, Miss Molly" and "Tutti Fruitti."

JOHN CALE, Wales, 1940. Singer and multi-instrumentalist with The Velvet Underground, an original member of the band with Lou Reed, later recorded solo and produces records.

MIKE SMITH, London, England, 1943. Singer and keyboardist with The Dave Clark Five.

Notes:

ROCK FROM THE DEVIL! Four die at a Rolling Stones concert at Altamont Speedway near San Francisco, including 18-year-old Meredith Hunter who is stabbed to death by a Hell's Angel security guard. Both the concert and murder are captured in the film *Gimme Shelter,* which premieres in New York exactly one year later. (1969)

1965   **The Rolling Stones** record "19th Nervous Breakdown" and "Mothers Little Helper" at RCA Studios in London.

1965   The **Beatles** *Rubber Soul* LP and the single "Day Tripper" are released in the U.S.

1967   **The Rolling Stones** are awarded a Gold Record for the LP *Their Satanic Majesties Request,* on advance sales.

1970   National Educational Television broadcasts its first rock show, "San Francisco Rock: Go Ride The Music," mostly a compilation of film clips of **The Jefferson Airplane** in rehearsal.

1978   The FBI coordinates raids in five cities and confiscates $100 million in bootleg record cutting equipment, virtually wiping out half the U.S. counterfeit recording industry.

Birthdays:

JONATHAN KING, London, England, 1948. Singer and songwriter best known for the single "Everyone's Gone To The Moon."

Notes:

DECEMBER 7

DRESS WITH SUCCESS! The Apple Boutique opens at 94 Baker Street in London and is immediately mobbed by fans who want to be close to anything the Beatles are involved with. Hot items include the marching band jacket styles worn by the Fab Four on *Sgt. Pepper's.* (1967)

1955 **The Teddy Bears** "To Know Him Is To Love Him," a **Phil Spector** song, is #1 in the U.S.

1974 South African, **Ricky Fataar,** quits **The Beach Boys.**

1978 **Sid Vicious** is arrested for assaulting **Patti Smith's** brother, **Todd,** with a beer mug in a Manhattan night club. Vicious was free on bail and awaiting trial for the murder of his girlfriend, **Nancy Spungen.**

🎵RECORD RELEASES include **The Trashmen** "Surfin' Bird" (1963) . . . **Diana Ross & The Supremes** and **The Temptations** "I'm Gonna Make You Love Me" (1968) . . . and **Linda Ronstadt** "You're No Good" (1974).

Birthdays:

TOM WAITS, Pomona, California, 1949. Singer and songwriter best known for his gravel-voiced, smoky-bar style songs.

HARRY CHAPIN, New York City, 1942. Singer and songwriter best known for his story-telling in songs like "Taxi" and "Cat's In The Cradle." Heavily involved in benefit work for World Hunger.

Notes:

343

LOST AND GONE FOREVER! John Lennon is shot and killed outside the Dakota Apartments in New York City after he and Yoko return from a recording session for their next single. Murderer, Mark David Chapman, fires four shots at Lennon after calling out his name. (1980)

1961 **The Beach Boys'** first single, "Surfin'," is released on Candix Records and becomes a local hit in Los Angeles. The group chooses its name to fit the song.

1967 **Traffic's** debut LP *Mr. Fantasy* is released.

1969 **Jimi Hendrix** testifies before an all-male jury in Toronto Supreme Court on charges of possession of heroin and hashish found in a flight bag during a routine search at Toronto International Airport. After three days of testimony, Hendrix is acquitted.

1970 **Jim Morrison** records his original poetry, which becomes his final album *An American Prayer.* **The Doors** lead singer tapes the mostly death-oriented verse on his 27th and last birthday.

1972 **Carly Simon** is awarded a Gold Record for the LP *No Secrets.*

1975 **Bob Dylan's Rolling Thunder Revue** winds up its concert tour at Madison Square Garden in New York.

1975 Record executive, **Ken Moss,** pleads guilty to charges of involuntary manslaughter in the drug-induced death of **Average White Band** drummer **Robbie McIntosh.**

🎵 **RECORD RELEASES** include **Lloyd Price** "Staggerlee" (1958).

Birthdays:

JIM MORRISON, Melbourne, Florida, 1943. Singer and songwriter, founding member of The Doors, one of the top bands of the sixties with "Light My Fire" and "Riders On The Storm." The Doors music surged into popularity again in the early eighties ten years after the band's demise.

GREGG ALLMAN, Nashville, Tennessee, 1947. Keyboardist and singer with The Allman Brothers Band, a founding member with his brother Duane.

BOBBY ELLIOTT, Lancashire, England, 1942. Drummer with The Hollies as replacement for Don Rathbone in 1963.

Notes:

WHO KNOWS BETTER NOW! *Tommy* premieres in London, the first stage presentation of The Who's classic rock opera. The cast includes Rod Stewart, Keith Moon, Peter Sellers, Steve Winwood, Maggie Bell, Merry Clayton and Roger Daltry. Ticket prices are $50 and more and *Tommy* is the hottest item on the social calendar in London. The reviews are dismal. (1973)

1967   **Jim Morrison** is maced backstage in New Haven, Connecticut, by a security officer who mistakes the singer for a fan. Morrison retaliates with verbal abuse of the officer on stage and dragged off and jailed, his first in a series of busts at **Doors** concerts.

1967   **Cream's** *Disreali Gears* LP enters the charts.

1971   **Carole King** is awarded a Gold Record for her LP *Music.*

1972   **Helen Reddy's** "I Am Woman" is #1 in the U.S.

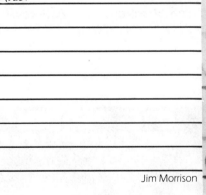 **RECORD RELEASES** include **Elton John** "Crocodile Rock" (1972) . . . and **The Blues Brothers** "Soul Man" (1978).

Birthdays:

RICK DANKO, Ontario, Canada, 1943. Bassist with The Hawks, which evolved into The Band, later pursued a solo career.

Notes:

Jim Morrison

LOVE IS DANGEROUS! Frank Zappa is attacked on stage during a concert in London by 24-year-old Trevor Howell, who shoves Zappa into the orchestra pit causing a broken leg and ankle and a fractured skull. "I did it because my girlfriend said she loved Frank!"—Trevor Howell. (1971)

1949 **Fats Domino** records "The Fat Man" in New Orleans.

1966 **The Beach Boys'** "Good Vibrations" is #1 in the U.S. replacing "Winchester Cathedral."

1967 **Otis Redding** and four of the **Bar-Kays** are killed in a plane crash near Madison, Wisconsin.

1968 **Robin Gibb** of **The Bee Gees** marries **Molly Hullis** after two years of living together.

1973 **Frank Zappa's** "Roxy And Elsewhere" is recorded live at The Roxy in Hollywood.

1976 Guitarist, **Tommy Bolin,** is buried wearing the same ring worn by **Jimi Hendrix** the day he died, a present from **Deep Purple's** manager.

🎵 **RECORD RELEASES** include **The Blues Magoos** "We Ain't Got Nothin' Yet," **The Electric Prunes** "I Had Too Much To Dream Last Night," **Keith** "98.6," and **The Monkees** "I'm A Believer" (1966) . . . and **The Bee Gees** "Stayin' Alive" (1976).

Birthdays:

CHAD STUART, Durham, England, 1943. Half of singing duo Chad & Jeremy.

Notes:

Otis Redding

THE FINAL SEND-OFF! Sam Cooke is shot and killed under sordid circumstances by a 22-year-old woman he allegedly was trying to rape. A court later ruled the shooting was justifiable homocide in self defense. Cooke was 34. (1964)

1968 **John Lennon** takes part in the filming of **The Rolling Stones'** "Rock And Roll Circus" TV program.

1970 Two *Plastic Ono Band* LPs are released on the same day, one by **John** and the other by **Yoko.** John's features "Mother" and "Working Class Hero."

1973 **James Brown** is arrested and charged with disorderly conduct following a concert in Knoxville, Tennessee. The charges are dropped when the soul singer threatens to sue the city for $1 million, claiming he was beaten by the police.

1976 **Kiss** guitarist, **Ace Frehley,** is nearly electrocuted when he touches a short-circuited railing light that had fallen to the floor during a concert in Lakeland, Florida. Frehley recovers ten minutes after being carried from the stage and finishes the set.

♫ **RECORD RELEASES** include **Carly Simon** "Anticipation" (1971) . . . **Al Stewart** "Year Of The Cat" and **Bob Seger** "Night Moves" (1976).

Birthdays:

BRENDA LEE, Atlanta, Georgia, 1944. Singer best known for her 1961 hit "I'm Sorry."

JERMAINE JACKSON, Gary, Indiana, 1954. Singer with The Jackson Five.

DAVID GATES, Tulsa, Oklahoma, 1940. Singer and multi-instrumentalist, originally a studio musician before co-founding Bread in 1969.

Notes:

DECEMBER 12

BIG TROUBLE IN A SMALL PACKAGE! Jerry Lee Lewis secretly marries 13-year-old Myra Lewis, the daughter of his cousin, J.W. Brown. The marriage takes place a full five months before Lewis is divorced from his second wife and is such a major scandal that it nearly ruins his career. (1957)

1966   Pink Floyd performs their first concert in a large hall, a special benefit for Oxfam called "You're Joking?" at Royal Albert Hall in London.

1967   Brian Jones wins the appeal of his recent drug conviction and is given three years probation instead of nine months in prison.

1969   Plastic Ono Band makes its concert debut at The Toronto Peace Festival, starring the hastily assembled **Eric Clapton, Klaus Voorman, Alan White** and **John & Yoko.** The group had never played live together before hitting the stage.

1973   Emerson, Lake & Palmer are awarded a Gold Record for the LP *Brain Salad Surgery.*

1975   Alice Cooper becomes the first internationally known rock act to headline The Sahara Tahoe Hotel and he treats the gambling crowd to his "Welcome To My Nightmare" show.

🎵 **RECORD RELEASES** include **The Righteous Brothers** "You've Lost That Lovin' Feeling" (1964) . . . and **Steve Stills** "Love The One You're With" (1970).

Birthdays:

DIONNE WARWICK, East Orange, New Jersey, 1941. Singer known for numerous hits including "Walk On By" and "Do You Know The Way To San Jose."

CONNIE FRANCIS, Belleville, New Jersey, 1938. Singer who first topped the charts in 1958 with "Who's Sorry Now."

PAUL ROGERS, Yorkshire, England, 1949. Singer with Bad Company, an original member of the group after his involvement with Paul Kossoff in Free.

DICKY BETTS, West Palm Beach, Florida, 1943. Guitarist and original member of The Allman Brothers, with a brief solo career in the late seventies.

CLIVE BUNKER, England, 1946. Drummer with Jethro Tull.

Notes:

LUNCH WITH JERRY AND GEORGE! George Harrison becomes the first rock artist ever to receive an official greeting at The White House by a President of The United States, when he lunches with President Ford. The meeting is arranged by Ford's son, Jack, and coincides with Harrison's concert in Washington D.C. The former Beatle and the President exchange buttons . . . George's "OM" button for a Ford "WIN" button. (1974)

♪ **GOLD RECORDS** include **The London Symphony Orchestra** for "Tommy" (1972) . . . and **Bachman-Turner Overdrive** for "You Ain't Seen Nothin' Yet" (1974).

♪ **RECORD RELEASES** include **Shocking Blue** "Venus" (1969) . . . **David Bowie** "Golden Years" and **Foghat** "Slow Ride" (1975).

Birthdays:

JEFF BAXTER, Washington, D.C., 1948. Guitarist with Steely Dan, then with The Doobie Brothers.

TED NUGENT, Detroit, Michigan, 1949. Guitarist and singer with The Lourdes, then co-founder of The Amboy Dukes before launching a successful solo career.

George Harrison

FIRST ONE TO LEAVE ALIVE! Mick Taylor quits The Rolling Stones while the rest of the band is recording in Munich. The lead guitarist had replaced Brian Jones five years earlier and would move on to form a new group with Cream bassist, Jack Bruce, leaving the way open for Ron Wood to join The Stones. (1974)

1968 **Iron Butterfly** is awarded a Gold Record for their 17-minute classic "In-A-Gadda-Da-Vida," from an LP that would stay on the charts two years and become one of the biggest grossing albums of all time.

1971 **John Lennon** and **Yoko Ono** perform at a farewell dinner for UN secretary general U Thant.

1972 **Seals and Crofts** are awarded a Gold Record for the single "Summer Breeze."

1973 **Gordon Sinclair** records *The Americans,* the famous pro-American essay backed by a chorus of "My Country 'Tis Of Thee."

1974 **The Baker-Gurvitz Army** is formed with former **Cream** drummer, **Ginger Baker,** and the **Gurvitz Brothers, Adrian and Paul.**

♬ **RECORD RELEASES** include **Tommy James and The Shondells** "Crimson & Clover" (1968) . . . and **Styx** "Lady" (1974).

Notes: _____

_____

_____

_____

_____

_____

_____

DECEMBER 15

TO LAUGH THE TRAGIC LAUGH! *The First Family* by John Kennedy impressionist, Vaughn Meader, is #1 on the U.S. album charts and is accepted by the President as a good piece of American humor. When Kennedy is assassinated two years later, both the LP and Meader drop from sight. (1961)

1964 The *Beatles '65* LP is released in the U.S.

1967 The **Beatles** are awarded a Gold Record for the *Magical Mystery Tour* LP.

1969 **John** and **Yoko** perform a benefit concert for UNICEF at the Lyceum Gallery in London. The concert sets the stage for the world-wide billboard campaign to spread the message "War Is Over/If You Want It/Happy Christmas . . . John and Yoko." **George Harrison** and **Delaney & Bonnie** join the **Plastic Ono Band** for the event.

1977 **The Who** perform a secret concert for *The Kids Are Alright* movie.

🎵 **RECORD RELEASES** include **Ringo Starr** "You're Sixteen" (1973).

Birthdays:

JOHN HAMMOND, 1915. Columbia Records executive who is responsible for signing label deals with Bob Dylan, Bruce Springsteen and many others.

ALAN FREED, Pennsylvania, 1922. Famous fifties DJ who coined the phrase "rock 'n' roll" and whose career ended with payola scandals of 1960.

DAVE CLARK, Tottenham, England, 1942. Drummer and founder of The Dave Clark Five, a band formed to raise money for Clark's rugby team.

CARMINE APPICE, Staten Island, New York, 1946. Drummer and founding member of Vanilla Fudge in 1966, then Cactus and later Beck, Bogert & Appice. In the eighties he performed with Rod Stewart and Ted Nugent as well as his own Carmine Appice & Friends band.

Notes:

DECEMBER 16

ENTER JOHN TRAVOLTA AND DISCO! *Saturday Night Fever* premieres and the gateway to the American disco movement is opened. The film becomes one of the biggest box office draws ever and the soundtrack LP sets a new record for the most weeks at #1 on Billboard's Hot 100 chart. It also launches John Travolta's acting career in film. (1977)

1966 "Hey Joe," the first single by **Jimi Hendrix,** is released and gets instant airplay on both U.S. and British radio.

1967 **Pink Floyd's** first performance at The Middle Earth Club, one of London's major rock venues.

1971 **Don McLean's** "American Pie" is released and becomes a smash hit, even though the lyrics are hazy, at best.

1972 **Joan Baez** witnesses the American bombing of Hanoi as she arrives in the city by invitation of The Committee For Solidarity With The American People, (just as U.S. bombers deliver their payload).

1973 **Steve Stills** becomes the father of a two-year-old boy when he loses a paternity suit filed against him by **Harriet Tunis** of Mill Valley, California. She refused Stills' suggestion that they settle quietly out of court.

1974 **Ian Hunter** quits **Mott The Hoople** to form another band with guitarist, **Mick Ronson.**

♪ **GOLD RECORDS** awarded to **Creedence Clearwater Revival** for their debut LP (1968) . . . and for their single "Bad Moon Rising" (1970).

♪ **RECORD RELEASES** include **The Lemon Pipers** "Green Tambourine" (1967) . . . and **Paul McCartney** "Hi, Hi, Hi" (1972).

Birthdays:

ANTHONY HICKS, Lancashire, England, 1945. Guitarist with The Hollies.

BENNY ANDERSON, Stockholm, Sweden, 1946. Singer and pianist with Abba, a founding member of the group.

Notes:

_____

_____

_____

_____

WHAT'S IN A NAME? Clifford Davis claims ownership of the name of the group he manages and, angered because Fleetwood Mac is taking a break from performing, assembles a company of unknowns to tour as "Fleetwood Mac." When the fraud is discovered by Mick Fleetwood, he files suit to keep the bogus band from further touring. (1973)

1955   Carl Perkins writes "Blue Suede Shoes."

1968   The Pink Floyd single "Careful With That Axe, Eugene" is released.

1970   The Beach Boys perform for Princess Margaret at Royal Albert Hall in London.

1971   *Hunky Dory,* **David Bowie's** American debut LP, is released.

1977   Elvis Costello makes a rare TV appearance, performing on *Saturday Night Live* when **The Sex Pistols** fail to show.

🎵 **RECORD RELEASES** include **The Lovin' Spoonful** "Nashville Cats" and **The Royal Guardsmen** "Snoopy & The Red Baron" (1966).

Birthdays:

EDDIE KENDRICKS, Birmingham, Alabama, 1939. Singer and original member of The Temptations, then pursued a solo career.

PAUL BUTTERFIELD, Chicago, Illinois, 1942. Singer, pianist, harmonica player with an early history with Howlin' Wolf, Magic Sam and Little Walter before forming his own Butterfield Blues Band.

Notes:

A CONCERT FOR ALL! Rod Stewart is broadcast live-in-concert from the Los Angeles Forum, a performance televised in 23 countries and simulcast in stereo on FM stations in many U.S. cities. The viewing audience alone numbers nearly 35 million. (1981)

1969 **Tiny Tim** marries **Miss Vicky** on **The Tonight Show.** Tiny is 40 . . . Miss Vicki just 17.

1970 The **Beatles** last recording is released, a Christmas LP for their fan club titled *From Them To Us.*

1975 **The Faces** disband when **Rod Stewart,** at a press conference in London, announces his plans to leave the group, "I was outgrowing them a bit and I thought it was time for us to move . . . time for me to move, anyway."—Rod.

1981 **Sting** of **The Police** rams his hand through a window during a filming of his movie *Brimstone and Treacle.*

🎵 **GOLD RECORDS** awarded to **America** for the *Homecoming* LP and **The Moody Blues** for the single "Nights In White Satin" (1972) . . . and to **Lynyrd Skynyrd** for the debut LP *Pronounced Leh-nerd Skin-nerd* (1974).

🎵 **RECORD RELEASES** include **Harry Nilsson** "Without You" (1971) . . . **The Eagles** "New Kid In Town" and the **Steve Miller Band** "Fly Like An Eagle" (1976).

Birthdays:

BRYAN "CHAS" CHANDLER, Newcastle-on-Tyne, England, 1938. Bassist with The Animals, then known for bringing Jimi Hendrix to London for better exposure to press and fans. In 1970, the manager of Slade.

KEITH RICHARDS, Kent, England, 1943. Guitarist and singer with The Rolling Stones, a founding member and co-author of most Stones tunes.

SAM ANDREW, Taft, California, 1941. Guitarist with Big Brother & The Holding Company, a founding member.

Notes:

MASSAGING THE MEDIUMS! John Lennon and Marshal McLuhan, two of the most powerful communicators of the spoken word through lecture and lyric, are together on a 45 minute television discussion program for CBS-TV. (1969)

1955 **Carl Perkins** records "Blue Suede Shoes" at Sam Phillips' Studios in Memphis.

1967 **The Strawberry Alarm Clock** is awarded a Gold Record for "Incense and Peppermints."

1969 **Mick Jagger** is busted for pot possession in London. He's fined 200 pounds sterling and sent on his way.

🎵 **RECORD RELEASES** include **Neil Sedaka** "Calendar Girl" (1960).

Birthdays:

ZALMAN YANOVSKY, 1944. Singer and guitarist with The Mugwumps before joining John Sebastian to form The Lovin' Spoonful.

PHIL OCHS, El Paso, Texas, 1940. Singer and songwriter best known for his folk protest songs of the sixties, particularly "I Ain't Marchin' Anymore."

ALVIN LEE, Nottingham, England, 1944. Guitarist with Britain's Largest Sounding Trio with Leo Lyons before forming Ten Years After, then The Alvin Lee Band in the seventies.

MAURICE WHITE, Chicago, Illinois, 1941. Singer, percussionist and producer with Earth, Wind & Fire, the founding member.

Notes:

_____

_____

_____

_____

_____

_____

_____

_____

FAME FROM ANOTHER'S NAME! Singer, Ian Anderson, and bassist Glen Cornick leave The John Evan Band to form Jethro Tull. The name is taken from a book that Anderson has seen in manager, Terry Ellis', home library . . . Jethro Tull, an 18th century agriculturist. Guitarist Mick Abrahams and drummer Clive Bunker round out the early line-up. (1967)

1968 "Leavin' On A Jet Plane" by **Peter, Paul & Mary** is #1 in the U.S.

1969 The new bootleg LPs appear on the record racks in Chicago. **Bob Dylan's** *Stealin'* sounds like out-takes lifted from the Columbia Records vaults and **The Rolling Stones** *Liver Than You'll Ever Be* has been illegally recorded live from performances at The Forum in Los Angeles and The Oakland Coliseum.

1973 **Bobby Darin** dies of a heart attack in a Los Angeles hospital at age 37 during his second open-heart operation in two years.

1975 **Joe Walsh** joins **The Eagles** as replacement for guitarist **Bernie Leadon.**

🎵 **RECORD RELEASES** include **The Hollies** "He Ain't Heavy (He's My Brother)" (1967) . . . **The Guess Who** "No Time" (1969) . . . **Eric Carmen** "All By Myself," **The Eagles** "Take It To The Limit," and **Paul Simon** "50 Ways To Leave Your Lover" (1975).

Birthdays:

PETER CRISS, New York City, 1947. Drummer and original member of Kiss until his departure in 1980 to pursue a solo career.

Notes:

_____

_____

_____

_____

_____

_____

_____

COVERING THEIR STYLE! The Rolling Stones release *Their Satanic Majesties Request,* the psychedelic concept LP with a plastic 3-D photograph of the band on the cover, costing $50,000 to produce. (1967)

1964   *Ode To A High Flying Bird* is published. Written in 1961 by **Rolling Stones** drummer, **Charlie Watts,** the book is a tribute to jazz great **Charlie "Bird" Parker.**

1968   **Crosby, Stills & Nash** unite in California to form one of rock's finest acoustic supergroups.

1970   **Tim Rice** and **Andrew Lloyd Webber** are awarded a Gold Record for the rock opera *Jesus Christ Superstar.*

1979   **The Frank Zappa** film *Baby Snakes* premieres in New York on his 39th birthday, and receives warm reviews.

🎵 **RECORD RELEASES** include **The Ronettes** "Baby, I Love You" (1963) . . . **The Bee Gees** "I Started A Joke" and **Bob Seger** "Ramblin' Gamblin' Man" (1968) . . . and **The Doobie Brothers** "Black Water" (1974).

Birthdays:

FRANK ZAPPA, Baltimore, Maryland, 1940. Singer, songwriter, multi-instrumentalist and producer, founding member of The Mothers Of Invention in 1964. Noted for his avant-garde compositions, with more than thirty LPs recorded and various film credits including *200 Motels.*

CARL WILSON, Hawthorne, California, 1946. Guitarist and original member of The Beach Boys.

The Doobie Brothers

WHO'S NEW IN THE WHO? Kenny Jones joins The Who, replacing drummer, Keith Moon, four months after his death. Jones makes his official Who recording debut on the *Quadrophenia* movie soundtrack, although he has appeared on Roger Daltry solo LPs and the movie soundtrack of *Tommy* (1978)

1975 **Ike** and **Tina Turner** are robbed of a suitcase containing $86,000 cash in concert receipts.

1976 Singer and composer, **Isaac Hayes,** files for bankruptcy.

1981 A "Rock 'n' Roll Auction" in London finds buyers for **John** and **Cynthia Lennon's** marriage certificate ($850), an autographed program from the world premiere of *Help!* ($2,100), **Mitch Mitchell's** drum kit ($450), and a letter of introduction from **Buddy Holly** to Decca Records ($2,000).

Birthdays:

ROBIN and **MAURICE GIBB,** Isle of Man, 1949. With older brother, Barry, they formed The Blue Cats, which evolved into The Bee Gees when the family moved to Australia in the late fifties.

Notes:

Maurice and Robin Gibb

FOUR FOR THE FUTURE! Elton John begins his collaboration with lyricist, Bernie Taupin, arranger, Paul Buckmaster, and producer, Gus Dudgeon, when the four meet for the first time to discuss Elton's recording career. The teamwork is responsible for some of the biggest hits of the seventies. (1969)

1964   Radio London begins regular transmission and becomes one of the top pirate radio stations for Great Britain.

1966   *Ready Steady Go*, England's premiere rock and roll show in which numerous stars got their start, including **The Rolling Stones, Donovan** and **David Bowie,** airs for the last time.

1966   **Pink Floyd** performs for the first time at The UFO club, one of their earliest regular venues. The club becomes a London hot spot.

1972   **John Lennon's** "Imagine" is world premiered on U.S. television.

1974   **The Faces** set an attendance record for the most successful rock tour of Britain for the year.

1980   **John McVie** and wife, **Julie,** are busted at their resort home in Honolulu and charged with possession of cocaine when a drug-sniffing dog alerts police to the contents of a package addressed to the McVie's.

🎵 **RECORD RELEASES** include **Tom & Jerry (Simon & Garfunkel)** "Hey! Schoolgirl" (1957) . . . **The Classics IV** "Spooky" and **The Jimi Hendrix Experience** "Foxy Lady" (1967) . . . and **Rod Stewart** "Do Ya Think I'm Sexy" (1978).

Birthdays:

JORMA KAUKONEN, Washington, D.C., 1940. Guitarist with the original Jefferson Airplane, then founding member of Hot Tuna.

RON BUSHY, Washington, D.C., 1945. Drummer with Iron Butterfly, well known for his lengthy drum solo in the 17-minute classic, "Inna-Gadda-Da-Vida."

TIM HARDIN, Eugene, Oregon, 1940. Singer, songwriter and guitarist who wrote for Bobby Darin, Johnny Cash, Joan Baez and The Youngbloods before pursuing a solo career.

LUTHER GROSVENOR, Worchestershire, England, 1949. Guitarist with Spooky Tooth, an original member.

Notes:

LOTS OF CHRISTMAS CHEERS! The Beatles' Christmas Show fills the Hammersmith Odeon in London, also starring The Yardbirds, Freddie and The Dreamers and The Mike Cotton Sound. (1964)

1961 **The Tokens'** "The Lion Sleeps Tonight" is #1 in the U.S., a song that will be a hit ten years later by **Robert John** with **Hank Medress,** one of the original Tokens, producing.

1966 **Tommy James and The Shondells** record "I Think We're Alone Now," which will become the group's third hit single.

1972 Fans riot at a **Manfred Mann** concert at The University of Miami when police pull the plug on the group at the 11 PM curfew. Students stage an unruly two-hour protest.

1973 **Tom Johnston** of **The Doobie Brothers** is arrested for possession of marijuana in Visalia, California. In the spirit of Christmas, police release him to his own custody.

1974 **James Taylor, Carly Simon, Joni Mitchell** and **Linda Ronstadt** make the rounds of the streets in Hollywood singing Christmas carols.

🎵 **RECORD RELEASES** include **The Seeds** "Pushing' Too Hard" (1966).

Birthdays:

JAN AKKERMAN, Netherlands, 1946. Guitarist with Focus.

Notes:

THE CHRISTMAS PROMISE! Paul McCartney announces his engagement to Jane Asher, sister of singer-producer, Peter Asher, but in eight months the couple will call it quits without ever reaching the altar. (1967)

1954   Singer, Johnny Ace, shoots himself in a game of Russian Roulette backstage at City Auditorium in Houston, Texas.

1969   **Robbie Bachman** gets his first drum set for Christmas and, years later, will become drummer for **Bachman-Turner Overdrive.**

Birthdays:

O'KELLY ISLEY, Cincinnati, Ohio, 1937. Singer and original member of The Isley Brothers.

HENRY VESTINE, Washington, D.C., 1944. Guitarist with The Mothers Of Invention, then with Canned Heat.

NOEL REDDING, Kent, England, 1945. Bassist with local bands before joining The Jimi Hendrix Experience, later pursued a solo career.

Notes:

A TREAT FOR THE DAY AFTER! The Beatles *Magical Mystery Tour* premieres on British television (BBC-1), a film produced entirely by the Beatles. The band thought they could do a better quality movie if they controlled all the elements, but it didn't impress the critics. (1967)

1970   George Harrison's "My Sweet Lord" is #1 in the U.S.

♬ RECORD RELEASES include The Kinks "All Day and All Of The Night" (1964).

Birthdays:

PHIL SPECTOR, New York City, 1940. Songwriter and record producer for numerous artists including The Teddybears (his own group), The Crystals, The Ronettes, Elvis Presley and the Beatles. Recognized for developing the "wall of sound" recording technique. Film credits include the role of the coke dealer in *Easy Rider.*

Notes:

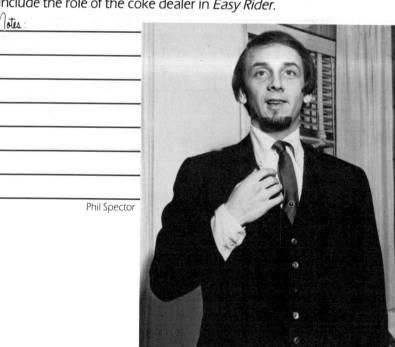

Phil Spector

DECEMBER 27

WITH A LITTLE HELP FROM HIS BROTHER! Bob Dylan re-records several tracks on his *Before The Flood* LP with assistance from his brother, Dave Zimmerman. The two rent a studio in Minneapolis and rework "Lily, Rosemary and the Jack of Hearts," "Tangled Up In Blue," and four other tunes. (1974)

1963 The London *Times* music critic, **William Mann,** hails the **Beatles** as "the outstanding composers of 1963."

1968 **The MC 5** make their concert debut at The Fillmore East in New York.

1969 **The Rolling Stones'** LP *Let It Bleed* enters the U.S. charts.

1969 *Led Zeppelin II* is #1 in the U.S.

1976 Blues great, Freddie King, dies after becoming ill at a Christmas Day concert in Dallas, Texas.

1976 **Queen's** *A Day At The Races* is released, featuring the hit single "Somebody To Love" and a retail price of $7.98, a dollar higher than most current LP prices.

🎵 **RECORD RELEASES** include **The Bee Gees** "Fanny" and **The Four Seasons** "December, 1963 (Oh What A Night)" (1975).

Birthdays:

MIKE PENDER, Birmingham, England, 1941. Keyboards and singer with The Moody Blues, an original member of the band.

MICK JONES, London, England, 1944. Guitarist and singer with Spooky Tooth, then formed Foreigner in 1976.

PETER QUAIFE, Devonshire, England, 1943. Bassist and original member of The Kinks.

Notes:

GUNTIME FOR GONZO! Ted Nugent faces the barrel of a .44 Magnum in the hands of a concert goer in Detroit who shoves his way to the front of the stage with the weapon. Nugent's band beats a hasty retreat to safety behind the wall of amps, but Nugent plays on. Lawrence Thompson is arrested by security guards before anyone is harmed. (1975)

1957 "At The Hop" by **Danny and The Juniors** is #1 in the U.S.

1968 The **Beatles** *White* LP is #1 in the U.S.

1971 **Who** drummer, **Keith Moon,** MCs a **Sha Na Na** concert at Carnegie Hall in New York City, dressed in a specially tailored gold lamé suit.

1981 WEA Records (Warner-Elektra-Atlantic) boosts the price of 45 RPM singles from $1.69 to $1.98, an 18% increase. Other labels follow suit.

RECORD RELEASES include **The Doors** "Touch Me" (1968).

Birthdays:

EDGAR WINTER, Beaumont, Texas, 1946. Guitarist with his brother, Johnny, in Black Plague before forming White Trash, then The Edgar Winter Group.

Notes:

DECEMBER 29

NO REASON TO BELIEVE! Tim Hardin is found dead in his Hollywood apartment from a heroin overdose. The prolific singer-songwriter rose to prominence with such songs as "If I Were A Carpenter" and "Reason To Believe." He was 40. (1980)

1967 **Dave Mason** quits **Traffic** shortly after the group's debut LP *Mr. Fantasy* enters the charts. It is the first of three times that Mason departs from the band.

1975 **Grace Slick** and **Paul Kantner** call it quits after living together for seven years. Though never married, they have a daughter, China, and shortly after the separation, Grace marries **Jefferson Starship** lighting director, **Skip Johnson.**

🎵 **RECORD RELEASES** include **Paul & Paula** "Hey Paula" (1962).

Birthdays:

MARIANNE FAITHFUL, 1946. English folksinger first recognized in 1964 with "Come and Stay With Me," followed by a highly publicized relationship with Mick Jagger and later, a renewed solo career in 1979.

RAY THOMAS, Stourport-on-Severn, England, 1941. Flute and sax player, an original member of The Moody Blues.

Grace Slick

PARTING COMPANY WITH A NEW SUIT! Paul McCartney sues John Lennon, George Harrison and Ringo Starr to dissolve the Beatles partnership and gain control of his interest in it. Paul claims the suit is nothing personal, strictly business, but it touches off a bitter feud between he and Lennon. (1970)

1973 **John McLaughlin** and **The Original Mahavishnu Orchestra** perform their final concert at The Masonic Auditorium in Detroit.

1974 The **Beatles** partnership officially dissovles exactly four years after Paul initiates his lawsuit.

1978 **XTC** performs their U.S. concert debut in Philadelphia.

🎵 **RECORD RELEASES** include **The Fireballs'** "Bottle Of Wine" (1968).

Birthdays:

BO DIDDLEY, born Ellas McDaniel, McComb, Mississippi, 1928. Singer, songwriter and guitarist noted for his influence on The Rolling Stones, The Who and others. Legendary for his early rock stage style and guitar riffs.

MICHAEL NESMITH, Dallas, Texas, 1942. Guitarist with The Monkees as an original member of the TV show, then pursued a solo career, including record producing on his own label and video production.

JEFF LYNNE, Birmingham, England, 1947. Guitarist, synthesizer and singer with The Electric Light Orchestra after work with The Move.

DECEMBER 31

A NEW CAREER FOR THE NEW YEAR! Mick Fleetwood telephones Stevie Nicks and Lindsay Buckingham and invites them to join Fleetwood Mac. They accept. "He called us up sight unseen. We could've been the two heaviest jerks he'd ever seen."—Stevie Nicks. (1974)

1961 **The Beach Boys** perform their first concert with that name at The Ritchie Valens Memorial Center in Long Beach, California.

1964 **Jerry Garcia** and **Bob Weir** play music together for the first time.

1966 **The Monkees** "I'm A Believer" is #1 in the U.S.

1969 **Jimi Hendrix** introduces the **Band Of Gypsies** at The Fillmore East in New York City, featuring **Buddy Miles** on drums and **Billy Cox** on bass.

1971 **Bob Dylan** and **The Band** spend New Year's Eve in concert at The New York Academy of Music, recording the *Rock Of Ages* LP.

1973 **David Bowie** is given an award for having five different LPs on the British rock charts at the same time.

1974 **Harry Chapin** is awarded a Gold Record for "Cat's In The Cradle."

1975 **Elvis Presley** performs before a crowd of 60,000 at The Silver Dome in Pontiac, Michigan, in a show that grosses $800,000, a world record take for a single concert by a single artist.

1976 **The Cars** make their concert debut at Pease Air Force Base in New Hampshire.

1978 Winterland closes with a final concert by promoter, **Bill Graham,** starring **The Grateful Dead** and **The Blues Brothers.** The famed theater housed the best known rock acts during its day, including the first and last concerts by **The Band.**

♫ **RECORD RELEASES** include **The Buckinghams** "Kind Of A Drag" and **The Spencer Davis Group** "Gimme Some Loving"(1966).

Birthdays:

JOHN DENVER, born Henry John Deutschendorf, Roswell, New Mexico, 1943. Singer and guitarist with The Chad Mitchell Trio before a solo career in 1969, including numerous television specials and film credits in *Oh God.*

BURTON CUMMINGS, Winnipeg, Canada, 1947. Singer and multi-instrumentalist, founding member of The Guess Who.

TOM HAMILTON, Boston, Massachusetts, 1951. Bassist and original member of Aerosmith.

Notes:

_____

_____

_____

_____

_____

_____

_____

_____

ABOUT THE AUTHOR

DAN FORMENTO is producer and anchor of Today In Rock History on NBC's *The Source,* heard daily on 120 radio stations of the young adult Network.